Girls' Education in the 21st Century

Gender Equality, Empowerment, and Economic Growth

Mercy Tembon and Lucia Fort
Editors

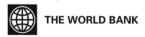 THE WORLD BANK

This volume is a product of the staff of the International Bank for Reconstruction and Development / The World Bank. The findings, interpretations, and conclusions expressed in this volume do not necessarily reflect the views of the Executive Directors of The World Bank or the governments they represent.

The World Bank does not guarantee the accuracy of the data included in this work. The boundaries, colors, denominations, and other information shown on any map in this work do not imply any judgement on the part of The World Bank concerning the legal status of any territory or the endorsement or acceptance of such boundaries.

ISBN-13: 978-0-8213-7474-0
eISBN-13: 978-0-8213-7475-7
DOI: 10.1596/978-0-8213-7474-0

Cover photo: © World Bank/Curt Carnemark

Library of Congress Cataloging-in-Publication Data

Girls' education in the 21st century : equality, empowerment, and growth.
    p. cm.
  1. Women--Education--Developing countries. 2. Women--Education--Economic aspects--Developing countries. 3. Educational equalization--Developing countries. I. Title: Girls' education in the twenty-first century.
  LC2572.G57 2008
  371.822--dc22
                          2008029785

Contents

Figures

Tables

Boxes

Foreword

"The surest way to keep a people down is to educate the men and neglect the women. If you educate a man you simply educate an individual, but if you educate a woman you educate a family."

— Dr. J. E. Kwegyir Aggrey, a visionary Ghanian educator
(1875–1927)

Gender equality is not just a women's issue, it is a development issue. Women's economic empowerment is essential for economic development, growth, and poverty reduction not only because of the income it generates, but also because it helps to break the vicious cycle of poverty. Educating girls and women is critical to economic development. Research conducted in a variety of countries and regions has established that educating girls is one of the most cost-effective ways of spurring development. Female education creates powerful poverty-reducing synergies and yields enormous intergenerational gains. It is positively correlated with increased economic productivity, more robust labor markets, higher earnings, and improved societal health and well-being.

For developing countries in particular, women represent a previously untapped source of human capital, and countries that have adopted aggressive policies to promote gender equality in education can be expected to reap higher social and economic benefits. Greater investment in girls' education is vital for increasing female participation and productivity in the labor market, especially in nonagricultural wage employment. Greater productivity means higher economic growth and more effective reduction of poverty.

Whether self-employed or earning wages, working women help their households escape poverty. When women have more schooling, the returns flow not only to themselves, but to the next generation as well. Indeed, studies have shown that giving women more access to education, markets (labor, land, credit), and new technology, as well as greater control over household resources, often translates into greater well-being for the household. When women have greater control over resources in the family, they are more likely than men to allocate more resources to food, children's health care, and education—a finding from as diverse a set of countries as Bangladesh, Brazil, Côte d'Ivoire, Ghana, Indonesia, and South Africa. Simply put, limiting women's economic options is a missed opportunity; it wastes resources and it slows progress on poverty reduction.

Well-documented evidence shows that educating girls and women also yields significant social and health benefits. Educated women are more likely to send their daughters to school. Countries with higher levels of female secondary-school enrollment have lower infant mortality rates, lower fertility, lower rates of HIV and AIDS, and better child nutrition. More education reduces the rate of violence against women, enables them to leave abusive relationships, and empowers them to reject adverse cultural practices, such as female genital mutilation. Eliminating gender disparities in primary and secondary education (Millennium Development Goal [MDG] 3) also may help countries attain other MDGs, including achieving universal primary education (MDG 2), reducing the under-five mortality (MDG 4), improving maternal health (MDG 5), and reducing the likelihood of contracting HIV/AIDS (MDG 6). Promoting gender equality in education is therefore key to sustainable global development as well as to greater well-being.

There has been steady progress in most of the world's poorest countries in women's and girls' education levels. Gender parity at the primary level has improved from 92 percent to 94 percent. Furthermore, between 1999 and 2004, the number of out-of–school girls fell by 24 percent, compared with 18 percent for out-of-school boys. There was also a sharp increase in the number of children starting school, with the highest gains registered in Sub-Saharan Africa (19 percent) and South Asia (11 percent). Efforts need to be made to sustain progress in education goals and to help women contribute to economic growth and share in its benefits. Promoting equality in educational opportunities involves entering the education system at the primary level, progressing to higher levels, and making the transition to the labor market. Restricting women's access to services (be it education, health, or transportation) and their economic opportunity is unfair: life chances should not be preordained at birth. In economic terms, restricting women reduces their well-being and the welfare of families. It limits economic growth and slows down progress in poverty reduction.

This book presents compelling evidence of the challenges for educational development and the determining factors for gender inequalities—in education particularly and society more broadly. It also presents examples of country-level experiences that help us understand issues and reaffirm the business case for investing more in female education. The book is a useful reference for researchers, policy makers, and development practitioners. We hope that the key messages, examples, and recommendations summarized in its chapters will help countries implement strategic policies and actions to accelerate the move toward gender equality and the empowerment of women by 2015.

Joy Phumaphi
Vice President
Human Development Network
The World Bank

Danny Leipziger
Vice President
Poverty Reduction and Economic Management Network
The World Bank

Preface

To re-energize efforts to promote equity in education, the World Bank convened an international, multidisciplinary symposium on gender, education, and development on October 2–3, 2007. The event, titled Education: A Critical Path to Gender Equality and Women's Empowerment, brought together high-level government officials from Afghanistan, the Arab Republic of Egypt, Nigeria, Turkey, and the Republic of Yemen; senior representatives from nongovernmental organizations and partner organizations, including the Rockefeller Foundation, Nike Foundation, the U.S. Agency for International Development, the United Nations Girls' Education Initiative, and the United Nations Children's Fund; as well as renowned academics and Bank staff. The event's keynote address was delivered by His Excellency Mr. Haneef Atmar, minister of education for Afghanistan.

The symposium sought to identify ways to accelerate the achievement of gender equity in education, and to promote shared growth, and to advance women's economic empowerment. It took stock of the progress made and lessons learned after nearly two decades of promoting gender equality in education; it brought out the nature and impact of challenges that blunt progress on achieving the Millennium Development Goals for gender equality and empowerment of women; and it explored ways of maintaining the focus on and accelerating the achievement of gender equality in education within the evolving development aid architecture and sectorwide approaches in education.

This book is based on the background papers developed for the symposium. Although the papers have been edited, their key messages remain intact, and the theme of the symposium respected. The overview chapter is a thematic paper prepared by the World Bank that brings out the main messages of the symposium. The subsequent chapters reflect the current state of education from a gender perspective and highlight the importance of and challenges to female education as well as the interdependence of education and development objectives. The final chapter presents five strategic directions for advancing gender equity in education.

Education and gender equality *are* intertwined: not only is education a critical path to gender equality and women's empowerment, but gender equality and women's empowerment are critical pathways for girls' education. We can no longer neglect the education, well-being, and intellectual advancement of half the human race. The time is right to synergize our efforts, generate that extra push, and include the excluded—so that we can ensure gender equality in education for our future generations.

Ruth Kagia
Director, Education
Human Development Network
The World Bank

Mayra Buvinic
Director, Gender and Development
Poverty Reduction & Economic
    Management
The World Bank

Acknowledgments

This book is based on a two-day symposium—Education: A Critical Path to Gender Equality and Women's Empowerment—held at the World Bank October 2–3, 2007. The symposium was organized by a team led by Mercy Tembon (Human Development Network, Education Group (HDNED)) and Lucia Fort (Poverty Reduction and Economic Management, Gender and Development Group (PRMGE)) under the direction of Ruth Kagia (Education Director, HDNED) and Mayra Buvinic (Gender Group, Director PRMGE). The chapters of the book reflect contributions by presenters at the symposium.

The team expresses its appreciation to all of the speakers and session chairs and chapter contributors to this book. A special note of gratitude goes out to His Excellency Haneef Atmar, minister of education of Afghanistan, and Nancy Birdsall, president of the Center for Global Development, for presenting the keynote address and opening statements at the symposium. Thanks are also extended to Sister S. M. Cyril of the Loreto Day School Sealdah in Kolkata, India, who could not attend the symposium but sent useful materials, including a video and PowerPoint presentation on "A School that Challenges Myths."

The World Bank would like to thank the Dutch government for providing the funding for the analytic work on girls' education as well as for the symposium, through its Bank-Netherlands Partnership Program. Thanks also go to the Inter-American Development Bank, the International Labour Organization (ILO), the Organisation for Economic Co-operation and Development (OECD), the United Nations Girls' Education Initiative (UNGEI), the United Nations Children's Fund (UNICEF), the government of Norway, the Academy for Educational Development (AED), the Center for Global Development, the Children's Defense Fund, the Forum for African Women Educationalists (FAWE), the Save the Children Fund, the Rockefeller and Nike Foundations, and Winrock International for their active participation at the symposium.

For their perspective and constructive guidance during preparation for the symposium and compilation of this book, the team would like to express its gratitude to the World Bank staff members, including Ruth Kagia, Robin Horn, Robert Prouty, Phillip Hay, Maureen Lewis, Mayra Buvinic, Elizabeth King, Yaw Ansu, Jee Peng Tan, Chris Thomas, Mamta Murthi, Mourad Ezzine, Eduardo Velez, Michelle Riboud, and Julian Schweitzer.

For logistic and technical support, before, during, and after the symposium, special thanks go to Fahma Nur and Seemeen Saadat, who went beyond the call of duty and worked tirelessly from the concept stage to the end.

Thanks also go to Veronica Grigera, Jung-Hwan Choi, Olivia Elee, Long Quach, Ashkan Niknia, Inosha Wickramaskera, and Hana Yoshimoto (HDNED); and Arunima Dhar, Gisela Garcia, and Shwetlena Sabarwal, (PRMGE) for their support.

Contributors

Michelle Akpo, Center for Gender Equity, Academy for Educational Development (AED)

Monazza Aslam, Department of Economics, University of Oxford

Felipe Barrera, Human Development Network, World Bank

Nazmul Chaudhury, Human Development, South Asia Region, World Bank

Codou Diaw, Forum for African Women Educationalists (FAWE)

Deon Filmer, Development Economics, World Bank

Eric Hanushek, Hoover Institution, Stanford University

Richard Johanson, Human Development, Africa Region, World Bank

Geeta Kingdon, Institute of Education, London University

Jackie Kirk, McGill University

Marlaine Lockheed, Center for Global Development

Changu Mannathoko, Education, United Nations
Children's Fund (UNICEF)

Harry Patrinos, Human Development Network, World Bank

Eija Pehu, Agriculture and Rural Development Department,
World Bank

Catherine Ragasa, Agriculture and Rural Development, World Bank

William Saint, Human Development, World Bank Institute, World Bank

Mans Söderbom , School of Economics at Göteborg University

Mercy Tembon, Human Development Network, World Bank

Sakena Yacoobi, Afghan Institute of Learning (AIL)

Abbreviations

AARI	average annual rate of increase
AET	agricultural education and training
AME	Association des Meres Educatrices (Mothers' Association)
APE	Association des Parents d'Eleves (Parents' Teacher Association)
AGORA	Access to Global Online Research in Agriculture
CA	classroom assistant
CAFS	conflict-affected fragile states
CCT	conditional cash transfer
CFS	child-friendly schools
COE	Center of Excellence
DHS	demographic and health surveys
ECDE	early childhood development and education
EFA	Education for All
FAWE	Forum for African Women Educationalists
FTI	fast-track initiative

GAD	gender and development
GBV	gender-based violence
GDP	gross domestic product
GER	gross enrollment ratio
GPI	gender parity index
GTT	gender task team
IASC	inter-agency standing committee
IDP	internally displaced person
IHS	integrated household survey
IRC	International Rescue Committee
INEE	Inter-Agency Network for Education in Emergencies
LIC	low-income country
LSMS	living standards measurement study
MDG	Millennium Development Goal
MICS2	End-of-Decade Multiple Indicator Cluster Surveys
MoE	ministry of education
MOU	memorandum of understanding
MSc	Master of Science
MTRF	medium-term results framework
NEPAD	New Partnership for African Development
NGO	nongovernmental organization
NWFP	North West Frontier Province (Pakistan)
OECD	Organisation for Economic Co-operation and Development
OLF	out of the labor force
PCR	primary school completion rate
PIHS	Pakistan Integrated Household Survey
PISA	Programme for International Student Assessment
RECOUP	Research Consortium on Educational Outcomes and Poverty
SMT	science, mathematics, and technology
STD	sexually transmitted disease
SWAp	sector wide approach
SWG	sub–working group
TEEAL	The Essential Electronic Agricultural Library
UIS	UNESCO Institute of Statistics
UNAIDS	Joint United Nations Programme on HIV/AIDS

UNESCO   United Nations Educational, Scientific, and
          Cultural Organization
UNGEI   United Nations Girls' Education Initiative
UNHCR   United Nations High Commissioner for Refugees
UNICEF   United Nations Children's Fund
UNSCR   United Nations Security Council Resolution
USAID   U.S. Agency for International Development
WID   Women in Development

Education Quality, Skills Development, and Economic Growth

CHAPTER 1

Overview

Mercy Tembon

Much has been done to increase gender equality in education over the past 15 years. National governments and the international community have followed through on promises made in various international forums to increase investments in girls' education.[1] Overall female enrollment at the primary level in low-income countries has accordingly grown from 87 percent in 1990 to 94 percent in 2004, considerably shrinking the gender gap. This progress is the result of recognition of the centrality of girls' education in development and the overall progress made under the Education for All (EFA) agenda. Making girls' education a high priority and implementing a range of interventions—including scholarships, stipends, conditional cash transfers, female teacher recruitment, and gender-targeted provision of materials—have proved effective in increasing the enrollment of girls in school.

These achievements notwithstanding, progress on the ground remains slow and uneven—despite more than two decades of evidence of what works in improving gender equality in education. In many countries, many more boys than girls are enrolled in school. However, in certain parts of Latin America and the Caribbean, the Middle East, North Africa, and Southern Africa, many more girls than boys are enrolled. In 2005, some 72 million children remained out of school, the majority of whom (41 million) were girls from groups with multiple disadvantages living mainly in Sub-Saharan Africa and South Asia.

Gender differences are now widest at the level of secondary education, where the acquisition of cognitive skills is crucial for national economic growth. Many children attending secondary school are failing to master the skills and competencies needed to succeed in today's labor market. Measured in terms of learning achievement, the quality of educational services in most developing countries remains low. Gender inequalities in both learning and earning outcomes persist. Although school graduates face significant challenges entering the labor market, men still tend to find employment faster than women, irrespective of their level of education. And gender inequality in both education and the workplace are exacerbated by HIV/AIDS, violent conflict, and emergency situations.

The Human Development and the Poverty Reduction and Economic Management Networks of the World Bank organized a symposium in October 2007 in Washington, DC, to discuss these issues. The symposium built on the 2006 World Bank Gender Action Plan (World Bank 2006), which addresses economic aspects of gender equality and recognizes education as the most critical pathway to its achievement. The meeting brought together more than 100 participants, including high-level government officials, academics, senior representatives from nongovernmental organizations (NGOs) and partner organizations, and World Bank staff to

- take stock of nearly two decades of efforts to achieve gender equality in education
- discuss the nature and impact of challenges that are constraining progress toward the Millennium Development Goals (MDGs) of gender equality and the empowerment of women
- explore ways to accelerate gender equality in education within the evolving architecture of development aid, including sectorwide approaches to education
- identify priority areas for future action, including strategic and operational approaches that draw on proven, innovative practices

The symposium facilitated evidenced-based discussions on five core issues that continue to hamper the achievement of gender equality in education and the effectiveness of education systems in many developing countries to do so. These five core issues are educational quality; access and retention; postprimary education; the transition from school to work; and emerging issues such as HIV/AIDS, violence, and conflict.

The presentations clearly demonstrated that female education is essential for economic growth and poverty reduction. In addition to helping generate additional income and breaking the vicious cycle of poverty, investments in female education have other economic and social benefits. Educated women tend to have fewer children, which reduces dependency ratios and raises per capita spending, eventually lifting households out of poverty. Increased maternal education also transmits intergenerational benefits by boosting the survival rate, educational level, and nutritional status of children.

It also came out clearly that achieving gender equality would require investing in the education of both girls and boys, while maintaining a balance between them. The country case studies presented showed that even within the context of gender equality, boys' education cannot be ignored. Efforts to improve the education of girls in some countries have resulted in significant increases and progress in female enrollments, but a slight regression in male enrollment and participation is becoming a cause for concern. Boys in Bangladesh, for example, are dropping out of school in much larger numbers than girls, a phenomenon that is now the country's biggest gender challenge—to the point where girls now account for 60 percent of enrollment in some schools, especially in rural areas.

Other key messages that emerged from discussions and are expounded upon in the chapters of this book are as follows:

- There remains a strong business case for investing in female education.
- The returns to female education are the largest, and gender disparities the widest, at the secondary level.
- Educational quality, not completion rates alone, improves economic outcomes.
- Education systems in developing countries are failing to reach, and to teach, large numbers of children.
- Gender disparities intensify the impact of structural impediments to education.
- The solution to gender inequality in education goes beyond the education sector, requiring a multisectoral strategy that addresses education as well as law, health, agriculture, and infrastructure. (See Box 1.1 for examples.)

Box 1.1

Interventions That Have Worked to Improve Girls' Education

A number of interventions being implemented in developing countries have proven successful in raising female enrollment and completion rates. These varied interventions seek to

- *increase demand* by such means as eliminating user fees and providing stipends and conditional cash transfers to girls
- *sharpen or focus attention on gender inequality* by means of advocacy and better impact evaluation research
- *address cultural and social constraints* to girls' education (for example, gender isolation, gender violence, and conflict) through community action attuned to local societal values and norms, as in Afghanistan
- *improve the economic returns to female education,* such as raising education standards and quality
- *promote postprimary education for girls* via the kind of fiscal incentives that helped modernize the madrassas of Bangladesh
- *genderize postbasic education* to improve national economic competitiveness via such initiatives as modernizing agricultural education at the graduate level
- *develop and disseminate gender-sensitive school and pedagogy models,* such as the regional programs of the Forum for African Women Educationalists

Structure of the Book

The chapters of this book, all of which are based on research and analysis or concrete practical experience, provide useful information on gender equality in education. The book is organized into three parts. Part I examines issues related to education quality, skills development, and economic growth. Part II looks at equity in education, and Part III documents practical experience of what works in promoting gender equality on the ground. The last chapter elaborates the main findings and conclusions of the preceding chapters and provides a forward-looking discussion, including needed World Bank actions to further advance gender equality in education.

Part I: Education Quality, Skills Development, and Economic Growth

There is no doubt that education has social and economic benefits for the general public and private individuals. However, many children today are completing primary, and even secondary, school without acquiring basic reading, writing, and arithmetic skills. Improving the quality of education not only improves individual children's quality of life, it also promotes economic growth. Encouraging greater female participation in labor markets worldwide will thus lead to gains in productivity. Labor market distortions and other social factors that impede women's wage employment in certain countries ultimately affect girls' access to education and retention rates in schools, given a higher perceived rate of return to education for boys. Chapters 2–5 examine these issues and their implications for future action.

In chapter 2, Eric Hanushek provides evidence that the quality of education (that is, what students know or how well they perform on standardized tests), not educational attainment (that is, how long students stay in school), determines the economic success of individuals and economies. This quality affects the education and income outcomes of both girls and boys. He presents solid empirical evidence linking educational quality to educational attainment, economic growth, and better economic institutions. Research in both developed and developing countries also underscores the prime importance of educational quality, as measured by tests of cognitive achievement, for raising earnings. It is the cognitive skills of a population, not mere school attainment, that are powerfully related to individual earnings, income distribution, and economic growth. In the United States, for example, a one standard deviation increase in mathematics performance at the end of high school is associated with 12 percent higher annual earnings. In primary schools in Brazil and Egypt, higher scores on tests of cognitive skills, which are indicative of better-quality schooling, are associated with lower repetition rates.

In developing countries, however, the level of material inputs allocated to schools on a per student basis and the level of efficiency with which these inputs are managed often do a poor job of raising student achievement. Evidence from Ghana, for example, reveals that although 37 percent of students stay in school through ninth grade, only 5 percent are fully literate. In Brazil, fewer than 22 percent of students attend through ninth grade, and only 8 percent are deemed literate. Improving the quality of education is therefore crucial for improving the performance of both boys and girls and, consequently, achieving equality in educational outcomes.

These complementarities suggest that improving educational quality also increases educational attainment. Educational quality may, in fact, be even higher in developing countries than in developed ones. Empirical evidence from member countries of the Organisation for Economic Co-operation and Development (OECD) reveals that not only does the quality of education have a powerful effect on economic growth, but that *low-quality schooling appears to confer few benefits*. When educational quality is included in cross-country economic growth regressions, for example, school attainment appears to play little to no role. The policy implications are clear: time in school yields little payoff if the students are not learning. Merely building schools and increasing enrollment without ensuring quality is unlikely to help countries meet their human capital objectives.

The chapter cautions that *improving student performance takes decades*. Raising cognitive skills requires changes in schools that are generally achieved over 20 to 30 years. If reforms succeed, moreover, their impact on the economy is generally not felt until new graduates represent a significant portion of the labor force. The direct impact of such reforms on the economy is nevertheless a powerful impetus for supporting renewed and expanded efforts to provide quality education to both girls and boys.

In chapter 3, Andreas Schleicher extends the discussion on quality and learning outcomes started in chapter 2. He presents 2003 results from the Programme for International Student Assessment (PISA) in OECD countries in mathematics, reading, and science, while examining gender differences from a quality and equity perspective.

The results show that in reading, girls perform significantly better than boys in all OECD countries. However, in mathematics boys tend to outperform girls somewhat in most countries, but the differences are generally modest. Boys are overrepresented among top performers, but boys and girls are equally represented among low performers. In science the results are mixed. The chapter argues that gender differences in mathematics are not related to underlying cognitive abilities but rather to the fact that boys show more interest, engagement, and motivation in mathematics, while girls show greater anxiety about mathematics. The chapter concludes with a discussion of policy levers and recommendations for individual learners, classrooms, service providers, and education systems.

Using empirical literature, Harry Patrinos examines the returns to education from a gender perspective in chapter 4. He concludes that overall returns to female education are, on average, higher than those to male education, both in terms of wages and social benefits. Among the social benefits of educating girls are reductions in infant mortality, a higher probability that children will live beyond age 5, and, as the proportion of women with secondary schooling doubles, lower fertility rates.

Despite the fact that private returns to education are highest at the primary level, in many developing countries the returns to this level of education are lower for girls than boys. The reasons for this difference are not entirely clear and may include discrimination, male-female differences in schooling quality, or the types of jobs available to men and women with a primary education. Lower returns to female primary education may be acting as a major brake on efforts to equalize girls' participation in education. If the perceived private returns to this level of education are lower for girls, poor families may decide to send sons rather than daughters to school or choose not to support full primary education for daughters.

Patrinos also shows that the biggest payoff to female education is at the secondary level. Therefore, lack of access to this level of education limits women's earnings and represents a major barrier to human development, economic growth, and poverty reduction. Maximizing the benefits of female education can be achieved by improving educational quality, as girls benefit more than boys from quality improvements. It can also be achieved by increasing female enrollment in, and completion of, both primary and secondary school using incentives such as scholarships.

In chapter 5, Monazza Aslam, Geeta Kingdon, and Mans Söderbom cite data from Pakistan that confirm the findings of chapter 4: girls need to stay in school longer than boys before they can realize the full benefits of education. In Pakistan, however, conservative attitudes and cultural norms greatly diminish the returns to female education until almost the postsecondary level. The country has historically been a low outlier in gender gaps in education, with girls lagging behind boys in access, school quality, and outcomes. The gender gap in primary education, for example, rose by 30 percentage points in Pakistan between 1985 and 1995—superseding even Afghanistan, where the corresponding difference rose by 18 points over the same period.

Moreover, Pakistan's labor market is highly segregated by gender. In 1999, only 17 percent of Pakistani women participated in the labor force, compared to 87 percent of men, and men dominate the better-remunerated sector of wage employment. Women lag far behind men in labor market outcomes because they earn substantially lower wages. Within any given occupation, however, women reap far greater wage benefits from additional years of education than do men. The economic returns to secondary education are, for example, substantially greater for women than men in all occupations except agriculture.

Fewer than 10 years of education has little effect on women's earnings in Pakistan. However, the proportion of women who achieve this level of education increased from 13 percent in 1999 to 19 percent in 2007. The educational attainment required for women to earn positive labor market outcomes also fell from 10 to 8 years over the same period, while the number of uneducated women in the labor force grew from 20 to 40 percent.

Labor market returns to education may be biased toward men in Pakistan for two possible reasons. First, *the returns that accrue to parents are higher from a boy's education than a girl's*, because the country lacks a social security system and married women traditionally live with their in-laws. Second, *women tend to earn much less money over the long term than men.* If education is to become a strong pathway to gender equality in the labor market, Pakistan needs to address conservative attitudes toward the division of labor and the participation of women in the paid labor force, as well as develop policies that reduce gender-differentiated treatment of employees.

Part II: Equity in Education: What Is Holding Countries Back?
This part examines the factors that prevent countries from achieving gender equality in education and discusses innovative strategies for encouraging access, equity, and quality in education, particularly in situations of poverty and conflict.

In chapter 6, Deon Filmer discusses patterns of inequality in educational attainment within and across countries, based on a compilation of more than 220 household surveys from more than 85 countries. He argues that inequalities associated with economic status are far greater than those associated with gender, orphanhood, or rural residence, and that within-country educational gap associated with economic status can be truly enormous—as large as or larger than differences across countries. Only disability is more important than income in accounting for differences in educational attainment. The schooling gap between children with and without disabilities starts at grade 1 in all countries, suggesting that efforts to boost the enrollment of disabled children should begin early to avoid a cycle of long-run poverty.

Although the gender gap remains substantial in South Asia and North and West Africa, gender gaps in school completion through grade 6 are typically smaller than the gaps associated with economic status or urban or rural residence. In Bangladesh, Nepal, and Pakistan, for example, fewer than 40 percent of children in the poorest socioeconomic quintile complete primary school, compared to 70–80 percent in the richest quintile. In Sierra Leone, the figures are 20 percent and 70 percent, respectively. *Raising the primary education completion rates of poor children in many developing countries is therefore more likely to lead to larger increases in school attainment than simply increasing the completion rates of girls.*

Filmer finds that *schooling attainment patterns vary widely by country and require different policy solutions.* Where all children attend some school and the poor increasingly drop out over the course of the basic education cycle, for example, policies stimulating the demand for, rather than access to, schooling are likely to be more effective. Where there is a large gap between rich and poor upon school entry, a combination of demand and supply policies, including improvements to educational quality, are more likely to be suitable.

Chapter 7, by Marlaine Lockheed, is a good complement to chapter 6. It shows how education systems are failing to reach and teach large numbers of children, particularly girls. Based on regression analyses of the association between the school participation of girls and the degree of country heterogeneity in 120 countries, the chapter contends that within any given country, gender intensifies the impact of structural impediments to education. Girls from excluded social groups are less likely to enroll in school, complete fewer years of schooling, and are less likely to complete primary or attend secondary school. Among nonmajority ethnic groups in Nigeria, for example, Hausa-speaking girls are 35 percent less likely than Yoruba-speaking boys to attend school. In Pakistan, only 10 percent of rural girls in Baluchistan complete primary school, as compared to 40 percent of Baluchistani boys, 55 percent of urban Punjabi girls, or 65 percent of urban Punjabi boys.

The chapter presents a variety of creative approaches for reaching and teaching socially excluded girls. It then proposes actions on two fronts: improving and diversifying the supply of education, and creating incentives for households to send girls to school. *On the supply side, education policies need to address discrimination and broaden school options.* Parental concerns about the physical safety of their daughters may make community and nonformal alternative schools, for example, more attractive than regular public schools. In Rajasthan, India, community schools employing paraprofessional teachers and part-time workers who escort girls from excluded groups to school have increased their enrollment, attendance, and test scores relative to those of regular public schools. Preschool programs in Bolivia, Brazil, and Turkey that involve both mothers and children from excluded groups have been effective in reducing children's subsequent dropout rates from primary school, as well as boosting their achievement.

On the demand side, proposed incentives for households to send girls to school include conditional cash transfers, scholarships, stipends, and school feeding programs. Although the middle-income countries of Chile, Malaysia, and Mexico have pioneered initiatives to reach excluded social groups, low-income countries will need external support to finance needed initiatives, such as creating Girls' Education Evaluation Funds. Such efforts would help expand the knowledge base about what works in reaching excluded girls, especially in Africa, where 40 percent of such girls reside.

In chapter 8, Changu Mannathoko examines the *various frameworks that have been used to help meet EFA and MDG education goals.* Specifically, she describes how the application of the women in development (WID), gender and development (GAD), poststructural, and rights-based approaches contribute differently to gender equality and quality education.

The WID framework focuses on access, that is, on expanding schooling to ensure that girls and women are educated and can therefore contribute more effectively to economic development and poverty reduction. This approach generates clear policy directives on issues such as the employment of more women teachers, tracking the number of girls and women in and out of school, overcoming barriers to girls' education, and realizing the benefits of schooling. One intervention championed in this approach is the creation of boarding facilities to allow girls in remote and sparsely populated areas to attend school.

The GAD framework highlights the complexities that surround changing education as a whole, as well as school institutions, to make schooling gender sensitive. Unlike WID, the GAD approach focuses on the impact of gender on the education of both boys and girls. This framework encourages such initiatives as the provision of complementary basic education programs for excluded girls; gender-sensitive and gender-equalizing curricula; gender-balanced make-up of teaching and nonteaching staff; making schools and school grounds physically and psychologically safe for girls; providing adequate facilities for personal hygiene; and policies to fight discrimination, harassment, and abuse.

The poststructural framework critiques schools as institutions that marginalize and diminish the power of local indigenous knowledge. This approach focuses on the fact that gender involves shifting processes of identification and questions the methodologies by which research participants objectify the identities of girls and women into gender "constructs." The approach argues that girls and boys should be given space to challenge such constructs and reclaim their power to be heard as experts on their own gender and sexuality.

The rights-based approach considers gender equality in education to be a function of the *right to education* (access and participation), *rights within education* (gender-sensitive environments, processes, and outcomes), and *rights through education* (that is, the links between quality education and wider gender justice in society). This approach is based on the major global agreements on human rights: the Universal Declaration of Human Rights, the Convention on the Rights of the Child, the Beijing Declaration, and the EFA Dakar Declaration.

The chapter concludes with a description of the child-friendly schools (CFS) initiative of UNICEF. Launched in the early 1990s, CFS is a holistic, comprehensive approach to quality education that addresses the major gender equality concerns of all four frameworks explored in the chapter. The initiative is being used by 50 countries worldwide to foster girl-friendly environments in education.

In chapter 9, Michelle Akpo discusses the perpetuation of gender-based violence in Benin, which remains culturally accepted despite the adoption of new laws to prevent the practice. Fearful of receiving poor marks or having to repeat a grade—or desperate for the monetary compensation they are offered—girls in Benin often submit to unwanted sexual advances from teachers. Such encounters often lead them to drop out of school; in many cases, the girls become pregnant, have unsafe abortions, contract HIV/AIDS and other sexually transmitted diseases, and even die. The prevalence of such violence in schools negatively affects not only girls' educational performance, but also their educational achievements, self-esteem, and health (physical and psychological). Ultimately, such treatment of women leads to a loss in national productivity.

The new laws on this social ill have not been adequately implemented or enforced, partly because the national judiciary system in Benin is very weak. Until recently, moreover, the subject of gender-based violence was considered taboo and not discussed. To date, there are no official channels through which victims of abuse can confidentially report incidents and get help. The general public is also largely unaware of citizens' rights, and victims often fail to understand that perpetrators of sexual violence have committed illegal acts. The chapter recommends aggressive public campaigns to achieve public awareness and behavioral change, as well engaging political leaders at the community level on the issue.

In chapter 10, Jackie Kirk discusses the enormous challenges of education in conflict-torn countries, concluding that *children must be educated even in the midst of emergencies and violent conflicts*. About half of all primary school-age children who are not in school live in conflict-affected or fragile states. Thousands more live in areas affected by natural disasters. The situation is particularly dire for refugees and internally displaced persons, only about 3 percent of whom have access to education.

All children living in crisis-affected countries suffer disadvantages, but the effects of crises on the schooling of girls are greater than on the schooling of boys. Of the 43 million children who live in crisis-affected countries worldwide and are not in school, more than half are girls. Practical, economic imperatives of survival and reconstruction take priority over education, especially for girls and women. The heightened risk of sexual violence, both during and after armed conflicts, also hurts the educational prospects of girls. Many parents consequently keep their daughters at home or marry them at young ages out of fear for their safety, with early marriage and motherhood generally putting an end to their schooling.

Crises and conflict may, however, create improved learning opportunities for girls, largely as a result of the involvement of community-based organizations and NGOs, as well as additional funding. In Pakistan, for example, opportunities for girls in many remote, mountainous communities are very limited. After the 2006 earthquake, however, many girls from these areas moved with their families to internally displaced persons camps in the valleys, where they attended school for the first time.

The Inter-Agency Network for Education in Emergencies (INEE) has created a set of minimum standards that provides a holistic framework for integrating gender equality and protection concerns across all aspects of education. In particular, the standards recognize the vulnerabilities of girls to sexual violence—violence that is more likely to occur if girls are attending school. The chapter concludes by recommending education programming in three specific areas: ensuring the strategic education of girls; integrating the issues of protection, proper restroom facilities, hygiene, and reproductive health into one programming area; and building the capacity of women as teachers and education leaders.

Part III: Experiences from the Field: How Was It Done?

Chapters 11–16 provide many examples of best practices for improving the education rates of girls worldwide, illustrating how different countries have addressed the economic and sociocultural issues that constrain girls' schooling. Efforts to improve access and quality are examined, together with the impact of school-based violence.

In chapter 11, Sakena Yacoobi describes a method of engaging communities to empower and educate women in Afghanistan. Successful implementation of this method in a Muslim culture is extraordinary—and holds great promise for other countries. As one of the most vulnerable groups of women in the world, Afghan women face multifaceted and complex problems on access to education. The chapter describes a successful program that offers health and education services to 350,000 women and children each year by operating within the context of Afghan culture and focusing at the grassroots level.

The main lesson of this program is that initiatives to empower and educate Afghan females must incorporate local cultural values and practices. In particular, the author argues that Western donors need to respect the strict custom of *purdah* (the veiling of women and segregation of the sexes in public) that prevails in Afghan villages and refugee settlements. She notes that, as practiced today, the custom is rooted in a combination of religious values, security concerns for women, and family honor. As Kaldor (1989) has observed, it is a tradition to be respected, *not a* problem to be solved.

The author counsels education programs that target women in Afghanistan to begin at the grassroots with locally identified needs, start with the least controversial service in the least conservative area, and take the time to build trust by forging personal relationships. More controversial educational programs should be offered only in a voluntary, culturally sensitive way after basic trust has been established.

In chapter 12, Filipe Barrera-Osorio compares the impact of abolishing school fees in several countries and concludes that *enrollment rates rise dramatically wherever fees are abolished, yet this change can be detrimental if schools do not receive compensation for the loss of needed resources.* Elimination of fees in Malawi in 1994, for example, increased net enrollment from 68 percent to 99 percent and gross enrollment from 89 percent to 113 percent in a single year. Yet the student-to-teacher ratio in the country soon reached 100 to 1, and the retention rate plunged to between 16 and 28 percent.

The chapter also argues that *user fees may increase efficiency and sustainability in the private sector.* Income targeting allows families that can afford higher fees to be charged accordingly, while low-income families are charged less. Fees, meanwhile, provide schools with the resources to finance everyday tasks and programs. Income-targeting instruments, argues the author, should have an important place in any discussion of abolishment of user fees. Other programs, such as conditional cash transfers and transportation programs, also reduce the direct costs of education. However, insufficient empirical evidence exists to determine the comparative cost effectiveness of the different types of programs.

In chapter 13, Mohammad Niaz Asadullah and Nazmul Chaudhury show how *financial incentives prompted madrassas (Islamic schools) in Bangladesh to modernize their curricula and open their doors to girls.* Concerned that the thousands of madrassas in the country were not preparing students for employment outside the religious sector, the government of Bangladesh offered madrassas cash incentives in the early 1980s on the condition that they teach science, mathematics, and English. A second reform, the Female Secondary School stipend program, introduced in the early 1990s, opened the madrassas to girls.

The modernization scheme converted many privately funded orthodox madrassas that eschewed the teaching of modern subjects into publicly funded schools that better suit national education goals. The converted madrassas are now registered with the government, follow state-mandated course outlines, use officially approved textbooks, and have become fiscally dependent on the state. Many employ female teachers (most of them graduates of secular schools) and educate girls, who make up almost half of their enrollees. These results suggest that with adequate incentives, religious educational institutions can play an important role in narrowing educational gaps—between genders, among economic classes, and between religious and secular schools—in countries with Muslim majorities.

In chapter 14, Richard Johanson and others examine the case for improving agricultural training, including that for women, in Africa. Strengthening the agricultural sector—which accounts for 40 percent of gross domestic product, 15 percent of exports, and 60–80 percent of employment in most African countries—is critical if Africa is to significantly raise living standards.

Agriculture education and training (AET) in African countries often does not respond to labor market demands for knowledge and practical competencies. The problem is particularly acute for skills in agribusiness, basic management, and problem solving. AET enrollment is declining, and only 20 percent of postsecondary students enrolled in agricultural science are women. Continuing neglect of agricultural training risks limiting both agricultural recovery and poverty reduction.

The authors conclude that a unique opportunity exists in Sub-Saharan Africa to support agricultural postsecondary education and improve the gender balance of this education at the same time. Among their recommendations are to train 1,000 new doctorates over the next 15 years and increase female enrollment in postsecondary agricultural programs through such instruments as quotas, earmarked scholarships, professional mentoring, and facilities that can accommodate women.

In chapter 15, Codou Diaw describes the achievements of the Forum for African Women Educationalists (FAWE), the leading NGO advocating for girls' education in Africa over the past 15 years. FAWE has established a strong network of grassroots organizations that promote the education of girls and women throughout Africa. The organization has mainstreamed gender-fair practices into national education policies in several countries, including reentry policies for young mothers. FAWE also promotes girls' participation in science, mathematics, and technology and has created gender-responsive school and pedagogy models.

The FAWE models have enabled many schools in Africa to become more sensitive to gender issues, enhancing the ability of teachers to make teaching and learning processes more inclusive for girls and boys. Promoting general equity in education is, however, an uphill endeavor that requires institutional and community-based partnerships. FAWE needs to continue to forge institutional relationships with Ministries of Education, preferably by means of memoranda of understanding on gender-fair education. At the same time, it must turn its focus to the community level—where the barriers to girls' education are most acute—by building the capacity of national FAWE chapters to conduct community-based advocacy.

In chapter 16, Tawfiq A. Al-Mekhlafy describes the achievements and challenges of improving the education of children, particularly girls, in Yemen—a country with an illiteracy rate of 45 percent (60 percent among women). Recognizing that universal primary education cannot be achieved by expanding access at the expense of quality, policy makers are seeking to improve both simultaneously. The government has accordingly built new schools and additional classrooms, rehabilitated others, and added lavatories (which make schools more acceptable to girls and their families). It has also launched cash and noncash incentive programs based on school attendance and offers certain incentives, such as exemption from fees for textbooks, specifically to increase girls' enrollment and retention rates. The government has also hired more female teachers and created a Girls' Education Sector in the Ministry of Education, headed by a (female) deputy minister.

The jump in educational enrollment rates in Yemen has been impressive, particularly by girls, whose enrollment at the basic school level (grades 1–9) grew 86 percent between 1997 and 2003. The corresponding gain in boys' enrollment was more modest, at only 14 percent. Growth in enrollment in secondary school over the same period was similarly lopsided: 162 percent for girls and 60 percent for boys. In the wake of this huge expansion, however, schools are starting to complain about budget shortages resulting from the abolition of textbook fees.

The author considers the gender gap in education in Yemen to be more truly a problem of development. He concludes that the sustainability of its education reforms, as well as progress in poverty reduction, will depend on the economic development of rural areas, which make up 70 percent of the country.

Conclusion

In chapter 17, Mercy Tembon discusses the implications of the previous chapters and makes recommendations for future World Bank operations to improve girls' education. Specifically, she presents an evidence-based plan framed around five strategic directions:

- *Quality:* developing an outcomes approach to gender equality in education
- *Access and equity:* scaling up good practices and focusing on the neediest and excluded groups of girls
- *Postprimary education:* investing in postprimary education for girls
- *Research and analysis:* investing in gathering and analyzing the empirical data needed to inform policy and decision making
- *Partnerships:* promoting partnerships with development agencies, as well as nonprofit organizations and the private sector, to more effectively enable developing countries to improve equity and quality in education

On educational *quality*, stakeholders are advised to establish standards that define what boys and girls should learn and be able to do at various levels of education, and then define outcome indicators to measure the achievement of those standards. Improving the quality of teachers at both the primary and secondary levels—particularly training instructors in more participative and gender-sensitive pedagogical methods—is a crucial aspect of raising educational quality. Addressing school-based violence through grassroots initiatives involving community organizations, as well as equipping girls and boys with the behavioral skills to protect themselves from HIV/AIDS, are other critical interventions needed to improve educational quality.

On *access and equity*, Tembon recommends the development of comprehensive, inclusive educational policies at the national level, together with relevant implementation strategies. Specifically, both public and private educational resources need to be targeted at marginalized groups; otherwise, programs have no chance of succeeding. Creating links between the nonformal and formal education sectors will also expand educational access, particularly for children and adolescents who have dropped out of school or never enrolled. Building and equipping schools in remote and low-enrollment areas may also be needed to enable girls to attend schools located at a culturally acceptable distance from home.

Postprimary education for girls needs to be expanded, particularly in remote regions, a task that will require mobilizing additional resources from both the public and private sectors. Secondary education, where the returns to female education are highest, is particularly important if girls are to acquire the skills and competencies needed to enter the labor market and become economically empowered. A combination of incentives that stimulates both demand for this level of education (for example, stipends, scholarships, free textbooks and learning materials, safe and affordable transportation schemes, community awareness campaigns) and its supply (for example, building more secondary schools in remote areas or, alternatively, building boarding facilities for existing schools) is recommended to increase girls' educational attainment. Moreover, education at the secondary level should encourage more girls to study science, technology, and mathematics—perhaps through cross-curricular programs that confound traditional gendered associations. Furthermore, linking secondary education directly to local work opportunities is necessary to improve graduates' employment prospects and, accordingly, enrollment demand.

Expanded *research and analysis*, both of current and future interventions in education, is urgently needed to investigate what does and does not work in improving the status of education in developing countries. The most serious knowledge gaps about gender inequalities in education need to be identified and filled. Little, for example, is understood about the social and cultural determinants of girls' enrollment. Education interventions also need to establish effective monitoring and evaluation systems to identify and resolve problems during project implementation. Rigorous impact studies, and the funding to conduct them, are needed to determine the results of such interventions.

More coherent *partnerships* (among development agencies, governments, NGOs, and the private sector) are needed to address gender equality in education more effectively, avoid duplication of efforts, and maintain a focus on girls' educational achievement. Partnerships between schools and communities—particularly partnerships at the grassroots level that directly involve mothers in the education of their daughters—will both reduce the financial cost of educating girls and increase accountability and sustainability. Forging partnerships with the media to communicate messages about the importance of girls' education and its benefits is also critical for building societal support for female education goals.

Tembon concludes by examining the implications of these five strategic directions on World Bank operations. They require that gender considerations become a part of the design and implementation of all education sector programs. The author argues in particular for the Bank to switch its primary gender-equality focus to secondary education, while maintaining programs to improve equity and quality at the primary level. For research and analysis, the Bank needs to establish systems for gathering gender-disaggregated data on educational projects and conduct more impact studies of education interventions. Without sustained efforts to study impact, she contends, it will be difficult to determine whether successful projects can be replicated in other countries or regions. Finally, the way forward for the Bank means working in close partnership with other development agencies engaged in improving education in the developing world, and with businesses and philanthropic organizations.

Note

1. Third World Conference on Women in Nairobi in 1985, Fourth World Conference on Women in Beijing in 1995, and Fifth World Conference on Women in Beijing +10 in 2005.

References

Kaldor, K. 1989. "Assisting Skilled Women." *Afghan Studies Journal* 1 (2): 21–34.

UNESCO (United Nations Educational, Scientific, and Cultural Organization). 2006. *Education for All: Literacy For Life.* EFA Global Monitoring Report. Paris: UNESCO.

World Bank. 2006. *Gender Equality as Smart Economics: A World Bank Group Action Plan.* Washington, DC: World Bank.

CHAPTER 2

Schooling, Gender Equity, and Economic Outcomes

Eric A. Hanushek

Improving schools is frequently high on the policy agenda of both developed and developing countries. The nature of the policy focus, however, differs across countries, with some emphasizing increasing school attainment and others focusing on quality concerns. Until recently, little evidence was very useful in helping decision makers formulate appropriate schooling policies. In the past decade, however, there has been a dramatic increase in useful information about the role of human capital in development.[1] The benefits of investing in human capital are especially pertinent for women in developing countries, where gender equity in education is often lagging.

This chapter reviews evidence on the economic impact of human capital investment, considering in particular where investment decisions might be made. Although the beneficial impact of investment is quite clear, the evidence on how best to make that investment is less clear. Specifically, recent research underscores the prime importance of educational quality, as measured by cognitive achievement, and the much lower importance of pure school attainment. This research spans both developed and developing nations.

Many arguments support policies of investments in schooling for girls and women, not the least of which is that basic equity demands it. But perhaps the easiest case is made in terms of the simple economic benefits. The first-order analysis is that women are equal to men in their potential contribution to economic outcomes, and this equality implies a huge untapped reservoir of talent in many developing countries.

There are additional arguments that point to the greater impact of investments in female education. First, such investments lead to increased labor force participation and a subsequent expansion of the economy. Second, a variety of positive health outcomes for women and their families are known to flow from increased education. Third, education generally leads to lower fertility rates. Fourth, as primary caregivers, women have a key role in the intergenerational transmission of knowledge.

As powerful as these additional benefits may be, the case for increased investments in girls' education is nonetheless easy to make on the simple benefits to the economy. The remainder of this chapter documents these key economic outcomes and relates them directly to policy choices.

Schooling as an Investment in Human Capital

Governments around the world place considerable emphasis on investments in human capital through the provision of schooling. And this focus carries through to international agencies such as the World Bank, which also emphasizes the provision of schooling. The underlying message is that human capital is important for individuals and for nations. At the same time, human capital—identified as the stock of productive skills of an individual—is an abstract concept. Both researchers and policy makers must transform the concept into practical terms that can be studied and translated into policy.

The genius of early researchers, led by Jacob Mincer (1970, 1974), was to recognize that different amounts of schooling signified different amounts of human capital and thus could be a clear measure of the abstract idea of human capital. From a research perspective, various census and survey databases routinely provide school attainment information that can be linked to incomes and other individual outcomes. From a policy perspective, school attainment is also a concrete notion—leading virtually all countries of the world to devote attention to rates of school completion and the promotion of access to further schooling.

The worldwide quest to improve schooling is highlighted in the developing world by the establishment of the Education for All (EFA) movement (headed by the United Nations Educational, Scientific, and Cultural Organization,UNESCO) and the Millennium Development Goals (MDG) of the United Nations. The EFA initiative grew out of the World Summit on Education in 1990 and was given more specificity in the Dakar Summit in 2000. The key elements of the EFA initiative (all to be accomplished by 2015) are

- expand early childhood care and education;
- provide free and compulsory primary education for all;
- promote learning and life skills for young people and adults;
- increase adult literacy by 50 percent;
- achieve gender parity by 2005 and gender equality by 2015; and
- improve the quality of education.

While each of the goals has received attention in annual monitoring reports (see, for example, UNESCO 2005), it is clear that schooling attainment largely drives the movement. The eight MDGs, developed in 2000, cover a range of issues, including health, nutrition, and the environment, but the second goal is achieving universal primary education.[2] Again the focus is raising school attainment to at least the primary schooling level everywhere.

This discussion begins with a review of the evidence on the value of added years of schooling.[3] The discussion then turns to issues of educational quality. The perspective taken is that school attainment is just one possible proxy for human capital and that other plausible proxies may be superior, particularly in an international context. Specifically, using cognitive achievement tests in math and science provides a superior measure of international differences in human capital. Moreover, focusing on cognitive skills changes the policy issues noticeably.

The Impact of School Attainment on Economic Growth

Policy debates rarely devote much time to discussing the importance of increasing school attainment. It is, after all, well known that further schooling has a large payoff. The innovative analyses by Mincer (1970, 1974) considered how investing in different amounts of schooling affects individual earnings, and over the last 30 years, literally hundreds of such studies have been conducted around the world. These studies have been reviewed in many interpretative articles, including Psacharopoulos (1994); Psacharopoulos and Patrinos (2004); and Heckman, Lochner, and Todd (2006).

By all accounts, the rate of return to additional years of schooling is large. In estimates of Mincer earnings functions for 98 countries, Psacharopoulos and Patrinos (2004) found that average returns for the world are above 17 percent, and they are systematically higher in developing countries (see table 2.1).[4]

These findings have been reinforced in analyses of the relationship between schooling and economic growth. The standard method to estimate the effect of education on economic growth is to estimate cross-country growth regressions where countries' average annual growth in gross domestic product (GDP) per capita over several decades is expressed as a function of measures of schooling and a set of other variables deemed to be important for economic growth.

The problem, of course, is that cross-country comparisons of average years of schooling implicitly assume that a year of schooling delivers the same increase in knowledge and skills regardless of the education system. For example, a year of schooling in Peru is assumed to create the same increase in productive human capital as a year of schooling in Hong Kong. Moreover, this measure assumes that formal schooling is the primary (sole) source of education and, again, that variations in the quality of non-school factors have a negligible effect on education outcomes. This neglect of cross-country differences in the quality of education is probably the major drawback of such a quantitative measure of schooling, and we come back to this issue in great detail below.

Table 2.1   Private Rates of Return to Investment in Education, by Level and Region
(percent)

Region or group	Primary	Secondary	Higher
Asia[a]	20.0	15.8	18.2
Europe, Middle East, and North Africa[a]	13.8	13.6	18.8
Latin America and the Caribbean	26.6	17.0	19.5
OECD countries	13.4	11.3	11.6
Sub-Saharan Africa	37.6	24.6	27.8
World	26.6	17.0	19.0

Source: Psacharopoulos and Patrinos 2004.

Note: a. Excluding member countries of the Organisation for Economic Co-operation and Development.

The Impact of Educational Quality on Economic Growth

Researchers are now able to document that the earnings advantages to higher cognitive skills, as measured by achievement on standardized tests, are quite substantial. These results are derived from different specific approaches, but the basic underlying analysis involves estimating a standard Mincer earnings function and adding a measure of individual cognitive skills.

Three U.S. studies provide direct and consistent estimates of the impact of test performance on earnings (Lazear 2003; Mulligan 1999; Murnane and others 2000). These studies employed different nationally representative data sets from the United States that followed students after they left school and entered the labor force. When test scores are standardized, they suggest that one standard deviation increase in mathematics performance at the end of high school translates into 12 percent higher annual earnings.[5]

Measures of Educational Quality in Developing Countries. Questions remain about whether the clear effects of educational quality in the United States generalize to developing countries. The literature on returns to cognitive skills in developing countries is restricted to a relatively limited number of countries: Ghana, Kenya, Morocco, Pakistan, South Africa, and Tanzania.

The evidence for developing countries is difficult to summarize easily.[6] Nonetheless, the available estimates permit a tentative conclusion that the returns to quality may be even larger in developing countries than in developed countries (Hanushek and Wößmann, forthcoming). This, of course, would be consistent with the range of estimates for returns to quantity of schooling (Psacharopoulos 1994; Psacharopoulos and Patrinos 2004), which are frequently interpreted as indicating diminishing marginal returns to schooling.

Evidence also suggests that educational quality is directly related to school attainment in developing countries. In Brazil, a country plagued by high rates of grade repetition and ultimate school dropouts, Harbison and Hanushek (1992) showed that higher cognitive skills in primary school lead to lower repetition rates. Further, Hanushek, Lavy, and Hitomi (2008) found that lower-quality education, measured by lower value-added to cognitive achievement, lead to higher dropout rates in Egyptian primary schools. Thus, as found for developed countries, the full economic impact of higher educational quality comes in part through greater school attainment.

This relationship between educational quality and school attainment also means that actions that improve quality of education will yield a bonus in meeting goals for attainment. Conversely, simply attempting to expand access and attainment—for example, by starting a large number of low-quality schools—will be self-defeating to the extent that low quality prompts reactions (such as dropping out) that affect the attainment results.

The estimates of the individual earnings functions show relative earnings within each country associated with both school attainment and achievement. They do not, however, permit direct comparisons across countries in the value of skills. For country comparisons, it is appropriate to return to differences in aggregate growth rates—focusing, however, on the cognitive skills of individuals in different countries.

Cognitive Skills Tests as Measures of Quality. Since the mid-1960s, international agencies have conducted many international tests of students' performance in cognitive skills such as mathematics and science. The different tests contain both "academic" questions related to the school curricula and "life skill" questions requiring practical applications to real-world phenomena. There have been 12 testing occasions that present results from a total of 36 separate test observations at different age levels and in different subjects. As discussed below, these results are difficult to put on a common scale. Nevertheless, it becomes obvious that the students from developing countries that participated in the tests performed dramatically worse than students from any country in the Organisation for Economic Co-operation and Development (OECD). The variation in the quality of education that exists among OECD countries is already substantial, but the magnitude of the difference in developing countries in the average amount of learning that has taken place after a given number of years of schooling dwarf any within-OECD difference.

Cognitive Skills and Economic Growth. Over the past 10 years, empirical growth research has demonstrated that consideration of the quality of education, measured by the cognitive skills learned, dramatically alters the assessment of the role of education in the process of economic development. When using the data from the international student achievement tests through 1991 to build a measure of education quality, Hanushek and Kimko (2000) found a statistically and economically significant positive effect of the quality of education on economic growth in 1960–1990 that dwarfs the association between quantity of education and growth. Thus, even more than in the case of education and individual earnings, ignoring quality differences very significantly misses the true importance of education for economic growth. Their estimates suggest that one country-level standard deviation higher test performance would yield around one percentage point higher annual growth rates.

This analysis has been extended to a larger group of countries and to economic performance through 2000 in Jamison, Jamison, and Hanushek (2007). The growth estimation relies upon the development of a consistent set of achievement estimates that rescale the various international tests to be comparable; those rescaled estimates are being developed in Hanushek and Wößmann (in process).[7] Hanushek and Wößmann (forthcoming) also use these data to extend the analysis of growth in a variety of ways.

The Hanushek and Wößmann (forthcoming) measure of the quality of education is a simple average of the math and science scores over all the international tests between 1964 and 2003. They interpret these data as a proxy for the average education performance of the whole labor force. This measure encompasses overall cognitive skills, not just those developed in schools. Thus, whether skills are developed at home, in schools, or elsewhere, they are included in the growth analyses.[8] After controlling for the initial level of GDP per capita and for years of schooling, the test-score measure features a statistically significant effect on the growth in real GDP per capita in 1960–2000. According to this basic specification, test scores that are larger by one standard deviation (measured at the student level across all OECD countries in the Programme for International Student Assessment [PISA]) are associated with an average annual growth rate in GDP per capita that is two percentage points higher over the whole 40-year period.

Moreover, once educational quality is included in the cross-country growth regressions, school attainment appears to have little or no role in growth. This finding is extraordinarily important and the subject of the policy discussion below.

Three issues are particularly important for understanding the role of human capital on economic performance in developing countries. First, educational quality is surely not the only thing that is important in determining growth, and many have emphasized the role of economic institutions. Second, the cross-country analysis is dominated by developed countries, and the impacts of educational quality may not be the same across all countries. Third, concentrating on just the average cognitive skills of a population can mask significant variations in educational quality within countries, particularly within developing countries.

The Role of Economic Institutions. While the evidence confirms an independent effect of educational quality on economic growth, this effect may differ depending on the economic institutions of a country. North (1990), for example, emphasized that the institutional framework plays an important role in shaping the relative profitability of piracy versus productive activity. If the available knowledge and skills are used in piracy , the effect on economic growth is likely to be substantially different than if they were used in production—and may even be negative. Similarly, Murphy, Shleifer, and Vishny (1991) showed that the allocation of talent between rent seeking and entrepreneurship matters for economic growth: countries with relatively more law students grow faster, and countries with relatively more engineering majors grow more slowly. Easterly (2002) argued that education may not have much impact in the less-developed countries that lack other facilitating factors, such as functioning institutions for markets and legal systems. In a similar way, Pritchett (2001, 2006) suggested that deficiencies in the institutional environment might render the average effect of education on growth across all countries negligible.

To address these issues, both Jamison, Jamison, and Hanushek (2007) and Hanushek and Wößmann (forthcoming) incorporate measures of economic institutions in their analyses. These measures include the openness of a country's economy over the latter half of the 20th century and the strength of property rights in the country. Two findings emerge from these extensions. First, economic institutions are indeed important. But, second, the role of educational quality remains, even in the face of different economic institutions. If anything, economic institutions and educational quality are complementary: better economic institutions leads to stronger impacts of educational quality.

An important issue is whether the role of educational quality holds for developing countries. If the sample is separated into OECD countries and non-OECD countries, the results of the analysis are remarkably similar (see Hanushek and Wößmann, forthcoming). The effect of educational quality on economic growth does not differ significantly between the two groups of countries. The results remain qualitatively the same when openness and quality of institutions are again added as control variables. Alternatively, it is possible to divide the sample into countries above and below the sample median of initial GDP per capita. Educational quality remains significant in both subsamples, but the effect of quality is considerably larger in the low-income countries. Thus, if anything, the effect of educational quality is larger in developing countries than in developed countries.

Gender Equity. It is useful at this point to return to the question of gender equity and investments in girls' education. The simple idea here is that females represent an untapped resource in many countries. There have been dramatic gains in reducing the disparity of school attainment by girls (UNESCO 2005). It is also clear that the gains have not been uniform across countries.

There are some inconsequential cognitive skill differences between boys and girls (OECD 2004). In almost all countries, girls are found to read better, but boys do better at math. However, for economic purposes, the differences appear to net out to zero. It brings the discussion back to the starting point: changing educational quality is most important and applies equally to boys and girls.

Education Reforms to Improve Quality

The previous estimation provides information about the long-run economic implications of improvements in educational quality. These analyses provide a means for linking policy reforms directly to the pattern of economic outcomes. Two aspects of any education reform plan are important: the magnitude of the reform that is accomplished and the time it takes for any reform to achieve its results.

Consider a schooling reform that yields a moderately strong improvement in average achievement of school completers (defined technically to mean an improvement of 0.5 standard deviation). Moving the average achievement of students in Brazil, Indonesia, Mexico, and Thailand, for example, would close half the gap with the average OECD student and would be considered a moderately strong improvement.

The timing of the reform is also important, and two aspects of timing are crucial. First, improvements in student performance cannot be achieved instantaneously; they require changes in schools that will be accomplished over time (for example, by systematic replacement of teachers through retirements and subsequent hiring). The timeline of any reform is difficult to specify, but achieving an improvement of 0.5 standard deviation for an entire nation may realistically take 20 to 30 years. Second, if the reforms succeed, their impact on the economy will not be felt until the new graduates become a noticeable portion of the labor force.

Figure 2.1 simulates the impact on the economy of reform policies taking 10, 20, or 30 years for a moderately strong (0.5 standard deviation) improvement in student outcomes at the end of upper secondary schooling. For the calibration, policies are assumed to begin in 2005, so that a 20-year reform would be complete in 2025.[9]

The figure indicates how much larger the level of overall GDP is at any point after the reform policy has begun compared with the level that would prevail with no reform. In other words, the estimates suggest the increase in GDP expected over and above any growth resulting from other factors.

Obviously, for any magnitude of improvement in achievement, a faster reform will have larger impacts on the economy. But figure 2.2 shows that even a 20- or 30-year reform plan has a powerful impact on GDP. For example, a 20-year plan would yield a GDP that was 5 percent greater in 2037 (compared with where the economy would be with no increase in educational quality). The figure also plots educational spending as 3.5 percent of GDP, an aggressive spending level in many countries of the world. An increase of 5 percent of GDP is significantly greater than the typical country's spending on all primary and secondary schooling—a significant change that would permit the growth dividend to more than cover *all* primary and secondary school spending. But even a 30-year reform program (which would not be fully accomplished until 2035) would yield more than 5 percent higher real GDP by 2041. Over a 75-year horizon, a 20-year reform yields a real GDP that is 36 percent higher than would occur with no change in educational quality.

Policy Objectives

Governments generally have multiple objectives when they develop schooling policies. They are concerned about the economic well-being of citizens and the nation as a whole. But they are also concerned about the distribution of economic outcomes.

The previous analysis has suggested educational quality should be the primary focus—because quality is the dominant factor affecting economic outcomes. However, the push to expand access clearly has deep roots in the distributional objective of governments by making sure that all citizens can obtain schooling. Clearly, the absence of schools means that government policy toward promoting human capital cannot be effective.

Figure 2.1   Improved GDP with Moderately Strong Knowledge Improvement

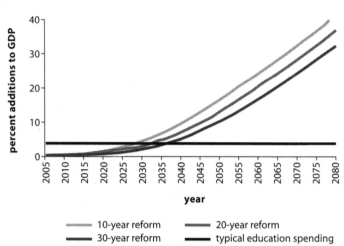

Source: Author's calculations based on data described in text.

Note: Moderately strong knowledge improvements are those with standard deviation of 0.5 or more.

Two aspects of the distributional side of governmental schooling policy are important. First, the strong message of the existing empirical work is that time in school has little payoff if the students are not learning. The student who attends eight years of school but comes away unable to read adequately is unlikely to reap many rewards from the schooling.

Second, the distribution of cognitive skills appears to be closely related to the distribution of earnings. Nickell (2004), employing the International Adult Literacy Survey data, finds a close association between skill variation and earnings variation. As seen in figure 2.2, the spread of earnings mirrors the spread of cognitive skills. Although this does not establish causation, it is highly suggestive of the role of educational quality.

All of this suggests that merely erecting schools without concern for educational quality is unlikely to meet the human capital objectives of governments. Indeed, as suggested previously, low-quality schools may make it even more difficult to increase attainment because students respond to lack of quality.

Figure 2.2   Inequality of Educational Quality and Earnings

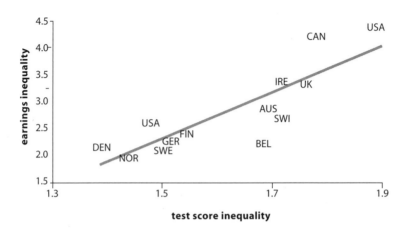

Source: Hanushek and Wößmann, forthcoming, as adapted from Nickell 2004.

Note: Measure of inequality is the ratio of ninth decile to first decile in both cases; test performance refers to prose literacy in the International Adult Literacy Survey.

The question, of course, is what portion of this evidence is relevant for developing countries. We know, for example, that the developing world is noticeably behind the rest of the world in terms of simple school enrollment rates. Table 2.2 provides recent information on net enrollment rates in primary school and gross enrollment rates for tertiary schooling. Developing countries are significantly behind others in primary schooling, and not surprisingly, this gap expands in tertiary schooling.

Don't these numbers show that the access and attainment problems should be paramount? The answer again is that low-quality schooling appears to confer few benefits. And the quality issue is real. For a selection of developing countries, Hanushek and Wößmann (forthcoming) calculate the proportion of recent students who both finish grade 9 *and* are minimally literate by OECD standards on the PISA tests. These calculations suggest that fewer than 10 percent of 15–19 year olds achieve that level in Brazil, Ghana, or South Africa. Fewer than 15 percent meet that standard in Peru, even though almost half of the population completes grade 9.

Table 2.2   Enrollment Rates by Development Status, 2004
(percent)

Group	Net enrollment rate in primary school	Gross enrollment rate in tertiary school
World	85.8	23.7
Countries in transition	90.7	54.2
Developed countries	95.8	64.9
Developing countries	84.6	16.2

Source: UNESCO 2007.

Thus, by all accounts, efforts to expand school attainment—which have been significant in recent years—may do little to meet the human capital goals of many developing countries.

Conclusion

Virtually every government is concerned about investments in human capital. These objectives must be put within context, because schooling is different from many publicly provided goods. First, schooling has direct implications for individual outcomes, for national aggregate outcomes, and for the distribution of outcomes across society. Thus, there is a direct economic relationship between government spending and the returns on investments. Second, schooling is not a homogenous commodity, but varies considerably in quality. The simple message of existing research is that the quality dimension is overwhelmingly important. Third, policies toward schools are heavily laden with politics that emanate both from students and parents, and from teachers and school personnel, making the specific policies quite contentious at times. It is ultimately very important for economic growth that countries pursue policies that are successful, even if they may be less popular in the short run.

All of these conclusions apply with greater force to a concentration on the education of girls. In simplest terms, women represent a vast additional resource for many economies. By effectively educating more women—that is, providing more women with a high-quality education—more will enter the labor market, and the economy will show the favorable results. Other justifications for educating women include the expected benefits for labor force participation, health, and children's education. But the simple direct impacts on the economy support a renewed and expanded effort to provide quality education to girls.

Notes

1. The relevance of information about human capital for development policy is described in Hanushek and Wößmann (2007).

2. The Millennium Declaration has eight objectives, initially set by a UN resolution in 2000 and adopted by 189 world leaders during the World Summit in 2005: eradicate extreme poverty and hunger; achieve universal primary education; promote gender equality and empower women; reduce child mortality; improve maternal health; combat HIV/AIDS, malaria, and other diseases; ensure environmental sustainability; and develop a global partnership for development.

3. Details of the underlying statistical analyses plus an extended set of references can be found in Hanushek and Wößmann (forthcoming).

4. The Mincer earnings function relates the logarithm of earnings to years of schooling, potential labor market experience, and other factors specific to individual studies (Mincer 1974). The coefficient on years of schooling in this regression can, under specific circumstances, be interpreted as the rate of return to schooling. However, Heckman, Lochner, and Todd (2006) offer a critique and interpretation of these analyses.

5. Because the units of measurement differ across tests, it is convenient to convert test scores into measures of the distribution of achievement across the population. A one-half standard deviation change would move somebody from the middle of the distribution (the 50th percentile) to the 69th percentile; a one standard deviation change would move this person to the 84th percentile. Because tests tend to follow a normal distribution, the percentile movements are largest at the center of the distribution.

6. See Alderman and others 1996; Angrist and Lavy 1997; Behrman, Ross, and Sabot 2008; Boissiere, Knight, and Sabot 1985; Glewwe 1996; Jolliffe 1998; Knight and Sabot 1990; and Moll 1998.

7. The rescaling uses performance of U.S. students over time (as measured by the National Assessment of Educational Quality, or NAEP) to calibrate the U.S. scores on different international tests. Then, by setting the variance of each test according to an OECD standardization group, each country and test can be equated.

8. Details of the data and analysis are found in Hanushek and Wößmann (forthcoming). The source of the income data is version 6.1 of the Penn World Tables (see also Heston, Summers, and Aten 2002), and the data on years of school-

ing are extended versions of the Cohen and Soto (2007) data described in Jamison, Jamison, and Hanushek (forthcoming).

9. The actual reform policy is presumed to operate linearly. So, for example, a 20-year reform that ultimately yielded achievement of 0.5 standard deviation improvement would see the performance of graduates increasing by 0.025 standard deviations each year over the period. It also assumes that the impact is proportional to the average achievement levels of prime-age workers, based on workers in the first 35 years of their working life.

References

Alderman, Harold, Jere R. Behrman, David R. Ross, and Richard Sabot. 1996. "The Returns to Endogenous Human Capital in Pakistan's Rural Wage Labor Market." *Oxford Bulletin of Economics and Statistics* 58: 29–55.

Angrist, Joshua D., and Victor Lavy. 1997. "The Effect of a Change in Language of Instruction on the Returns to Schooling in Morocco." *Journal of Labor Economics* 15 (S1): S48–S76.

Behrman, Jere R., David Ross, and Richard Sabot. 2008. "Improving the Quality versus Increasing the Quantity of Schooling: Estimates of Rates of Return from Rural Pakistan." *Journal of Development Economics* 85 (1–2): 94–104.

Boissiere, Maurice X., John B. Knight, and Richard H. Sabot. 1985. "Earnings, Schooling, Ability, and Cognitive Skills." *American Economic Review* 75 (5): 1016–1030.

Cohen, Daniel, and Marcelo Soto. 2007. "Growth and Human Capital: Good Data, Good Results." *Journal of Economic Growth* 12 (1): 51–76.

Easterly, William. 2002. *The Elusive Quest for Growth: An Economist's Adventures and Misadventures in the Tropics.* Cambridge, MA: The MIT Press.

Glewwe, Paul. 1996. "The Relevance of Standard Estimates of Rates of Return to Schooling for Educational Policy: A Critical Assessment." *Journal of Development Economics* 51: 267–290.

Hanushek, Eric A., and Dennis D. Kimko. 2000. "Schooling, Labor Force Quality, and the Growth of Nations." *American Economic Review* 90 (5): 1184–1208.

Hanushek, Eric A., Victor Lavy, and Kohtaro Hitomi. 2008. "Do Students Care about School Quality? Determinants of Dropout Behavior in Developing Countries." *Journal of Human Capital* 1 (2): 69–105.

Hanushek, Eric A., and Ludger Wößmann. 2007. *Education Quality and Economic Growth.* Washington, DC: World Bank.

———. Forthcoming. "The Role of Cognitive Skills in Economic Development." *Journal of Economic Literature.*

————. In process. *The Human Capital of Nations*.

Harbison, Ralph W., and Eric A. Hanushek. 1992. *Educational Performance of the Poor: Lessons from Rural Northeast Brazil*. New York: Oxford University Press.

Heckman, James J., Lance J. Lochner, and Petra E. Todd. 2006. "Earnings Functions, Rates of Return and Treatment Effects: The Mincer Equation and Beyond." In *Handbook of the Economics of Education*, eds. Eric A. Hanushek and Finis Welch. Amsterdam: North Holland.

Heston, Alan, Robert Summers, and Bettina Aten. 2002. *Penn World Table Version 6.1*. Philadelphia: Center for International Comparisons, University of Pennsylvania.

Jamison, Eliot A., Dean T. Jamison, and Eric A. Hanushek. 2007. "The Effects of Education Quality on Mortality Decline and Income Growth." *Economics of Education Review* 26 (6): 772–789.

Jamison, Jamison, and Hanushek. 2007. "The Effects of Education Quality on Income Growth and Mortality Decline." *Economics of Education Review* 26 (6), 777–788.

Jolliffe, Dean. 1998. "Skills, Schooling, and Household Income in Ghana." *World Bank Economic Review* 12 (1): 81–104.

Knight, John B., and Richard H. Sabot. 1990. *Education, Productivity, and Inequality: The East African Natural Experiment*. New York: Oxford University Press.

Lazear, Edward P. 2003. "Teacher Incentives." *Swedish Economic Policy Review* 10 (3): 179–214.

Mincer, Jacob. 1970. "The Distribution of Labor Incomes: A Survey with Special Reference to the Human Capital Approach." *Journal of Economic Literature* 8 (1): 1–26.

————. 1974. *Schooling Experience and Earnings*. New York: National Bureau for Economic Research.

Moll, Peter G. 1998. "Primary Schooling, Cognitive Skills, and Wages in South Africa." *Economica* 65 (258): 263–284.

Mulligan, Casey B. 1999. "Galton versus the Human Capital Approach to Inheritance." *Journal of Political Economy* 107 (6): S184–S224.

Murnane, Richard J., John B. Willett, Yves Duhaldeborde, and John H. Tyler. 2000. "How Important Are the Cognitive Skills of Teenagers in Predicting Subsequent Earnings?" *Journal of Policy Analysis and Management* 19 (4): 547–568.

Murphy, Kevin M., Andrei Shleifer, and Robert W. Vishny. 1991. "The Allocation of Talent: Implications for Growth." *Quarterly Journal of Economics* 106 (2): 503–530.

Nickell, Stephen. 2004. "Poverty and Worklessness in Britain." *Economic Journal* 114 (494): C1–C25.

North, Douglass C. 1990. *Institutions, Institutional Change and Economic Performance.* New York: Cambridge University Press.

OECD (Organisation for Economic Co-operation and Development). 2004. *Learning for Tomorrow's World: First Results from PISA 2003.* Paris: Organisation for Economic Co-operation and Development.

Pritchett, Lant. 2001. "Where Has All the Education Gone?" *World Bank Economic Review* 15 (3): 367–391.

———. 2006. "Does Learning to Add Up Add Up? The Returns to Schooling in Aggregate Data." In *Handbook of the Economics of Education,* eds. Eric A. Hanushek and Finis Welch. Amsterdam: North Holland.

Psacharopoulos, George. 1994. "Returns to Investment in Education: A Global Update." *World Development* 22: 1325–1344.

Psacharopoulos, George, and Harry A. Patrinos. 2004. "Returns to Investment in Education: A Further Update." *Education Economics* 12 (2): 111–134.

UNESCO (United Nations Educational, Scientific and Cultural Organization). 2005. *Education for All: The Quality Imperative.* EFA Global Monitoring Report. Paris: UNESCO.

———. 2007. *Strong Foundations—Early Childhood Case and Education.* EFA Global Monitoring Report. Paris: UNESCO.

CHAPTER 3

Student Learning Outcomes in Mathematics from a Gender Perspective: What Does the International PISA Assessment Tell Us?

Andreas Schleicher

Introduction

Individuals and countries that invest heavily in education benefit economically and socially from that investment. Moreover, among the 30 member countries of the Organisation for Economic Co-operation and Development (OECD) with the largest expansion of college education over the last decade, most still see rising earnings differentials for college graduates, suggesting that an increase in knowledge workers has not led to a decrease in their pay (as has been the case for low-skilled workers). Skills are also a major factor driving economic growth and broader social outcomes, both in the world's most advanced economies and in those experiencing rapid development. The long-term effect of one additional year of education on economic output in the OECD ranges between 3 and 6 percent (OECD 2007a).

Technological developments also play a key role in economic growth, but these, too, depend closely on educational progress—and not just because tomorrow's knowledge workers and innovators require high lev-els of education. A highly educated workforce is a prerequisite for adopt-ing new technologies and increasing productivity. Together, skills and technology have flattened the world: all work that can be digitized, auto-mated, and outsourced can now be performed by the most effective and competitive individuals or enterprises, wherever they are located on the globe.

Although most countries have responded to the increasing demand for better skills by significantly raising qualification levels, these trends have been highly uneven among countries. Two generations ago, the Republic of Korea had the economic output of Afghanistan today and ranked 24 in terms of educational output among the OECD countries of today. Today Korea is the top OECD performer with regard to the proportion of suc-cessful school leavers, with 96 percent of each age cohort obtaining an upper secondary degree (see figure 3.1). In contrast, the United States slipped from rank 1 among OECD countries on this measure for adults born in the 1940s to rank 13 among those born in the 1970s, not because completion rates declined but because they have risen so much faster elsewhere.

Dramatic increases in the educational attainment of females underlie the fundamental changes that have taken place in the global talent pool. Indeed, in most industrial countries, women now are attaining university degrees at a higher rate than men. This trend reverses the pattern of two generations ago, when educational attainment was considerably higher among males (see figure 3.2). In the United States, for instance, 32 per-cent of men ages 55–64 years—the cohort that was of school age two gen-erations ago—have university degrees, compared with 27 percent of women. In contrast, today 25 percent of American men ages 25–34 years—people who went to school in recent years—have university degrees, while 33 percent of women in that same age group do. And in Japan, where male educational attainment still outstrips that of women, the gap has narrowed. Two generations ago, 22 percent of Japanese men and 5 percent of Japanese women had university degrees; today the rates are 35 and 21 percent, respectively (OECD 2007a).

Figure 3.1   Growth in Baseline Qualifications

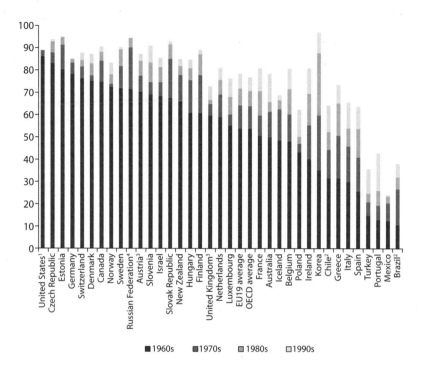

Source: OECD education database.

Note:
1. Excluding ISCED 3C short programs.
2. Year of reference is 2004.
3. Including some ISCED 3C short programs.
4. Year of reference is 2005.

Gender Differences in Mathematics Performance

As noted above, females have made significant progress over the past 40 years in reducing historic educational disparities relative to males. In more than two-thirds of OECD countries with comparable data, university-level graduate rates for women equal or exceed that of men. However, gender differences in mathematics and computer science graduates remain persistently high. On average, only 30 percent of OECD females graduate with a mathematics or computer science degree.

Figure 3.2   Gender Differences in University Attainment, in Percentage Points

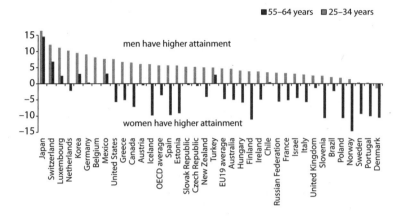

Source: OECD education database.

To some extent, this is reflected in the mathematics performance of 15-year-old males and females. The OECD Programme for International Student Assessment (PISA), the most comprehensive international effort to test student knowledge and skills, regularly compares the quality of learning outcomes across the principal industrial countries, which make up roughly nine-tenths of the world economy. The results from the PISA 2006 assessment show that in reading, girls were far ahead of boys in all OECD countries (figure 3.3); in mathematics, boys tended to outperform girls somewhat in most countries, even if gender differences in mathematics performance were generally modest, with boys overrepresented among top performers and boys and girls equally represented among low performers (figure 3.4). In science, the gender differences were mixed.

It is important to note that when students were assessed separately for analytical reasoning and problem-solving skills—some of the essential ingredients of mathematics performance—females tended to perform significantly better and, in many countries, outperformed male 15-year-olds in problem-solving (OECD 2004). This finding suggests that the lower performance of females in mathematics cannot be attributed to weaknesses in the cognitive competencies that underlie mathematics. More likely, it reflects the way in which these cognitive competencies are contextualized in mathematics instruction at school. This has important implications for educational policy and practice.

Figure 3.3   Performance of Males and Females on the Mathematics Scale in PISA 2006

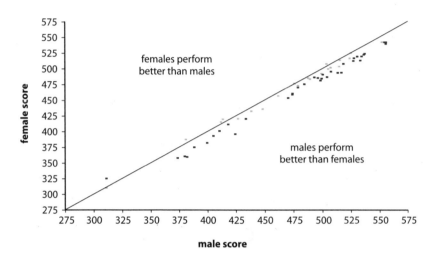

Source: OECD PISA 2006 database.

In most countries that are compared by PISA 2003 and 2006, gender differences are also larger within schools than they are overall, reflecting that females tend to attend higher-performing, academically oriented tracks and schools at a higher rate than males. Within these tracks and schools, however, females often perform significantly below males (OECD 2007b). From a policy perspective—and for teachers in class-rooms—gender differences in mathematics performance, therefore, warrant continued attention.

Figure 3.5 expresses gender differences in terms of effect sizes, so that results can be compared across a variety of measures, with an effect size of 0.20 used as a criterion to establish differences that warrant attention by policy makers. While gender differences in student performance in mathematics tend to be moderate (they are generally statistically signifi-cant, but they are not large when measured in terms of effect sizes), PISA 2003 shows marked differences between males and females in their inter-est in and enjoyment of mathematics, their self-related beliefs, as well as their emotions and learning strategies related to mathematics.

Among the 41 countries compared in PISA 2003, males in 21 coun-tries express stronger levels of interest in and enjoyment of mathematics

Figure 3.4   Performance of Males and Females on the Reading Scale in PISA 2006

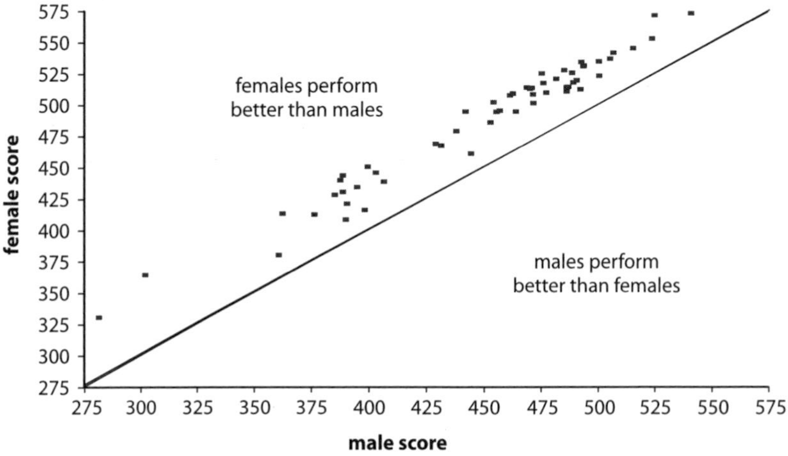

Source: OECD PISA 2006 database.

than females, with an average effect size of 0.21 (greater than 0.50 in Switzerland). Gender differences in instrumental motivation in mathematics tend to be even greater (the average effect size is 0.24) than the gender differences in interest in mathematics, suggesting that males may be more motivated to learn because they believe that mathematics will help them in their later careers.

A similar picture also emerges when looking at students' mathematics-related self-efficacy beliefs, self-concepts, and anxiety. Again, although females' performance is not much lower than males', females tend to report lower mathematics-related self-efficacy than males in almost all countries. The strongest effects are in Finland, the Netherlands, and Switzerland, as well as in the partner country Liechtenstein. Similar results emerge for students' self-concept in mathematics, where males tend to have a more positive view of their abilities than do females in most countries.

Females, for example, experience significantly greater feelings of anxiety, helplessness, and stress in mathematics classes than do males in 32 of 40 countries. Significantly higher levels of anxiety among females is also reported in Austria, Denmark, Finland, France, Germany, Luxembourg,

Macao-China, the Netherlands, Norway, Spain, Switzerland, and Tunisia.

For students' use of learning strategies, gender differences are less pronounced. Nevertheless, although gender patterns in the use of memorization are not widely apparent, in 28 of the 40 countries with available data, males consistently report using elaboration strategies more often than females. Conversely, females in 21 countries report using control strategies more often than males. This suggests that females are more likely to adopt a self-evaluating perspective during the learning process. Females might benefit from training in the use of elaboration strategies, and males might benefit from more general assistance in planning, organizing, and structuring learning activities (OECD 2004).

Policy Implications

For much of the past century, the content of school mathematics curricula was dominated by the need to provide the foundations for the professional training of a small number of mathematicians, scientists, and engineers. With the growing role of science, mathematics, and technology in modern life, however, the objectives of personal fulfillment, employment, and full participation in society increasingly require that all adults, not just those aspiring to a scientific career, should be mathematically, scientifically, and technologically literate. The performance of a country's best students in mathematics and related subjects may have implications for the role that that country will play in tomorrow's advanced technology sector and for its overall international competitiveness. Conversely, deficiencies among lower-performing students in mathematics can have negative consequences for individuals' labor-market and earnings prospects and for their capacity to participate fully in society.

Not surprisingly, policy makers and educators alike attach great importance to mathematics education. Addressing the increasing demand for mathematical skills requires excellence throughout education systems, and it is therefore essential to monitor how well countries provide young adults with fundamental skills in this area. The wide disparities in student performance in mathematics within most countries suggest that excellence throughout education systems remains a remote goal; countries need to serve a wide range of student abilities, including those who perform exceptionally well and those most in need. At the same time, international comparisons show that strong performance for both genders, and indeed improvement, is possible. Whether in Asia (for example, Japan or

Figure 3.5 Gender Differences in Mathematics and Other Learning Characteristics as Measured by Effect Sizes

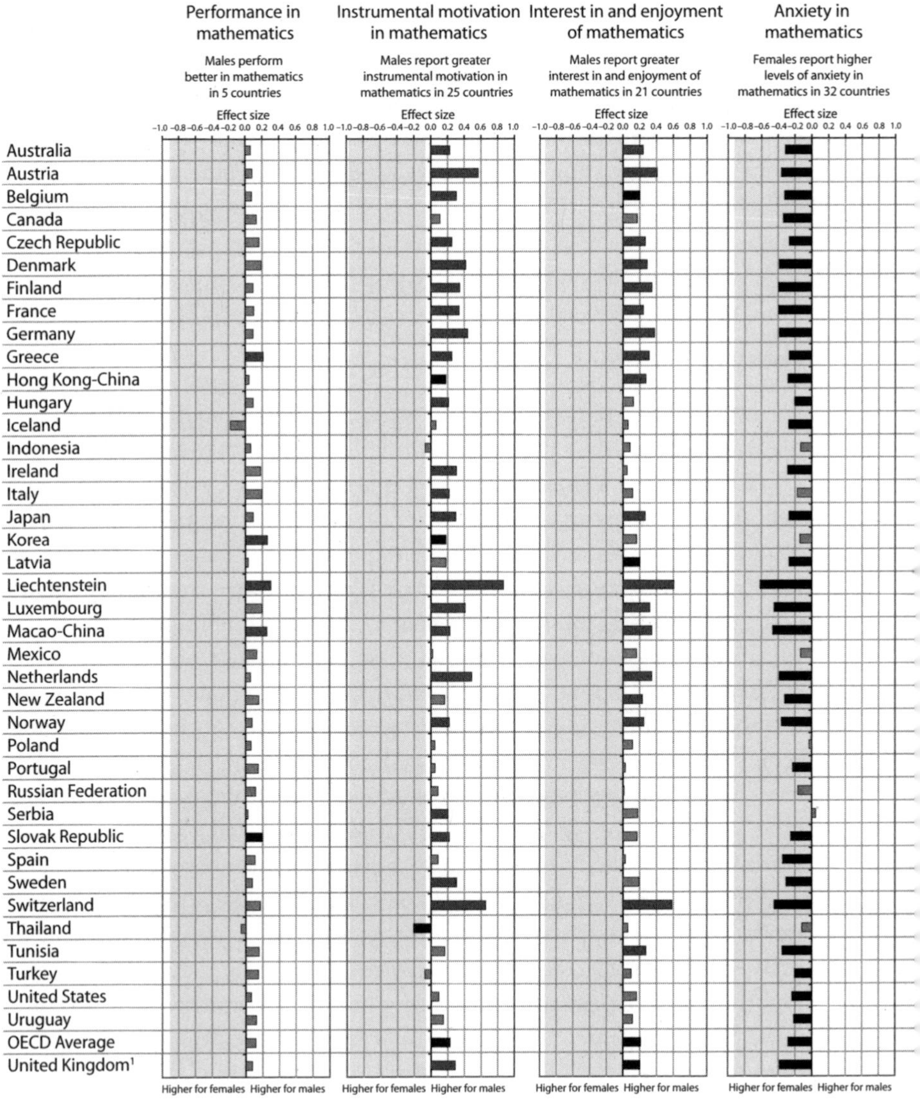
Performance in mathematics
Males perform better in mathematics in 5 countries
Instrumental motivation in mathematics
Males report greater instrumental motivation in mathematics in 25 countries
Interest in and enjoyment of mathematics
Males report greater interest in and enjoyment of mathematics in 21 countries
Anxiety in mathematics
Females report higher levels of anxiety in mathematics in 32 countries
Effect size
-1.0 -0.8 -0.6 -0.4 -0.2 0.0 0.2 0.4 0.6 0.8 1.0
Australia
Austria
Belgium
Canada
Czech Republic
Denmark
Finland
France
Germany
Greece
Hong Kong-China
Hungary
Iceland
Indonesia
Ireland
Italy
Japan
Korea
Latvia
Liechtenstein
Luxembourg
Macao-China
Mexico
Netherlands
New Zealand
Norway
Poland
Portugal
Russian Federation
Serbia
Slovak Republic
Spain
Sweden
Switzerland
Thailand
Tunisia
Turkey
United States
Uruguay
OECD Average
United Kingdom[1]
Higher for females
Higher for males

Source: OECD PISA 2003 database.

Note: Effect sizes equal to or greater than 0.20 are marked in darker color (see Annex A4).

1. Response rate too low to ensure comparability (see Annex A3).

Self-efficacy in mathematics	Self-concept in mathematics	Memorization strategies	Elaboration strategies	Control strategies
Males report greater efficacy in mathematics in 35 countries	Males report a stronger self-concept in mathematics in 5 countries	Males report greater use of memorization strategies in mathematics in 3 countries	Males report greater use of elaboration strategies in 28 countries	Females report greater use of control stategies in 8 countries
Effect size	Effect size	Effect size	Effect size	Effect size

Higher for females Higher for males   Higher for females Higher for males   Higher for females Higher for males   Higher for females Higher for males   Higher for females Higher for males

Korea), in Europe (for example, Finland) or in North America (for example, Canada), many countries display strong overall performance and, equally important, show that poor performance in school does not automatically follow from a disadvantaged socioeconomic background or relate to gender. Last but not least, some countries show that success can become a consistent and predictable educational outcome. In Finland, the country with the strongest overall PISA results, the performance variation between schools amounts to only 5 percent of overall student performance variation (OECD 2007b). Finnish parents can rely on high and consistent performance standards in whatever school they choose to enroll their children.

While females generally do not perform much below males in mathematics, they consistently report much lower interest in and enjoyment of mathematics, lower self-related beliefs, and much higher levels of helplessness and stress in mathematics classes. This reveals inequalities between the genders in the effectiveness with which schools and societies promote motivation and interest and, to an even greater extent, help students overcome anxiety about different subject areas. The performance of males and females at school, and their motivation and attitudes in different subject areas, can have a significant influence on their further educational and occupational pathways. These factors, in turn, may have an impact not only on individual career and salary prospects, but also on the broader effectiveness with which human capital is developed and used in economies and societies. At the same time, the wide variation in gender gaps among countries suggests that current differences are not the inevitable outcome of education and that effective policies and practices can overcome what were long taken to be the fixed outcomes of differences in interests, learning styles, and even underlying capacities between males and females.

Students' motivation, their positive self-related beliefs, and their emotions also affect their use of learning strategies. There are good grounds for this: high-quality learning is time and effort intensive. It involves controlling the learning process as well as explicitly checking relations between previously acquired knowledge and new information, formulating hypotheses about possible connections, and testing these hypotheses against the background of the new material. Learners are only willing to invest such effort if they have a strong interest in a subject or if there is a considerable benefit from high performance, with learners motivated by the external reward of performing well. Thus, students need to be willing to learn how to learn. From the perspective of teaching this implies that effective ways of learning—including goal setting, strategy selection, and the control and evaluation of the learning process—can and should be fostered by the educational setting and by teachers.

Research on ways of instructing students in learning strategies has shown that the development of learning expertise depends not only on the existence of a repertoire of cognitive and metacognitive information-processing abilities, but also on the readiness of individuals to define their own goals, to be proactive, to interpret success and failure appropriately, to translate wishes into intentions and plans, and to shield learning from competing intentions. A repertoire of strategies combined with other attributes that foster learning develops gradually through the practices of teachers who model learning behavior, through intricate activities aimed at building a scaffolding structure of learning for the student, and through analysis of the reasons for academic success and failure. During the process of becoming effective and self-regulated learners, students need assistance and feedback, not only on the results of their learning, but also on the learning process itself. In particular, the students with the weakest approaches to learning need professional assistance to become effective and self-regulated learners.

The links between students' self-related beliefs in mathematics and learning behaviors in mathematics that emerged from the analysis of the PISA 2003 results suggest that motivation and self-confidence are indispensable to outcomes that will foster lifelong learning. The combined effect of motivation and self-confidence on control strategies suggests that teaching a student how to learn autonomously is unlikely to work without strong motivation and self-confidence as a basis.

Finally, the finding that the profile of students' self-reported approaches to learning varies much more within schools than among schools also has policy implications, even if it does not imply that all schools are similar with regard to the learner characteristics of their intake. What it does highlight is the large variation in learner characteristics among students in each school. This underlines the importance for schools and teachers to be able to engage constructively with heterogeneity—not only in student abilities, but also in their characteristics as learners and their approaches to learning. It will not be sufficient to operate on the principle that "a rising tide raises all ships," since even in well-performing schools there are students who lack confidence and motivation and who are not inclined to set and monitor their own learning goals.

References

OECD (Organisation for Economic Co-operation and Development). 2004. *Problem Solving for Tomorrow's World—First Measures of Cross-Curricular Competencies from PISA 2003*. Paris: OECD.

———. 2007a. *Education at a Glance*. Paris: OECD.

———. 2007b. *PISA 2006: Science Competencies for Tomorrow's World*. Paris: OECD.

CHAPTER 4

Returns to Education: The Gender Perspective[1]

Harry Anthony Patrinos

"The most valuable of all capital is that invested in human beings."

— Alfred Marshall, 1890

Although the concept of human capital is not a new idea, recent studies of the return to investment in education have reaffirmed the importance of human capital theory. Since the 1950s, many estimates have been made of the rate of return to investment in education, and several reviews of the empirical literature have been written in attempts to establish patterns. Now, with the benefit of more estimates from a wide variety of countries—several extending over time and many using new econometric techniques designed to establish causality—education can clearly be viewed as an investment. This chapter reviews the empirical literature on rates of return to education, based mostly on the review by Psacharopoulos and Patrinos (2004). The literature shows that education should be a profitable investment for the individual. Moreover, the social benefits associated with schooling, particularly women's schooling, suggest that primary schooling investment is a priority. However, low economic returns to primary schooling for females in developing countries, especially those not yet having achieved universal primary schooling, may be a serious policy concern. To the extent that private rates of return to primary schooling inform family decisions about educating daughters, then action may be needed to ensure that girls' schooling draws adequate investments.

Calculating the Rate of Return to Education

In the past, typical estimates of the returns to schooling used age-earnings profiles and discounted earnings streams for a full or elaborate estimate of the internal rate of return. However, most recent estimates usually come from earnings functions. Such functions take into account the cost of schooling—the opportunity cost (or forgone earnings) as well as the direct costs (fees and so on). This estimate gives the individual, or private, rate of return to education. Figure 4.1 shows a typical graphic presentation of age-earnings profiles.

Using earnings functions, the rate of return to schooling is calculated from an equation such as the following:

Figure 4.1   Typical Age-Earnings Profiles

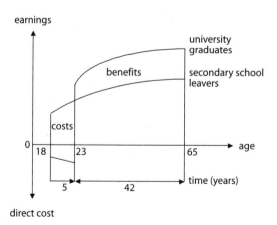

Source: Author's calculations based on data described in text.

$$ln\ W_i = \alpha + \beta S_i + \gamma_1 X_i + \gamma_2 X_i^2 + \varepsilon_i$$

where $ln\ W_i$ is the annual wage for an individual in logarithmic terms, α is a constant term, S is years of schooling, X and X^2 are years of labor market experience and its squared term, and ε_i represents the error term. The coefficients on experience and experience-squared are represented by γ and γ_2. The return to schooling is the coefficient on schooling, or β. Typical returns to an additional year of schooling across a number of countries are presented in figure 4.2. While returns might be low in some countries and higher in others, numerous studies have shown that the global average rate of return to schooling—estimated over time for 100 countries (see Psacharopoulos and Patrinos 2004)—is 10 percent.

On average, returns to schooling in developing countries (11 percent) are considerably higher than in industrial countries (7 percent), reflecting the relative scarcity of education in low-income countries. In developing countries, on average, the rate of return is highest at the primary level (see figure 4.3). This is also the priority area for public investment, given the many social benefits associated with primary schooling (see below).

The returns are higher in low-income regions. The same diminishing returns apply across countries: the more developed the country, the lower the returns to education at all levels. The high returns to education in

Figure 4.2   Rate of Return to Additional Years of Schooling in Selected Countries
(percent)

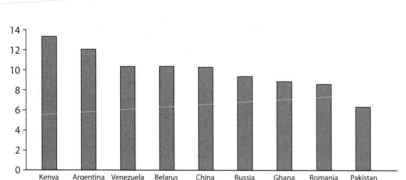

Source: Psacharopoulos and Patrinos 2004.

Figure 4.3   Returns to Education in Developing Countries, by Level of Education

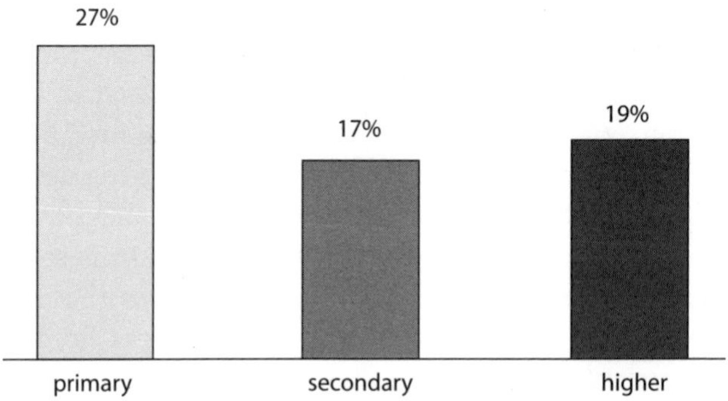

Source: Psacharopoulos and Patrinos 2004.

developing countries must be attributed to the relative scarcity of human capital. The average private returns to another year of schooling by region are presented in figure 4.4. The highest overall returns are found in Latin America, followed by Sub-Saharan Africa. The lowest returns are in the educationally advanced Organisation for Economic Co-operation and Development (OECD) countries and in the region including non-OECD Europe, the Middle East, and North Africa.

From 1970 to 2000, the returns to higher education have increased by about two percentage points, while the returns to primary schooling have decreased by approximately the same amount (Psacharopoulos and Patrinos 2004).

Given the recent expansion of schooling, it is not surprising that the average rate of return to a year of schooling has been declining in recent decades (see figure 4.5).

The profitability of education, according to estimates of private rates of return, is indisputable, universal, and global. It helps explain individual behavior in schooling enrollment decisions. The concept is also useful for analyzing the distributional effects of schooling policy—a good example is student loan financing. However, private rates of return to schooling are not sufficient for assessing funding policies overall. For that, one must turn to the social benefits of schooling.

Figure 4.4   Returns to Schooling, by Region

(percent)

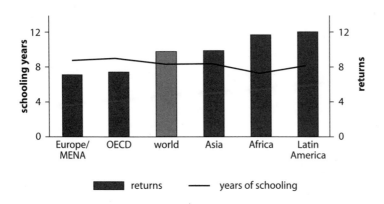

Source: Psacharopoulos and Patrinos 2004.

Note: MENA = Middle East and North Africa.

Figure 4.5   Declining Returns to Schooling, 1970–2000

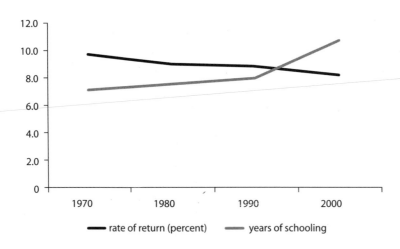

Source: Patrinos and Psacharopoulos 2007.

The Social Benefits of Schooling

Going beyond private benefits of increased productivity and private non-market effects, economists look at, for example, the externalities created by schooling, such as the impact of spillovers, the rate of innovation in a society, and the range of community benefits. A useful concept in this regard is the social rate of return to schooling. To estimate social returns, one needs access to social costs and social benefits. The costs are easy to assemble, based as they are on public spending on schooling. The social benefits include all private benefits, as the individual is part of society, but also benefits that accrue to others in society. Thus social benefits are much more difficult to assemble than social costs.

Theory would suggest that social benefits are higher than just the private benefits of schooling. In the empirical literature, given the usual absence of estimates of social benefits, estimates of social returns are lower than private returns. This is because most researchers have accurate information on costs, but only a vague idea of the social benefits, and they usually are not able to aggregate private and social estimates of the benefits of schooling. The few attempts to estimate social returns to education have produced interesting and useful insights. When analyzing the effect of investment in education on private wages, the social returns are higher than private returns (Acemoglu and Angrist 2000).

The empirically assessed social benefits are listed in table 4.1. When researchers include the known social benefits, the average social returns to schooling are twice as high as the estimated private returns (Haveman and Wolfe 1984). There are also intergenerational benefits associated with schooling. For example, parents with more schooling spend time with their children effectively, are better at assessing returns to schooling, and serve as role models.

Gender Differences

The social benefits of women's schooling are significant, especially in developing countries (Herz and Sperling 2004; Schultz 2002; Watson 2005). For example, a year of schooling for girls reduces infant mortality by 5 to 10 percent (Schultz 1993). Children of mothers with five years of primary education are 40 percent more likely to live beyond age 5 (Summers 1994). When the proportion of women with secondary schooling doubles, the fertility rate is reduced from 5.3 to 3.9 children

Table 4.1   Nonmarket and External Benefits of Education

Benefit type	Findings
Child education	Parental schooling affects child's schooling level and achievement.
Child health	Child's health is positively related to parental education.
Fertility	Mother's education is inversely related to daughter's births.
Own health	More education increases life expectancy.
Spouse's health	More schooling improves spouse's health and lengthens life expectancy.
Job search efficiency	More schooling reduces cost of search, increases mobility.
Desired family size	More schooling improves contraceptive efficiency.
Technological change	Schooling helps research and development and diffusion.
Social cohesion	Schooling increases voting and reduces alienation.
Crime	Education reduces criminal activity.

Source: Based on and adapted from Wolfe and Zuvekas 1997.

per woman (Subbarao and Raney 1995). Providing girls with an extra year of schooling increases their wages by 10 to 20 percent (Psacharopoulos and Patrinos 2004). There is evidence of more productive farming methods attributable to increased female schooling and a 43 percent decline in malnutrition (Smith and Haddad 1999). It has also been shown that educating women has a greater impact on children's schooling than educating men (Filmer 2006). In Brazil women's resources have 20 times more impact than men's resources on child health (Thomas 1990). Young rural Ugandans with secondary schooling are three times less likely to be HIV positive (De Walque 2007). In India women with formal schooling are more likely to resist violence (Sen 1999). In Bangladesh educated women are three times more likely to participate in political meetings (UNESCO 2000).

In terms of wages, women receive higher returns to their schooling investment: their return, on average, is 9.8 percent, compared with 8.7 percent for men (Psacharopoulos and Patrinos 2004), although results vary by country (see figure 4.6). Of the 95 estimates of male and female schooling returns, with coefficients from 49 countries, it has been shown that in 63 cases (66 percent) the returns are greater for females, in 3 they are equal, and in 23 the returns are higher for males.

On average, women obtain less schooling than men (see figure 4.7). The gap is much smaller in industrial countries, but a sizable gap remains in most developing countries.

Figure 4.6   Returns to Schooling in Selected Countries, by Gender

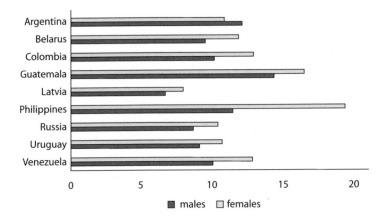

Source: Patrinos and Psacharopoulos 2007.

Figure 4.7   Gender Differences in Years of Schooling in Developing and Industrial Countries

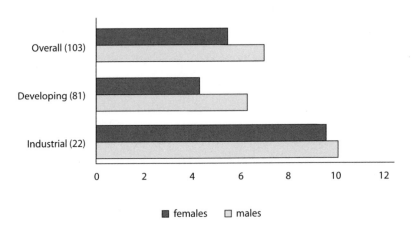

Source: Patrinos and Psacharopoulos 2007.

Note: Data in parentheses indicate the number of countries in the sample.

Returns to Schooling by Level

In developing economies, on average, the rate of return to primary education for women is lower than that of men. Women overtake men by secondary education. At the university level, on average, men's rate of return is about two percentage points higher than women's (see figure 4.8).

A Major Policy Concern: Low Returns to Girls' Primary Education

The lower private returns to girls' primary education could represent a major brake on efforts to increase and equalize girls' participation in schooling, especially in low-income countries that have yet to achieve universal primary schooling. Families may decide to send sons rather than daughters to school, or at least not to support full primary school completion for girls. This jeopardizes at least two of the Millennium Development Goals (MDGs): Goal 2—"ensure that all boys and girls complete a full course of primary schooling," and Goal 3—"eliminate gender disparity in primary and secondary education preferably by 2005, and at all levels by 2015." The low returns to primary education could jeopardize achieving Goal 2 if parents perceive the private returns as

Figure 4.8   Returns to Schooling, by Level and Gender

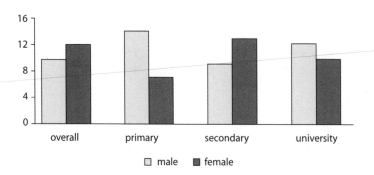

□ male   ■ female

Source: Patrinos and Psacharopoulos 2007.

meaning that schooling is less beneficial for girls. The low returns at the primary level also jeopardize achieving Goal 3, because one needs to complete primary schooling before entering secondary, even though the returns to secondary schooling are higher for girls than for boys. One could also argue that by extension, failure to meet Goals 2 and 3 jeopardizes achievement of other MDGs, such as eradicating extreme poverty and hunger; reducing child mortality; improving maternal health; and combating HIV/AIDS, malaria, and other diseases. The many social benefits of girls' education will not be achieved if parents perceive low private returns and decide to limit girls' education.

Lower returns to girls' primary schooling in developing countries is puzzling. In fact, the opposite situation is found in most transition countries. Potential explanations may include the detrimental impact of discrimination and other factors, which could cause women to accept wage offers that undervalue their characteristics (Dougherty 2005). Better-educated woman may be more able and willing to overcome sex handicaps and compete with men in the labor market. Or there could be male-female differences in the quality of schooling. Analyses of international test score achievements suggest that males rarely have much of an advantage. In fact, girls significantly outperform boys in reading (see figure 4.9).

In Chile, using the 1998 International Adult Literacy Survey, working women score higher than men on standardized tests: 219 versus 209

Figure 4.9   Average Scores on Subject Examinations of the 2003 Programme for International Student Assessment (PISA) in OECD Countries, by Gender

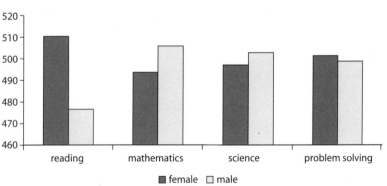

Source: OECD 2003.

points. In addition, women have more schooling than men: 10.5 versus 9.3 years. But women earn significantly less than men. They also receive lower returns to schooling and surprisingly lower returns to cognitive ability (see table 4.2).

Women may choose to work in sectors where education is relatively highly valued. An alternative explanation might be the option value of schooling. That is, because women are likely to perform better, they stay in school longer and experience higher returns for each year of schooling. In that case, the most able go beyond primary schooling, thus depressing the returns at that level (Dougherty 2005). In the United States, Dougherty (2005) found that education doubly affects the earnings of women. It increases their skills and productivity, and it reduces the gap in male and female earnings attributable to discrimination, which accounts for about half of the differential in the returns to schooling.

Lower return to primary schooling in developing countries may be evidence of discrimination, such that women need to achieve more schooling to earn sufficient wages. It is possible that differential returns are due to different job opportunities available to men and women at each schooling level. There is some evidence for this. In Thailand, for example, manufacturing jobs that pay more and require secondary schooling have grown more rapidly for women than for men (Hawley 2004; Kurian 1999; Phananiramai 1996). For jobs that require only primary schooling (for example, construction), the proportion of men may be higher because of tradition or labor intensity, so men have higher returns to primary schooling.

But do lower returns deter enrollments? In at least one case there is evidence that private monetary returns to schooling influence the schooling decisions of boys and girls. Kingdon and Theopold (2006) found that

Table 4.2   Returns to Schooling and Cognitive Ability, by Gender, in Chile

	Returns to schooling (%)		Returns to cognitive ability (%)	
	Males	Females	Males	Females
Returns to years of schooling	11.3	7.9	8.7	6.7
Standardized score on International Adult Literacy Survey			15.3	10.5

Source: From earnings functions that control for experience, supplied by Chris Sakellariou.

in the case of India, the returns to schooling have a positive and significant effect on school enrollment, although the cost of schooling is also a barrier for poor girls. To the extent that this is true for other countries, lower returns to girls' primary schooling could be a major barrier to universalizing primary school enrollment.

Conclusions

Overall, the returns to schooling are high, especially in developing countries. The high private and social returns justify public and private investment in schooling. However, differential returns signal problems in the labor market, and there is a need for further research to detect the barriers to female schooling. Further research should include evaluations of programs designed to increase girls' schooling.

Lower returns to girls' primary schooling in developing countries may be a major policy concern. It could be that the lower returns jeopardize achievement of at least two of the MDGs. While learning outcomes need to be improved—that is, quality is absolutely necessary—this will not be sufficient for equalizing returns or enrollment rates. In fact, enrollment incentives may be needed. There is now considerable evidence that scholarships can significantly increase girls' enrollment (see, for example, Arends-Kuenning and Amin 2004; Schultz 2004). In Bangladesh the scholarship program contributed to reversing the gender gap in school enrollment; today, more girls than boys attend school.

Note

1. Material in this chapter was originally presented at the World Bank's "Global Symposium: Education: A Critical Path to Gender Equality and Empowerment," October 2–3, 2007, in Washington, D.C. All views expressed are those of the author and should not be attributed to the World Bank Group.

References

Acemoglu, D., and J. Angrist. 2000. *How Large Are the Social Returns to Education? Evidence from Compulsory Attendance Laws.* NBER Macro Annual No. 15. Cambridge, MA: National Bureau for Economic Research.

Arends-Kuenning, M., and S. Amin. 2004. "School Incentive Programs and Children's Activities: The Case of Bangladesh." *Comparative Education Review* 48 (4): 295–317.

de Walque, D. 2007. "How Does the Impact of an HIV/AIDS Information Campaign Vary with Educational Attainment? Evidence from Rural Uganda." *Journal of Development Economics* 84 (2): 686–714.

Dougherty, C. 2005. "Why Are the Returns to Schooling Higher for Women Than for Men?" *Journal of Human Resources* 40 (4): 969–988.

Filmer, D. 2006. "Gender and Wealth Disparities in Schooling: Evidence from 44 Countries." *International Journal of Educational Research* 43 (6): 351–369.

Haveman, R. H., and B. L. Wolfe. 1984. "Schooling and Economic Well-Being: The Role of Nonmarket Effects." *Journal of Human Resources* 19 (3): 377–407.

Hawley, J. 2004. "Changing Returns to Education in Times of Prosperity and Crisis, Thailand 1985–1998." *Economics of Education Review* 23 (3): 273–286.

Herz, B., and G. B. Sperling. 2004. *What Works in Girls' Education: Evidence and Policies from the Developing World.* Washington, DC: Council on Foreign Relations.

Kingdon, G., and N. Theopold. 2006. "Do Returns to Education Matter to Schooling Participation?" GPRG Working Paper Series 052, Centre for the Study of African Economies, University of Oxford.

Kurian, R. 1999. "Women's Work in Changing Labour Markets: The Case of Thailand in the 1980s." In *Women, Globalisation and Fragmentation in the Developing World*, eds. H. Afshar and S. Barrientos. New York: St. Martin's Press.

Patrinos, H. A., and G. Psacharopoulos. 2007. "Returns to Education: An International Update." Unpublished paper, Human Development Network, World Bank, Washington, DC.

Phananiramai, M. 1996. "Changes in Women's Economic Role in Thailand." In *Women and Industrialization in Asia*, ed. S. Horton. London: Routledge.

Psacharopoulos, G., and H. A. Patrinos. 2004. "Returns to Investment in Education: A Further Update." *Education Economics* 12 (2): 111–134.

Schultz, T. P. 1993. "Investment in the Schooling and Health of Women and Men." *Journal of Human Resources* 28 (4): 694–734.

———. 2002. "Why Governments Should Invest More to Educate Girls." *World Development* 30 (2): 207–225.

———. 2004. "School Subsidies for the Poor: Evaluating the Mexican Progresa Poverty Program." *Journal of Development Economics* 74: 199–250.

Sen, A. 1999. *Development as Freedom.* New York: Alfred A. Knopf.

Smith, L. C., and L. Haddad. 1999. "Explaining Child Malnutrition in Developing Countries: A Cross-Country Analysis." Discussion Paper 60, International Food Policy Research Institute, Food Consumption and Nutrition Division, Washington, DC.

Subbarao, K., and L. Raney. 1995. "Social Gains from Female Education: A Cross-National Study." *Economic Development and Cultural Change* 44 (1): 105–128.

Summers, L. H. 1994. "Investing in All the People: Educating Women in Developing Countries." EDI Seminar Paper 45, World Bank, Washington, DC.

Thomas, D. 1990. "Intra-household Resource Allocation: An Inferential Approach." *Journal of Human Resources* 25: 635–664.

UNESCO (United Nations Educational, Scientific, and Cultural Organization). 2000. *Women and Girls: Education, Not Discrimination.* Paris: UNESCO.

Watson, C. 2005. *Addressing the MDGs and Targets for Education and Gender: Comments on Selected Aspects linked to the ICPD Programme of Action.* New York: UNICEF.

Wolfe, B., and S. Zuvekas. 1997. "Nonmarket Outcomes of Schooling." *International Journal of Educational Research* 27 (6): 491–502.

CHAPTER 5

Is Female Education a Pathway to Gender Equality in the Labor Market? Some Evidence from Pakistan[1]

Monazza Aslam, Geeta Kingdon, and Mans Söderbom

Can education be a path to gender equality in the labor market? The labor market benefits of education accrue both by increasing a person's knowledge and skills needed for entry into the more lucrative occupations, and by raising a person's earnings within any given occupation. For education to promote gender equality, however, it must benefit women equally if not more than men, given the history of discrimination against women and girls in schooling. We examine the case of Pakistan, where discrimination has been especially rampant, to gain insights into the relationships between education and labor market outcomes for women.

Pakistan has long been an international outlier in gender gaps in education. Girls lag behind boys in education access, in the quality of schooling available, and in the outcomes of education. Far from narrowing over time, the gender gap in primary enrollment rose by 30 percentage points

between 1985 and 1995, superseding even Afghanistan, where the corresponding gap rose by 18 percentage points over the same period (computed from Conly 2004). Although Pakistan's gender gap in gross primary
enrollment fell from 27 percent to 24 percent between 2000 and 2005,[2]
it remains stubbornly high. This persistence of gender inequality in access
to schooling jeopardizes achievement of the Millennium Development
Goals for education in Pakistan.

Given the magnitude of education disparities, it is unsurprising to find
stark gender differences in adult labor market outcomes, too: Pakistani
women lag far behind men in labor force participation, are concentrated
in a much narrower set of occupations, perform mostly unskilled jobs, and
have substantially lower earnings in employment than men, as we will
show later. Low education levels trigger a vicious cycle, wherein poorly
educated women are left ill-equipped to obtain well-paid jobs, and this,
in turn, reduces incentives for parents to invest in girls' schooling.

What can be done to reverse this trend? Education can benefit individuals in the labor market by facilitating entry into higher-earning occupations and by raising earnings within an occupation. It can also promote
gender equality in the labor market if these two benefits of education
accrue to women equally (or more than) to men. But the benefits of education depend on the quality of education. There is now almost universal
agreement that what is learned in school matters as much as, if not more
than, the years of schooling acquired.[3] The objective of this study is
achieved, therefore, by investigating whether education and the quality of
education (as measured by cognitive skills) act as vehicles of labor market success of both men and women.

We find that for men, education promotes entry into the more highly
remunerated occupations along the range of education levels. For women,
however, it does so only beyond 10 years of education. This is because
women's labor force participation increases with education only beyond
10 years of education. Moreover, while possession of cognitive skills facil-
itates both men's and women's entry into the more highly remunerated
occupations, the effect of skills is generally larger for men than women.
On the more positive side, however, the economic returns to education
and skills (the earnings increment from an extra year of education) are
substantially greater for women than men in all occupations except agriculture. As a result, the gender gap in earnings narrows sharply with education. Thus, we conclude that education is a pathway to gender equality

in Pakistan's labor market because it reduces gender gaps in earnings. Nonetheless, only a small proportion of Pakistani women take advantage of the equality-promoting benefits of education. This is because only 17 percent of women participate in the labor force and only 10 percent have 10 or more years of education, the level above which women's chances of wage employment increase with education. We also examine whether and how much the education–labor market relationship (by gender) has changed over an eight-year period from 1999 to 2007. Our findings show that education continues to have a limited impact on women's occupational choices in the labor market, although it has a slightly bigger role in 2007 than it did in 1999.

Examining the Education-Occupation Relationship in Pakistan

Unless otherwise stated, the data used in this chapter come from the third round of the Pakistan Integrated Household Survey (PIHS) conducted in 1998–99. Following a two-stage sampling strategy, the PIHS provides a nationally representative sample made up of around 16,000 households, which represent roughly 115,000 observations. The household questionnaire is composed of a number of detailed modules on such characteristics as income, education, health, maternity and family planning, consumption and expenses, housing conditions, and available services. In addition, there are modules that concentrate on household enterprises and agricultural activities—including associated expenses and revenues. Unless otherwise stated, the sample used throughout this study consists of individuals between 16 and 70 years old and not currently in school.

Because we are interested in the effect of education on both earnings and occupational attainment, all individuals in the labor market are classified into one of five occupational categories: wage employment, self-employment, agricultural employment, unemployment, and out of the labor force.[4] Unemployed individuals are those who seek employment and are available for it, while individuals who are out of the labor force (OLF) are those who do not seek employment, such as housewives and the retired.

The cognitive skills variable is based on a self-reported measure of whether the respondent can read and write (literacy) and do simple sums (numeracy). The link between skills and labor market outcomes among the relatively young deserves special policy attention. Accordingly, in most cases, we analyze labor market outcomes for the young age group (16- to 30-year-olds) separately from that for the older age group (31- to 70-year-olds). However, because of space constraints, not all findings for the older group are shown.

Table 5.1 shows summary statistics for selected variables highlighting the extent of gender asymmetry in Pakistan's labor market. Economic activity, as measured by the labor force participation rate, is extremely low for women—only 17 percent of working-age women participate in the labor market, compared with 87 percent of men. Conditional on employment, men's earnings are substantially higher than women's. This is partly explained by men being, on average, twice as likely to be literate and numerate and much better educated than women.

Table 5.2 summarizes statistics for the full sample and separately for men and women within each of the five occupation categories. Occupational attainment clearly differs by gender. Among the 17 percent of women who participate in the labor force, roughly the same proportions work in agriculture (8 percent) and wage employment (6 percent). Only 1 percent are self-employed. Men, in contrast, are concentrated in the relatively more lucrative wage employment sector (47 percent), followed by agriculture (23 percent), and self-employment (14 percent).

There are large differences in earnings across the three major occupations, particularly between wage employment and self-employment on the one hand, and agriculture on the other. Within each occupation, earnings differ sharply by gender; they are much lower for women (see figure 5.1). For women, earnings are highest in wage employment, followed by agri-

Table 5.1   Employment and Education Characteristics of Persons Ages 16–70 Who Are Not Enrolled in School in Pakistan, by Gender, 1999

Variable	All	Men	Women
Labor force participation (percentage)	49	87	17
Annual earnings (mean)	30,277	34,338	13,327
Annual earnings (median)	24,125	29,573	7,775
Years of education	3.35	4.85	2.07
Maths skills (percentage)	61	75	49
Reading and writing skills (percentage)	40	57	25
Married (percentage)	70	67	73

Source: PIHS 1989–1999.

Note: Earnings measured in 1998–99 Pakistan rupees. Sampling weights are used for these calculations.

Table 5.2 **Employment and Education Characteristics of Persons Ages 16–70 Who Are Not Enrolled in School in Pakistan, by Gender and Occupational Status, 1999**

	All		Self-employment		Agricultural employment		Wage employment		Unemployment		Out of the labor force	
	Men	Women	Men	Women	Men	Women	Men	Women	Men	Women	Men	Women
Annual earnings												
Mean	34,338	13,327	40,697	9,175	24,037	12,514	38,318	15,849	—	—		
Median	29,573	7,775	30,444	6,137	14,400	7,788	34,800	9,000			—	—
Log earnings												
Mean	10.02	8.77	10.17	8.27	9.47	8.87	10.30	8.79	—	—		
Median	10.29	8.96	10.32	8.72	9.57	8.96	10.46	9.10			—	—
Years of education	4.81	1.87	5.03	1.71	3.26	0.50	5.65	3.95	7.21	2.33	4.56	2.10
Age	35.69	33.89	36.50	31.22	38.27	35.02	33.89	33.07	27.94	32.12	42.37	34.92
Math skills (percentage)	75	47	83	46	66	40	78	59	86	49	67	49
Reading and writing skills (percentage)	57	21	62	22	43	09	63	37	77	32	53	26
Number of children younger than 12 in household	2.62	2.61	2.75	2.19	2.72	2.84	2.51	2.40	2.26	2.41	2.34	2.70
Number of persons older than 65 in household	0.21	0.22	0.20	0.14	0.25	0.25	0.19	0.19	0.19	0.16	0.31	0.26
Married (percentage)	70	72	73	63	71	79	68	63	33	69	51	73
Observations	22,041	25,763	3,013	320	4,990	2,076	10,283	1,479	810	603	2,945	21,285
Earnings observations	18,286	3,874	3,012	320	4,990	2,076	10,283	1,479	0	0	0	0

Source: PIHS 1989–1999.

Note: Data are means unless otherwise noted. Earnings are measured in 1998–99 Pakistan rupees. The U.S. dollar exchange rate over the sampling period is approximately 50. Sampling weights are used for these calculations.

Figure 5.1   Kernel Densities of Log Earnings, by Employment Status and Gender, 1999

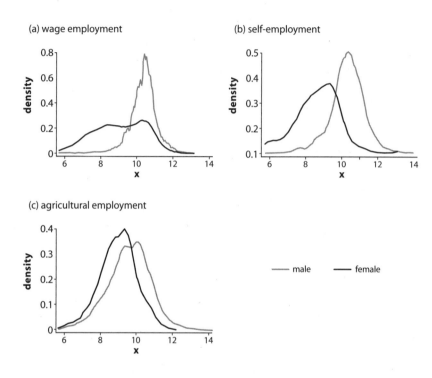

(a) wage employment

(b) self-employment

(c) agricultural employment

——— male   ——— female

Source: Authors' calculations.

Note: x = log of earnings.

culture, and they are lowest in self-employment. Men in self-employment and wage employment earn on average 67 percent more than men in agriculture, and this is mirrored by a similar differential in education and literacy and numeracy scores. Among women, the picture is not so clear-cut. Women in wage employment (where earnings are highest) are more educated and more literate and numerate than their counterparts in the other two occupations. However, self-employed women are paid significantly less than those in agriculture, despite being better educated or skilled. This is partly because for women, self-employment is very different than for men, involving mostly home-based, low-paid work. Women working in agriculture are less educated and have poorer literacy and numeracy skills compared even with women who are out of the labor force. The gender gap in earnings is extremely high in both self-employment and wage employment.

Although five occupation categories are distinguished in the data, for men the main difference with regard to skills and earnings is between wage employment and self-employment on the one hand, and agriculture and OLF status on the other. For men, therefore, skills matter a lot in determining which of these two broadly defined occupation groups individuals end up in. Unemployed men are well educated and clearly queue for suitable job opportunities in the labor market. Among women, there are substantial differences in skills and earnings across the three occupations, and the characteristics of women who are OLF or unemployed are somewhat similar to the self-employed. We now investigate the correlates of occupational outcomes in more detail.

Education, Labor Market Transitions, and Occupational Attainment

This section examines the relationship between education and occupation for men and women. Figure 5.2 illustrates the estimated association between years of education and the predicted likelihoods of occupational outcomes, for young men (panel a) and young women (panel b), evaluated at the sample mean values of the other explanatory variables in the model.[5] It is clear that for young men the likelihood of being employed for wages is relatively invariant to education level. By contrast, education is clearly associated with a lower likelihood of being involved in agriculture. Strikingly, the likelihood of not working (because of being either unemployed or OLF) increases with education. One possible reason for this is that individuals with a lot of education are willing to wait for a good job opportunity before taking paid employment. The likelihood of self-employment can be modeled as an inverse U-shaped curve, peaking at about eight years of education. Education clearly has an impact in determining occupational attainments of men.

For women the picture is very different, indeed. Panel b of figure 5.2 shows that women with up to 10 years of education have high chances of not working. Among women with no schooling at all, about 80 percent are OLF, and this increases to 90 percent for women with 8 to 10 years of education. After 10 years of education, women's labor force participation becomes increasingly responsive to extra education: as education increases beyond 10 years, women begin to join the labor force in larger numbers. However, the only occupation they enter is wage employment. (Coming out of the OLF state is mirrored exactly in joining wage employment for women in figure 5.2.) The probability that a woman with a postgraduate degree (approximately 18 years of education) has a wage job is approximately 50 percent. However, only about 10 percent of women had 10 or more years of education in 1998–99.

The fact that occupational outcomes vary with education level so much for men and so little for women suggests the strong influence of culture, conservative attitudes, and gender division-of-labor norms in Pakistan. Only education beyond 10 years begins to counter the effects of culture, but barely 10 percent of women are fortunate enough to have at least 10 years of education. This provides one element of the answer to the key question in this chapter: education has only limited potential to effect gender equality in the labor market because, as a result of cultural norms, occupational choices are invariant with respect to education up to

Figure 5.2   Estimated Probability of Occupation and Education for Young Men and Women in Pakistan

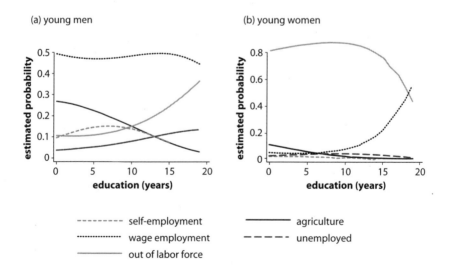

Source: Based on the multinomial logits reported in appendix 1 in Kingdon and Söderbom 2007a.

the end of lower secondary education, and only a small minority of Pakistani women have greater than 10 years of education.

Do transitions from education into the labor market differ substantially for men and women? Figure 5.3 plots the estimated occupation probabilities as a function of *age* for young adults, holding all other explanatory variables fixed at the sample mean values. Transitions into the labor market are noticeably different by gender. We see that occupation status changes a good deal with age for men but hardly at all for women. Although women very gradually begin to enter gainful employment after about age 25, men enter the labor force rapidly; by age 25, almost all men are labor force participants. (The OLF curve falls sharply between ages 15 and 25 for men and falls only very slowly for women, even after age 25.)

Thus, we find that both the transition from education to work and the relationship between education and occupational attainment vary dramatically by gender in Pakistan. These trends reflect entrenched

Figure 5.3   Estimated Probability of Occupation and Age for Young Men and Women in Pakistan

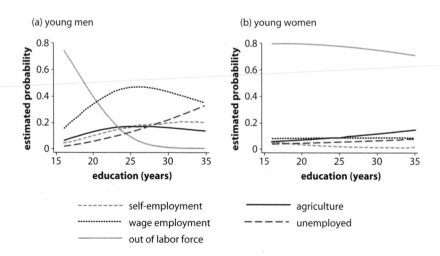

Source: Based on the multinomial logits reported in appendix 2 in Kingdon and Söderbom 2007a.

conservative attitudes toward women's work. Only wage employment appears to be an "acceptable" occupation for women, and even then, only for women with high levels of education. The very small proportion of women (only 10 percent) who have acquired 10 years of schooling or more suggests that the extent to which education can become a pathway to gender equality in economic outcomes is limited in Pakistan.

Are these findings applicable elsewhere? Figure 5.4 shows the relationship between years of education and the predicted likelihoods of being in different labor market states for men (panel a) and women (panel b) in Ghana, an African country for which we had comparable data.[6] Even though a direct comparison is not possible (because for Pakistan, we distinguish between the young and old, but not for Ghana because of its smaller sample size), it is clear that the role of education in occupational attainment in Ghana is extremely different from that in Pakistan. It is visually clear from figure 5.4 that the relationship between education and occupational choice is far more similar for men and women in Ghana than in Pakistan. These findings indicate a much lower degree of segmentation by gender in Ghana than in Pakistan and suggest that in Ghana, education is as much a vehicle for labor market success for women as it is for men.

A Static Labor Market?

Our assessment so far is based on 1998–99 data, and it is of interest to know whether the role of education in promoting gender equality in the labor market has improved in recent years. In this section, a comparison across time is made using data collected in Pakistan in 2006–07 under the auspices of the Research Consortium on Educational Outcomes and Poverty (RECOUP). These household-level data were collected using stratified random sampling in two provinces of Pakistan—Punjab and the North West Frontier Province (NWFP)—and yielded information on 1,194 households across nine districts. As one of the main objectives of data collection was to analyze economic outcomes of education, the survey contained questions on the labor market status of all household members (and detailed questions for individuals ages 15–60).

To render the PIHS 1998–99 and RECOUP 2006–07 data sets comparable, we limited the PIHS analysis to Punjab and NWFP only, and in both data sets we restricted analysis to individuals between ages 16 and 60.[7] As before, we distinguished between the young (16–30 years old) and the older (31–60 years old), although because of space constraints, we report findings only for the young.

Figure 5.4   Estimated Probability of Occupation and Education for Men and Women in Ghana

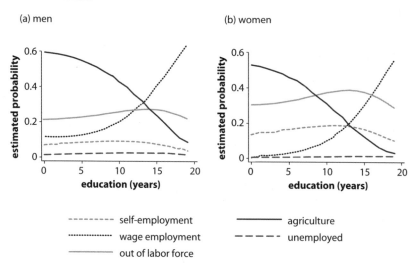

Source: Based on the multinomial logits reported in appendix 1 in Kingdon and Söderbom 2007b.

Table 5.3 presents summary statistics for men and women in 1999 and 2007. It shows a large increase in women's economic activity—from 19 percent in 1999 to 35 percent in 2007. However, the gender gaps in education and literacy levels are surprisingly persistent over this eight-year period. Although both men and women are more educated now, *gains* in men's education were greater, so that the gender gap in years of education rose (from 2.69 years to 2.98 years). On the positive side, though, gender gaps in literacy have declined from 31 percent to 27 percent, because literacy rate improvement was greater among women than among men (a 10-point increase for women compared with only 6 points for men).

Figure 5.5 illustrates the estimated association between years of education and the predicted likelihood of occupational outcomes for young men in 1998–99 (panel a) and in 2006–07 (panel b), evaluated at the sample mean values of the other explanatory variables in the model.[8] With some exceptions, the picture is quite similar between 1999 and 2007 for men. One conspicuous change, though, is that the probability that highly educated young men stay OLF has increased from 0.48 to

about 0.78 across this eight-year period. This suggests much greater levels of discouragement among the highly educated over the past decade,
perhaps because of an increase in the supply of skilled workers
unmatched by a corresponding increase in demand. Instead of remaining

**Table 5.3 Employment and Education Characteristics of Persons Ages 16–60
Who Are Not Enrolled in School in Punjab and North West Frontier Province,
by Gender, 1999 and 2007**

	Men		Women	
Variable	1999	2007	1999	2007
Labor force participation (percentage)	89	92	19	35
Years of education	4.89	6.41	2.20	3.43
Literate (percentage)	58	64	27	37
Married (percentage)	64	64	73	72

Source: Author's calculations based on PIHS data from 1998–99.

Note: Sampling weights are used for 1999 calculations. "Literate" is a dummy variable measuring whether individuals can read or write (1999 data) and whether individuals achieved a score of 1 or more in a short test of literacy administered to each individual.

**Figure 5.5   Estimated Probability of Occupation and Education for Young Men,
1999 and 2007**

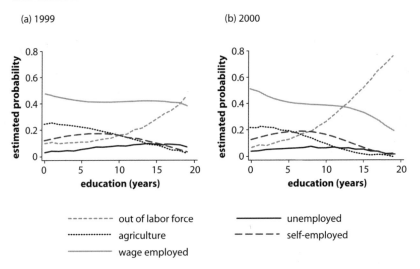

Source: Based on the multinomial logits available from the authors.

in the labor force and openly unemployed, highly educated young men appear to prefer to wait out of the labor force.

Figure 5.6 plots the likelihood of occupational attainment with respect to education for young women in 1999 (panel a) and 2007 (panel b). Here, there is suggestion of some encouraging changes over time. First, although 80 percent of women with no education were OLF in 1999, by 2007 only 60 percent of such women were OLF; that is, the labor force participation rate among uneducated women increased over this eight-year period. Second, and more important, women's occupational status became more responsive to education over time. In 1999 education beyond 10 years was needed for women to increasingly participate in the labor market, and then the rate at which education increased the chances of labor force participation was slow. But by 2007 education beyond about eight years[9] began to encourage participation in the labor force, and the rate at which it did so also increased considerably. As a result, the OLF and wage employment curves cross each other at about 15 years of education in 2007, rather than at the 18 years of education in 1999. Although in 1999 a woman with 15 years of education had a 22 percent chance of being wage employed, in 2007 a woman with 15 years of education was

Figure 5.6   Estimated Probability of Occupation and Education for Young Women, 1999 and 2007

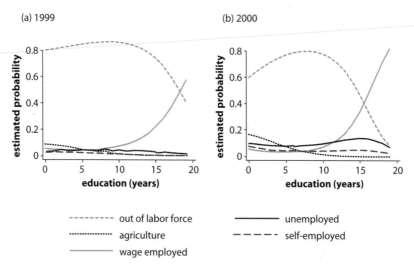

Source: Based on the multinomial logits available from the authors.

about 35 percent likely to be wage employed. At higher levels of education, up to 19 years, the escalation of employment opportunities between 1999 and 2007 is even more striking.

Overall, while a comparison across the eight-year period reveals a high degree of similarity in the education-occupation relationship between 1999 and 2007 for both men and women, there are some encouraging trends. In particular, there is a suggestion that in recent times, education is beginning to influence occupational outcomes of women from 8 years onward (rather than from 10 years onward, as in 1999) and to have a larger (steeper) impact on their chances of employment, even though wage employment continues as the only acceptable occupation for women. Another silver lining in the cloud is that the proportion of women with 10 years of education or more has risen over the eight-year period (from about 13 percent in 1999[10] to 19 percent in 2007). This suggests that a larger proportion of women can take advantage of the equality-promoting labor market benefits of education.

Skills and Occupational Attainment

What is learned in school may be more important than the years of schooling acquired. The extent to which literacy and numeracy skills promote entry into the more remunerative occupations is worth investigating. Table 5.4 presents the marginal effects of basic literacy and numeracy on the likelihood of being in different occupations (estimates based on PIHS 1999). The descriptive statistics discussed in table 5.2 made clear that for men, wage and self-employment are the well-paying parts of the labor market in Pakistan and agriculture is not. For women, wage employment offers the highest earnings, with agriculture coming in second best and self-employment faring worst.

Table 5.4 shows that possession of literacy promotes entry into a well-paying part of the labor market, namely wage employment, for all groups except young men. In the older group, the effect is three times as large for men as for women. Literacy skills strongly reduce the chances of ending up in the worst-paying part of the labor market for men (agriculture), and the effect is significantly higher for men than for women in both age groups. Moreover, although the effect is small, literacy reduces the likelihood of women (young and old) entering the worst-paying self-employment sector, while there is a weak suggestion that literacy promotes young men's entry into self-employment.

Surprisingly, being literate is associated with significantly *increased* chances of being either OLF or unemployed for all groups. Literate women either work in wage employment—which may be viewed as the respectable part of the labor market—or remain OLF (and to a lesser extent unemployed), perhaps as a result of cultural norms or their greater efficiency in the production of home goods.

Table 5.4   Effects of Literacy and Numeracy on Occupational Outcome, by Gender and Age Group

Occupational status and skill level	Young		Older	
	Men	Women	Men	Women
Self-employment				
Can solve simple math problem	0.028	−0.005	0.067	−0.001
	(2.18)**	(2.45)*	(5.95)**	(0.46)
Can read and write	0.020	−0.005	−0.002	−0.004
	(1.93)+	(2.09)*	(0.20)	(1.98)*
Agricultural employment				
Can solve simple math problem	0.010	0.013	0.006	0.003
	(0.78)	(2.19)*	(0.60)	(0.59)
Can read and write	−0.110	−0.078	−0.167	−0.081
	(11.42)**	(25.77)**	(21.37)**	(29.38)**
Wage employment				
Can solve simple math problem	−0.020	−0.003	−0.025	−0.003
	(1.14)	(0.47)	(1.90)+	(0.63)
Can read and write	0.017	0.031	0.119	0.041
	(1.15)	(4.05)**	(9.81)**	(4.80)**
Unemployed				
Can solve simple math problem	0.010	0.001	−0.002	−0.006
	(0.95)	(0.26)	(0.64)	(2.00)*
Can read and write	0.030	0.014	0.009	0.008
	(3.16)**	(2.71)**	(1.99)*	(1.65)+
Out of the labor force				
Can solve simple math problem	−0.028	−0.005	−0.045	0.007
	(2.28)*	(0.59)	(5.94)**	(0.82)
Can read and write	0.042	0.038	0.041	0.036
	(3.53)**	(4.05)**	(4.69)**	(3.63)**

Source: Results based on the multinomial logits reported in appendix 1 in Kingdon and Söderbom 2007a.

Note: t-values are in parentheses. + significant at 10 percent level; * significant at 5 percent level; ** significant at 1 percent level.

Numeracy, in contrast, is not related to the chances of being in wage employment, suggesting that many wage jobs are unskilled, not requiring numerate individuals. But numeracy has a high association with the chances of being in self-employment for men. This could be either because numeracy promotes entry into self-employment or because people in self-employment end up becoming numerate; that is, numeracy is learned on the job. As with literacy, numeracy reduces the likelihood of young women entering the ill-paying self-employment sector. Numeracy also reduces the chances of being OLF for men, but not for women. This could be to the result of cultural norms or because the earnings rewards of numeracy differ for men and women. We turn to these in the next section.

Education and Earnings

Thus far, we have examined whether and to what extent education can be a pathway to promoting gender equality through improving women's occupational attainment. However, the labor market benefits of education also accrue through a second channel, namely, by raising earnings within any given occupation. Education must raise women's earnings equally if not *more* than men's if it is to assist in reducing gender inequalities in the labor market.

In this section we investigate how the wage increment from each extra year of women's education compares with that from men's education. This is done by estimating and comparing the marginal rate of return to education for men and women, using the familiar Mincerian earnings function approach and the predictions of human capital theory. In an earnings equation, the coefficient on years of schooling measures the rate of return to each additional year of schooling acquired.

Returns to education have been estimated for almost every country in the world (see Psacharopoulos 1994; Psacharopoulos and Patrinos 2004), but estimates by gender are less common and the evidence is mixed. Among developed countries, returns to women's education are significantly higher than men's in Germany, Greece, Ireland, Italy, and the United Kingdom; they are lower in Austria, Denmark, the Netherlands, and Sweden (Harmon, Oosterbeek, and Walker 2000). The developing country evidence is equally mixed. Some studies found that returns to schooling do not differ significantly by gender (Behrman and Wolfe 1984; Schultz 1993). However, studies in Bangladesh (Asadullah 2006), India (Kingdon 1998; Kingdon and Unni 2001), Indonesia

(Behrman and Deolalikar 1995), and Pakistan (Aslam 2007a) found that returns to women's schooling are higher than men's.

Several authors have estimated returns to education in Pakistan (see Aslam 2007a for an annotated list of papers), in line with much of the international literature on economic returns to education, but these studies have estimated returns to education solely in wage employment. However, as shown in table 5.2, wage employment absorbs only about half of the total labor force and a very small proportion of women. The remaining half of the labor force is engaged in self-employment, both agricultural and nonagricultural. What are the returns to education in this major part of the labor market?[11]

Table 5.5 presents ordinary least squares estimates of the economic returns to education in Pakistan, by occupation, gender, and age group. It shows that the returns to education are very precisely determined, even in cases where sample sizes are very small. It is clear that returns to education are significantly and substantially greater for women than men in all occupations and in both age groups (except among the young in agriculture). In other words, within any given occupation, the increase in women's earnings with respect to education is much greater than the increase for men. The fact that returns to education in wage employment in Pakistan are about three to four times as high for women as for men (both young and older) could reflect the scarcity of educated women, combined with the existence of some jobs that require education and are predominantly female, such as nursing and primary school teaching. However, the reasons for the higher earnings premium for women than men in self-employment are less clear, even though the female premium over the male is not so high in self-employment as in wage employment.

Next we turn to earnings equations where education is replaced by our measures of cognitive skills. Table 5.6 shows strong returns to literacy among men and women in wage and self-employment and for men in agriculture. In most cases, the returns to literacy are dramatically larger for women than men, and this finding mirrors that of returns to additional years of education. The returns to literacy for women are more than six times as high as those for men in wage employment and about three times as high in self-employment. Part of the explanation for this finding is a scarcity premium, because far fewer women than men are literate. Fewer women than men have the years of schooling required to develop literacy skills, and women are likely to have attended poorer schools than men in Pakistan.[12] Significant positive returns to numeracy skills accrue to

Table 5.5   Effect of Age and Education on Earnings, by Employment Status and Gender

Age and education	Wage employment		Self–employment		Agricultural employment	
	Men	Women	Men	Women	Men	Women
Young						
Education	0.033	0.149	0.048	0.105	0.053	0.041
	(17.08)**	(20.02)**	(5.77)**	(3.39)**	(5.27)**	(1.17)
Age	0.165	0.021	0.043	0.130	0.152	0.331
	(6.31)**	(0.18)	(0.41)	(0.43)	(1.29)	(1.42)
Age squared	−0.002	0.001	0.000	−0.002	−0.001	−0.006
	(4.18)**	(0.24)	(0.08)	(0.30)	(0.56)	(1.28)
No. of individuals	4,844	732	1,230	161	2,027	973
Older						
Education	0.066	0.172	0.070	0.170	0.074	0.188
	(47.96)**	(28.99)**	(13.64)**	(6.92)**	(9.83)**	(4.07)**
Age	0.095	0.079	0.042	0.012	−0.019	0.016
	(11.98)**	(1.86)	(1.76)	(0.14)	(0.75)	(0.25)
Age squared	−0.001	−0.001	−0.001	0.000	0.000	−0.000
	(11.55)**	(1.68)	(2.10)*	(0.16)	(0.74)	(0.32)
No. of individuals	5,439	747	1,783	159	2,963	1,103

Source: Authors' calculations.

Note: Province dummy variables are included in all regressions. The estimation method is ordinary least squares. t-values are given in parentheses. + significant at 10 percent level; * significant at 5 percent level; ** significant at 1 percent level.

both older men and women in agriculture. The size of these returns is identical across gender.

The fact that returns to education and to cognitive skills are substantially larger for women than men presents the cheering scenario that education can be a path to gender equality in the labor market. It also suggests that there are really strong economic incentives for investment in girls' schooling, which ought to lead to gender equality in education or, if anything, to *pro-female* gender gaps in education, rather than what we actually observe—large pro-male gaps. This raises a puzzle as to why women have low levels of education when the economic incentives for educating them are so much stronger than for educating men.

One potential explanation is that parents may allocate less education to daughters than sons, even if the labor market rewards women's

Table 5.6 Effect of Literacy and Numeracy on Earnings, by Employment Status and Gender

Age and skills	Wage employment		Self–employment		Agricultural employment	
	Men	Women	Men	Women	Men	Women
Young						
Can solve simple	0.036	0.184	0.039	−0.433	0.339	0.077
math problem	(1.06)	(1.13)	(0.28)	(1.35)	(2.48)*	(0.41)
Can read and write	0.216	1.393	0.371	1.053	0.271	0.209
	(7.17)**	(8.97)**	(3.34)**	(2.86)**	(2.23)*	(0.82)
Age	0.192	0.180	0.089	0.080	0.186	0.336
	(7.21)**	(1.39)	(0.82)	(0.26)	(1.57)	(1.43)
Age squared	−0.003	−0.002	−0.001	−0.001	−0.002	−0.006
	(4.93)**	(0.84)	(0.33)	(0.12)	(0.81)	(1.30)
Number of individuals	4,844	732	1,230	161	2,027	973
Older						
Can solve simple						
math problem	0.076	0.047	0.132	0.208	0.341	0.356
	(3.22)**	(0.37)	(1.60)	(0.88)	(4.36)**	(2.34)*
Can read and write	0.486	1.901	0.454	1.285	0.251	0.445
	(22.65)**	(14.32)**	(6.86)**	(4.11)**	(3.26)**	(1.67)
Age	0.097	0.084	0.049	0.020	−0.017	0.016
	(11.21)**	(1.86)	(2.04)*	(0.22)	(0.65)	(0.25)
Age squared	−0.001	−0.001	−0.001	0.000	0.000	−0.000
	(11.11)**	(1.74)	(2.38)*	(0.04)	(0.59)	(0.33)
Number of individuals	5,439	747	1,783	159	2,963	1,103

Source: Authors' calculations.

Note: Province dummy variables are included in all regressions. The estimation method is ordinary least squares. t-values are given in parentheses. + significant at 10 percent level; * significant at 5 percent level; ** significant at 1 percent level.

education more, because the returns *accruing to parents* from a daughter's education are lower than those from a son's education. The absence of a social security system for old-age support, coupled with the social norm that girls live with their in-laws, implies that any economic benefits of education investments in daughters are reaped by their in-laws, while economic benefits of education investments in sons are reaped by parents in the form of old-age support. Thus, economic necessity may prompt greater investments in boys' education, despite higher labor market returns to women.

A second explanation for the puzzle is that while the return to each extra year of education and to cognitive skills may be much higher for women than men, the *total* labor market return from employment is much lower for women than for men because overall, employed women earn far less money than employed men. This is clear from the graph of predicted earnings for wage employees in figure 5.7. Although the slope of the education-earnings relationship is three times as steep for women as for men, the intercept of the wage regression is much higher for men; men enjoy earnings premiums at all levels of education. Aslam (2007a) showed that a large part of the gender gap in earnings is due to potential discrimination in the labor market and is not explained by differences in men's and women's productivity endowments, such as education and experience. Education of women helps to reduce that earnings gap— there is less gender discrimination among the educated in the Pakistan labor market.

The gender gap in earnings is widest among workers with no education and narrows as completed years of education increase, as seen in figure 5.7. This suggests that education is a pathway to reducing gender inequalities in Pakistan's labor market, because the gender gaps in earnings are substantially smaller among those with higher levels of education. Thus, education has mixed success as a vehicle to promote gender equality in the labor market. While women's occupational attainment is relatively invariant to education (except beyond 10 years of schooling), limiting the extent to which education can mitigate gender inequalities, education clearly does reduce gender gaps in earnings among those who are employed and thus plays a vital role in attenuating gender inequalities in labor market earnings.

Conclusion

The central research question addressed in this chapter is whether education and the quality of education (as measured by cognitive skills) are paths to reducing gender inequality in the labor market, either by promoting women's entry into lucrative occupations or by raising their earnings within a given occupation at least equally, if not more, than for men.

Figure 5.7   Predicted Earnings and Level of Education for Wage Employment

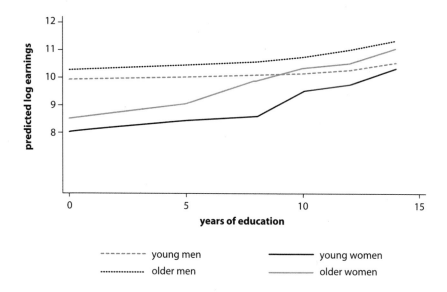

Source: Based on the results reported in table 5.5.

Our findings suggest that in Pakistan, education does increase gender equality in labor market outcomes, through both improved occupational attainment of women and reduced gender gaps in earnings in any given occupation. Nonetheless, these positive effects of education are limited by cultural norms that prevent a woman's occupational choice from being responsive to education until she has about 10 years of education, and by possible discrimination that a woman faces in both education and employment.

Based on the PIHS data from 1999, our results show that although education plays an important role in occupational outcomes for men from very low levels of education, women begin to take advantage of the benefits of education in earnest only after about 10 years of schooling when they begin to join the labor force and enter wage employment. Given the very small proportion of women (about 10 percent) who have completed 10 years or more of schooling, however, the extent to which education can promote gender equality within the labor market is limited. A comparison across an eight-year period using latest household data (RECOUP 2007) shows that education continues to have a limited impact on women's occupational choices in the labor market, although it had a slightly bigger role in 2007 than in 1999. Moreover, wage employment continues to be the only acceptable occupational choice for better-educated women. On a more positive note, however, in 2007 women's wage employment participation was responsive to education from about 8 years of education onward, suggesting some loosening of cultural norms. The proportion of women with 10 or more years of education has also risen over time, suggesting a larger number of women can take advantage of the labor market benefits of education.

Occupational attainment is largely invariant to years of schooling for women, but cognitive skills have substantially high payoffs. This is true for both men and women. In particular, literacy promotes entry into the lucrative parts of the labor market for both men and women—although the effect is larger for men, which once again limits the extent to which skills acquisition can help alleviate gender inequalities in the labor market.

A second channel through which education may promote gender equality in labor market outcomes is by narrowing gender gaps in earnings within any given occupation (by rewarding women's education and skills more than men's). We find that the economic returns to women's schooling and skills are indeed invariably and substantially higher than to men's in all occupations and among both age groups, so that the gender gap in earnings is substantially smaller among those with higher levels of education. Hence, education clearly reduces gender gaps in earnings and can play a vital role in attenuating inequalities in earnings in the labor market.

If education is to become a strong pathway to gender equality in the labor market, Pakistan must, first of all, address the conservatism of attitudes on the division of labor between men and women and the participation of women in the paid labor force. This may be possible through, for example, public education campaigns and media messages, including putting forward successful female role models. Second, given the suggestion of gender discrimination in the labor market, Pakistan can benefit from reforming labor market policies in ways that reduce gender-differentiated treatment by employers. Third, to strengthen the labor market equality-promoting benefits of education, Pakistan will need to ensure that a greater proportion of its women acquire secondary education and beyond.

For this, it may need to improve the supply of secondary and tertiary education and also ease credit constraints for girls, such as providing attendance-contingent cash transfers for staying enrolled in school.

Notes

1. An initial version of this paper was prepared as a background paper for a World Bank study, "Linking Education Policy to Labor Market Outcomes." The RECOUP 2007 data used in one section of this study was collected under the auspices of the Research Consortium on Educational Outcomes and Poverty (RECOUP), funded by DFID. The paper has benefited from the comments of participants of seminars at the Centre for the Study of African Economies, University of Oxford, and the Institute of Education, University of London.

2. Computed from http://stats.uis.unesco.org.

3. There is evidence that cognitive skills have economically large effects on individual earnings and on national growth. This literature was summarized in Hanushek (2005), which cited three U.S. studies showing quite consistently that a one standard deviation increase in mathematics test performance at the end of high school in the United States translates into 12 percent higher annual earnings. Hanushek also cited three studies from the United Kingdom and Canada showing strong productivity returns to both numeracy and literacy skills. Substantial returns to cognitive skills also hold across the developing countries for which studies have been carried out, that is, in Ghana, Kenya, Morocco, Pakistan, South Africa, and Tanzania. Hanushek and Zhang (2006) confirmed significant economic returns to literacy for 13 countries for which literacy data were available. A study in Pakistan (Behrman, Ross, and Sabot 2002) also found that cognitive skills have statistically significant payoffs in the labor market.

4. Earnings information is available only for the first three categories: wage employment, self-employment, and agricultural employment. Although earnings are available for the individual who is wage-employed, only household-level earnings are available for the self-employed and agricultural workers. Thus, while earnings functions can be estimated for individual wage employees, household-level functions are estimated for those in self-employment and agriculture. (See Kingdon and Söderbom 2007a for further details.)

5. These graphs are based on occupational outcomes modelled by means of a simple, parsimoniously specified multinomial logit. (Wage employment is the base category.) The explanatory variables are education, skills, basic individual and family characteristics (age, marital status, number of young children in the household, and number of elderly people in the household), and province

dummies. Because education and skills are highly correlated, whenever education is included as an explanatory variable, the literacy and numeracy variables are excluded, and vice versa. All regressions are estimated separately for men and women. Underlying regressions are available in Kingdon and Söderbom (2007a).

6. These estimates are based on the fourth round of the Ghana Living Standards Measurement Survey 1998–99 (GLSS4). The sample is restricted to individuals ages 16–70 and not enrolled in school. Graphs are based on multinomial logits with wage employment as the base category. Figure 5.4 shows the estimated association for men and women evaluated at the sample mean values of the explanatory variables in the model. See Kingdon and Söderbom (2007b) for underlying regressions.

7. The sampling for the RECOUP survey was intended to yield a representative sample at the province level, and we assume that it is representative and therefore comparable with the sample from the PIHS data set.

8. These graphs comparing occupational outcomes using the PIHS and RECOUP data sets are based on identical specifications of parsimoniously specified multinomial logits (OLF is the base category). The explanatory variables are years of education, education squared, age, age squared, number of children in the household under the age of 12, number of adults in the household over the age of 65, and a dummy variable depicting whether or not the individual is married. All regressions are estimated separately for men and women. Underlying regressions are available from the authors.

9. In 2007, 21.8 percent of women had more than eight years of education.

10. The figure was estimated on only the Punjab and NWFP sample of the 1999 PIHS.

11. As is common in the literature, we use the term "returns to education." Strictly speaking, however, the coefficient on the Mincerian earnings function is simply the gross earnings premium from an extra year of education and is not the "return" to education, because it does not take the cost of education into account.

12. Aslam and Kingdon (2006) showed that Pakistani girls receive significantly lower educational expenditures within the household than Pakistani boys. Aslam (2007b) found that girls also face poorer quality schooling than boys in Pakistan: they are very significantly less likely to be sent to private schools than their brothers, and private schools are more effective than public schools in imparting cognitive skills to students. Aslam's findings on the relative effectiveness of private and public schools are supported by other studies on Pakistan (Alderman, Orazem, and Paterno 2001; Andrabi, Das, and Khwaja 2002; Arif and Saqib 2003).

References

Alderman, H., P. F. Orazem, and E. M. Paterno. 2001. "School Quality, School Cost, and the Public/Private School Choices of Low-Income Households in Pakistan." *The Journal of Human Resources* 36 (2): 304–326.

Andrabi, T., J. Das, and A. Khwaja. 2002. "The Rise of Private Schooling in Pakistan: Catering to the Urban Elite or Educating the Rural Poor?" Background paper for the *Pakistan Poverty Assessment*, World Bank, Washington, DC.

Arif, G. M., and N. Saqib. 2003. "Production of Cognitive Life Skills in Public, Private, and NGO Schools in Pakistan." *Pakistan Development Review* 42 (1): 1–28.

Asadullah, M. N. 2006. "Returns to Education in Bangladesh." *Education Economics* 14 (4): 453–468.

Aslam, M. 2007a. "Rates of Return to Education by Gender in Pakistan." GPRG-WPS-064, Centre for the Study of African Economies, University of Oxford. Forthcoming in *Economic Development and Cultural Change.*

———. 2007b. "The Quality of School Provision in Pakistan: Are Girls Worse Off?" GPRG-WPS-066, Centre for the Study of African Economies, University of Oxford.

Aslam, M., and G. G. Kingdon. 2006. "Gender and Household Education Expenditure in Pakistan." CSAE Working Paper Series GPRG-WPS 025. University of Oxford. Forthcoming in *Applied Economics.*

Behrman, J. R., and A. Deolalikar. 1995. "Are There Differential Returns to Schooling by Gender? The Case of Indonesian Labour Markets." *Oxford Bulletin of Economics and Statistics* 57 (1): 97–117.

Behrman, J., D. Ross, and R. Sabot. 2002. "Improving the Quality Versus Increasing the Quantity of Schooling: Evidence from Rural Pakistan." Mimeo, University of Pennsylvania, Philadelphia.

Behrman, J. R., and B. Wolfe. 1984. "The Socio-economic Impact of Schooling in a Developing Country." *Review of Economics and Statistics* 66 (2): 296–303.

Conly, Shanti. 2004. "Educating Girls: Gender Gaps and Gains." Population Action International, http://www.populationaction.org/resources/publications/educating_girls/ggap_graph02.htm.

Hanushek, Eric A. 2005. "The Economics of School Quality." *German Economic Review* 6 (3): 269–286.

Hanushek, Eric A., and Lei Zhang. 2006. "Quality Consistent Estimates of International Returns to Skill." NBER Working Paper 12664, National Bureau of Economic Research, Cambridge, MA.

Harmon, C., H. Oosterbeek, and I. Walker. 2000. "The Returns to Education: A Review of Evidence, Issues and Deficiencies in the Literature." Mimeo, London School of Economics.

Kingdon G. G. 1998. "Does the Labour Market Explain Lower Female Schooling in India?" *Journal of Development Studies* 35 (1): 39–65.

Kingdon, G. G., and M. Söderbom. 2007a. "Education, Skills and Labor Market Outcomes: Evidence from Pakistan." Background paper prepared for "Linking Education Policy to Labor Market Outcomes," forthcoming in HDNED Working Paper Series.

———. 2007b. "Education, Skills and Labor Market Outcomes: Evidence from Ghana." Background paper prepared for "Linking Education Policy to Labor Market Outcomes," forthcoming in HDNED Working Paper Series.

Kingdon, G., and J. Unni. 2001. "Education and Women's Labour Market Outcomes in India." Education Economics 9 (2): 173–195.

Psacharopoulos, G. 1994. "Returns to Investment in Education: A Global Update." World Development 22 (9): 1325–1343.

Psacharopoulos, G., and H. Patrinos. 2004. "Returns to Investment in Education: A Further Update." *Education Economics* 12 (2): 111–134.

Schultz, T. P. 1993. "Returns to Women's Education." In *Women's Education in Developing Countries: Barriers, Benefits, and Policies*, eds. Elizabeth M. King and M. Anne Hill. Baltimore, MD: Johns Hopkins University Press.

PART II

Equity in Education:
What Is Holding Countries Back?

CHAPTER 6

Inequalities in Education: Effects of Gender, Poverty, Orphanhood, and Disability

Deon Filmer

Measured by the percentage of children who reach the last year of primary school, known as the primary completion rate, the world has made substantial progress toward reaching the Millennium Development Goal of enabling all children to "complete a full course of primary schooling."[1] The primary completion rate in low-income countries increased from 57 percent to 73 percent between 1991 and 2006, with growth in all of the poorer regions: Latin America and the Caribbean (82 to 99 percent), Middle East and North Africa (77 to 91 percent), South Asia (62 to 80 percent), and Sub-Saharan Africa (51 to 60 percent).[2]

There are, however, large inequalities in education across and, importantly, within countries. Documenting inequalities across countries is straightforward. So, while some countries are reaching 100 percent of children completing primary school, the rate is below 50 percent in many countries: a sizable group of children still fails to complete school. This failure is especially large in countries where progress has been slow, but also exists in countries where overall progress is being made.[3]

By analyzing a very large collection of household data sets, the work described here documents patterns of inequalities in educational attainment. There are four main findings. First, within-country gaps associated with economic status can be truly enormous—as large as, if not larger than, differences across countries. Second, the schooling attainment patterns that give rise to these inequalities vary substantially across countries—suggesting that country-specific policies will be the key to addressing shortfalls. Third, inequalities associated with economic status are typically larger than those associated with other commonly cited sources of education gaps—in particular gaps associated with gender and orphanhood. Fourth, disability, while affecting only a small share of the population, is associated with very large education deficits.

Data and Methodology

The results described here are derived from an ongoing project to compile household survey data sets and extract systematic information about education inequalities from them. (More details on this project as well as extensions of the project are at http://econ.worldbank.org/projects/edattain.) To date, the compilation covers more than 220 data sets from more than 85 countries. Country coverage is determined primarily by the availability of data. The data are from Demographic and Health Surveys (DHS); UNICEF's End-of-Decade Multiple Indicator Cluster Surveys (MICS2); as well as integrated household surveys (IHS), such as those from the World Bank's Living Standards Measurement Study (LSMS) project.

Measuring educational enrollment and attainment in poor countries is deceptively difficult. For example, children who are reported as enrolled by schools are frequently absent. Relying on household surveys is not a panacea: reported school enrollment can still mask large periods of absenteeism. Nevertheless, self-reported school outcomes are generally more reliable than administrative data. More important, to study school participation and attainment, one must use household surveys if one is to relate education outcomes to children's background characteristics and to integrate children and youth who are not in school into the analysis.

Many of the surveys analyzed (for example, all DHS and MICS2 data sets) do not include information on per capita household consumption expenditures—which is typically the preferred variable for use in poverty analysis. To overcome this limitation, the analysis uses an index based on consumer durables owned by households (such as a radio, television, or bicycle) as well as characteristics of the household's dwelling (such as the roofing and flooring material or the type of toilet facilities used) to derive population quintiles. The poorest 20 percent of the population live in the "poorest quintile," and the richest 20 percent live in the "richest quintile."[4]

Poverty

The gap in educational attainment between the richest and poorest quintiles in the same country can be truly staggering (see figure 6.1).[5] For example, in Sierra Leone roughly 20 percent in the poorest quintile complete grade 6, whereas more than 70 percent in the richest quintile do. Gaps are typically largest in Sub-Saharan African and South Asian countries (left side of figure 6.1).

Compared to countries in other regions, African countries have the lowest grade 6 completion rate among children from the richest quintile; and for African children in the poorest quintile, the completion rate is even lower. For example, in Burundi, Guinea, and Niger, only about 50 percent of children from the richest quintile complete grade 6, and fewer than 20 percent of children from the poorest quintile do. Even as attainment rises somewhat in the richest quintile, children from the poorest quintile often lag behind. For example, in Mozambique, where slightly more than 80 percent of children from the richest quintile complete grade 6, only about 30 percent of children from the poorest quintile do. In The Gambia, just more than 80 percent of children from the richest quintile complete grade 6, and again, only about 30 percent of children from the poorest quintile do. In several Sub-Saharan African countries where grade 6 completion exceeds 90 percent, the gap between rich and poor can remain quite large (for example, Nigeria, Tanzania, Uganda, and Zambia).

Inequality in grade 6 completion between the rich and poor is systematically large in countries in the South Asia region. For example, in Bangladesh, Nepal, and Pakistan, fewer than 40 percent of children in the poorest quintile complete grade 6, while between 70 and 80 percent of children in the richest quintile do. In India the gap is extremely large: virtually all children from the richest quintile complete grade 6, whereas only about 40 percent of those in the poorest quintile do.

In the Latin American countries covered in this analysis, children from the richest quintile typically complete grade 6, but there is substantial

Figure 6.1   School Completion through Grade 6, by Richest and Poorest Quintiles in Selected Countries

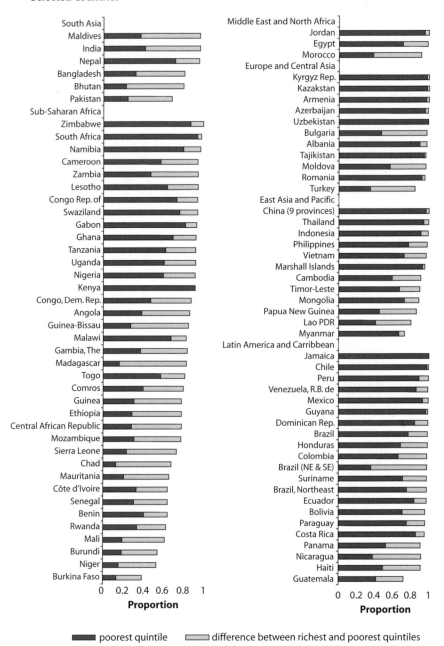

Source: Author's calculations from household surveys. See http://econ.worldbank.org/projects/edattain.

variability in the share of the poorest quintile who do. For example, in Nicaragua about 90 percent of those in the richest quintile complete grade 6, but fewer than 40 percent from the poorest quintile do. In Honduras, by contrast, where completion is similar to Nicaragua in the richest quintile, it is quite a bit higher in the poorest quintile (around 70 percent). In the East Asian countries, there is more variability among the richest quintile (ranging from about 80 percent in Cambodia, Lao People's Democratic Republic, and Papua New Guinea, to close to 100 percent in Indonesia and Thailand) and similar variability in the poorest quintile.

The Pattern of Educational Attainment: Survivor Profiles

The percentage of children and youth who complete grade 6—and within-country differences therein—is a useful summary of attainment. But important for policy is the pattern of how those children attain the grade they do, and where in the schooling cycle differences arise. Grade survival profiles show the whole pattern of school completion and give useful insights into problems in a country and possible policies to address them.

Compare, for example, Sierra Leone and Mozambique (figure 6.2). In both countries, about 25 to 30 percent of children from the poorest quintile complete grade 6. In Sierra Leone, however, roughly the same percentage complete at least one year of schooling, while in Mozambique almost 70 percent of children from the poorest quintile complete at least one year of schooling. Clearly, in Mozambique poor children are starting school and then either dropping out or repeating grades, whereas in Sierra Leone they are not enrolling in school at all. In both these countries, gaps between rich and poor start at enrollment and perpetuate through the basic education cycle.

In South Africa, where the vast majority of children complete grade 6 (and even grade 9), all children start school. To the extent that there is a gap between rich and poor, it emerges slowly across school years, accelerating progressively in upper primary and lower secondary school. This pattern is similar—although magnified—in Brazil, where virtually all children complete one year of schooling and inequalities grow consistently across the basic education cycle. In Tanzania, by contrast, a large gap in the percentage of children who complete even one year of schooling is exacerbated in the transition year from primary to lower secondary

Figure 6.2   Grade Survival Profiles: Proportion of Cohort from Each Income Quintile That Has Completed Grades 1–9 in Selected Countries

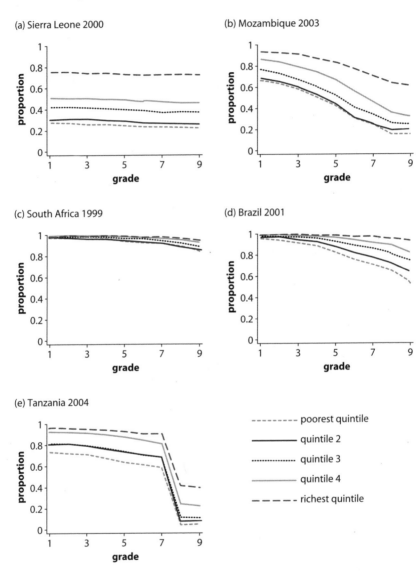

(a) Sierra Leone 2000

(b) Mozambique 2003

(c) South Africa 1999

(d) Brazil 2001

(e) Tanzania 2004

- - - - - - - poorest quintile
———— quintile 2
·············· quintile 3
———— quintile 4
— — — — richest quintile

Figure 6.2   Continued

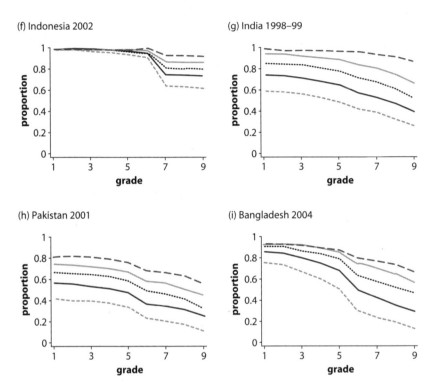

(f) Indonesia 2002

(g) India 1998–99

(h) Pakistan 2001

(i) Bangladesh 2004

Source: Author's calculations from household surveys. See http://econ.worldbank.org/projects/edattain.

Note: Graphs show Kaplan-Meier survival curve estimates of grade survival in the cohort of 10- to 19-year-olds.

school. Similarly, in Indonesia virtually all the gaps between rich and poor occur at the transition to lower secondary school—almost all children complete the primary cycle.

In India and Pakistan gaps between rich and poor remain fairly constant over the entire basic education cycle, including at the very beginning of schooling. In these countries it is not dropout and repetition that drive inequalities, but differences in the percentages of children who ever go to school. Bangladesh embodies all of these patterns simultaneously: inequalities in grade completion start at entry, they increase progressively over the primary school years as poor children drop out and repeat grades, and the gap between the two is exacerbated in the transition to secondary school.

The nine countries illustrated in figure 6.2 show how varied cross-country patterns in enrollment and dropout can be—and how inequalities between rich and poor manifest themselves in different ways. Clearly, addressing lack of completion (overall or within the poorest quintiles only) will require in-depth analysis of country-specific conditions, constraints, and opportunities. But the patterns illustrated by these nine countries point to some general lessons. First, when all children attend some school and then the poor increasingly drop out over the entire basic education cycle, it is unlikely that physical access to schooling is the primary determinant of dropout. Policies to stimulate the demand for schooling are likely to be the right starting point for addressing the issue. Note that this potentially includes increasing the quality of schooling, thereby making it more attractive and worthwhile to rich and poor alike. When there are large gaps even at entry, then it is more likely that a combination of demand and supply policies will be important. Second, in many countries (such as Brazil, India, Mozambique, Pakistan, Sierra Leone, and South Africa among the nine countries discussed above) there is no break in grade completion in the transition to the secondary cycle. Rather, the gap between rich and poor grows progressively larger in a smooth way. In these countries access to secondary school places is unlikely to be the main constraint on secondary schooling. Contrast these to countries where there is a sharp break in the transition (for example, India or Tanzania), where it is likely that rationing of secondary school places—either explicitly through an exam or implicitly through lack of facilities—creates a binding constraint on expansion beyond the primary cycle.

Urban or Rural Residence and Gender

Economic status is, of course, only one source of inequality in educational attainment. Children from excluded groups (such as ethnic minorities or lower castes in South Asia), orphans or other vulnerable children, or children with disabilities have lower attainment—even at the same level of economic well-being.[6] However, poverty status (or being in the poorest quintile) is associated with the largest education gaps when countries are far from having universal education.

Consider the relationship between the rich-poor gap in grade 6 completion and overall grade 6 completion (left panel of figure 6.3). As one

Figure 6.3   Inequalities in School Completion through Grade 6, by Household Economic Status, Urban or Rural Residence, and Gender

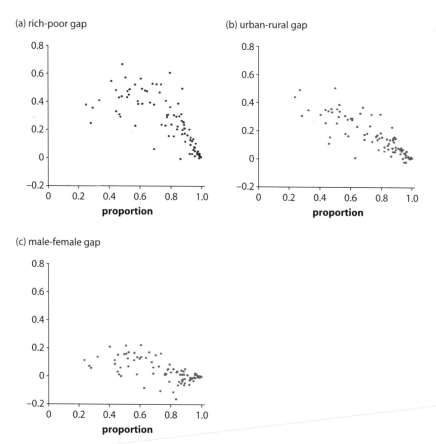

(a) rich-poor gap

(b) urban-rural gap

(c) male-female gap

Source: Author's calculations from household surveys. See http://econ.worldbank.org/projects/edattain.

deviates from universal completion (which would be indicated as a point with a value of one on the horizontal axis and zero on the vertical axis), the gap between the richest and poorest quintiles grows sharply. The gap between richest and poorest quintiles averages about 40 percentage points when overall completion of grade 6 is about 80 percent. Clearly, economic status is strongly related to shortfalls in attainment.

Urban and rural residence is likewise a strong correlate of shortfalls in completion (middle panel of figure 6.3). This is perhaps unsurprising because in most countries the majority of the population in the poorest quintile lives in rural areas. But the fact that the slope is flatter than the one associated with economic status indicates that poverty is a better predictor of inequality in completion than rural residence. This means that in many cases, poverty—be it urban or rural—is associated with shortfalls in schooling. Being female, another education risk factor, is a much weaker predictor of shortfalls in completion (right panel of figure 6.3). Gender gaps in school completion through grade 6 are typically much smaller than the gaps associated with economic status and urban or rural residence. Raising completion among the poor is therefore more likely to lead to larger increases in the aggregate than raising completion among girls.

Nonetheless, the gender gap is still substantial in countries in South Asia and North and West Africa. In countries where the gender gap is large among youth in the poorest quintile, it is not nearly as large in the richest quintile (see figure 6.4). For example, in Chad the male/female ratio in grade 6 completion is greater than 3 (that is, grade 6 completion of males is three times that of females) in the poorest quintile, but it is only 1.2 in the richest quintile. Other countries with high male/female

Figure 6.4 Inequalities in School Completion through Grade 6 in the Richest and Poorest Quintiles, by Gender

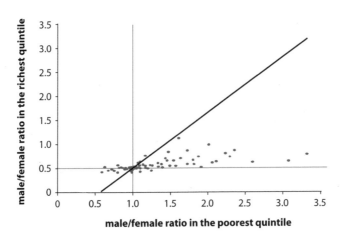

Source: Author's calculations from household surveys. See http://econ.worldbank.org/projects/edattain.

ratios in the poorest quintile are Guinea-Bissau (3.1), Turkey (2.6), Pakistan (2.4), and Niger (2.3). In all these countries the male/female ratio is lower than 1.3 in the richest quintile.

Orphanhood

The increasing number of orphans in developing countries—from the spread of AIDS and war—has increased attention on the human capital development of these vulnerable children.[7] Concerns that orphans will acquire less education, thus worsening their own life chances, are several: school-age children who have lost one or both parents may not be able to afford the costs of schooling; they may be needed for economic activities; or their guardians may simply invest less in their welfare. These concerns have prompted calls for governments to subsidize the schooling of orphans—although there is a limited amount of empirical evidence of systematic schooling shortfalls among orphans based on large-scale nationally representative surveys.

A subset of the data sets discussed above have the requisite information to study the links among orphanhood, poverty, and schooling. The data sets cover 102 nationally representative household surveys conducted since 1990 from 51 developing countries in Africa, Latin America, the Caribbean, and Asia. The sample includes countries with high and low HIV prevalence and orphan rates. Orphans are defined as children 7 to 14 years of age who have lost one or both parents for any reason. In these data sets most orphans had lost either their father (3–16 percent of children) or mother (1–7 percent of children); only 1.4 percent of children, on average, had lost both parents. The analysis of enrollment gaps associated with orphanhood controls for age and gender.

Enrollment among two-parent orphans is typically lower than among nonorphans (see figure 6.5). In most data sets the difference in enrollment between paternal orphans and nonorphans, or between maternal orphans and nonorphans, is not statistically significant once other factors are controlled for. In 38 percent of the data sets paternal orphans' enrollment is significantly lower than that of nonorphans; in 46 percent of the data sets maternal orphans' enrollment is significantly lower than that of nonorphans. For two-parent orphans, more than half of the data sets (58 percent) show a statistically significant enrollment deficit compared with nonorphans, while for the remaining 42 percent there was no statistically significant difference.

Figure 6.5   Differences in Enrollment of Children Ages 7–14, by Orphan Status

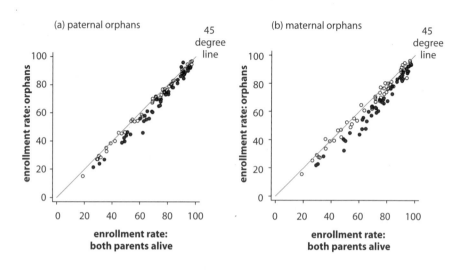

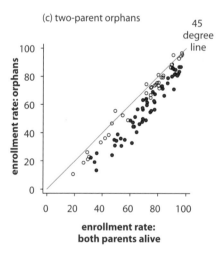

Source: Ainsworth and Filmer 2006.

Note: This figure compares enrollment among children with two parents living (horizontal axis) to children who have lost one or both parents (vertical axis). Each point represents findings from a single country. A point along the 45-degree line indicates enrollment rates that are equal for orphans and nonorphans, after controlling for other factors, including poverty. A point below the 45-degree line represents a data set in which orphan enrollment is lower than nonorphan enrollment. Points show predicted enrollment after controlling for sex, age, urban or rural residence, household economic status, and geographic region. Solid points indicate that the difference between orphans and nonorphans is significantly different from zero at the 5 percent level.

Figure 6.6   Differences in Enrollment of Children Ages 7–14, by Orphan Status and Economic Status, Conditional on Individual and Household Characteristics

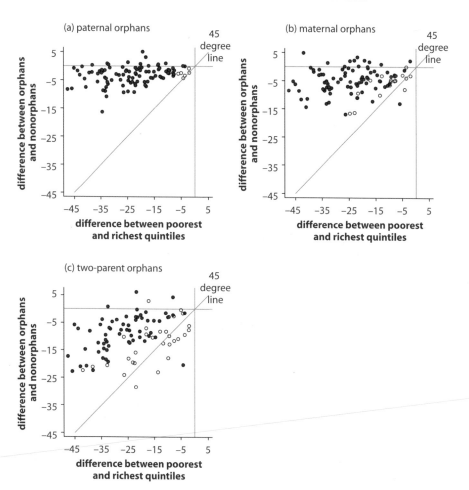

Source: Ainsworth and Filmer 2006.

Note: Points show differences in predicted enrollment between orphans and nonorphans and between children from the poorest and richest economic status quintiles after controlling for sex, age, urban or rural residence, and geographic region. Solid points indicate that the difference between the orphan differential and the economic status differential is significantly different from zero at the 5 percent level.

The size of the orphan enrollment gap is dwarfed by the gap in enroll-ment between children at the bottom and top of the distribution of eco-nomic status. Figure 6.6 compares the enrollment gap between orphans and nonorphans (the vertical axis) with the enrollment gap between children from the richest and poorest quintiles of the population (the horizontal axis). In almost all cases the gap between rich and poor is sta-tistically significantly larger than the gap between orphans and nonor-phans (solid points)—and substantially larger in magnitude.

It is clear from these results that the experience of countries hit hard-est by HIV/AIDS cannot be generalized to all countries. The education consequence of being an orphan depends on many country-specific fac-tors, including the overall poverty rate; the socioeconomic status of households that experience adult mortality; the mitigating effects of cus-toms and demographic factors, such as child fostering and the extended family; the demand for schooling; and the public policies already in place. The diversity in these underlying conditions is reflected in the diversity in the relation between orphan status and enrollment shortfalls.

As discussed above, not all countries have a deficit in enrollment or attainment among girls. But when such a deficit exists, it typically is no larger among orphans in this age group. Figure 6.7 illustrates the male-female gap among nonorphans on the horizontal axis and among orphans on the vertical axis. Points above the 45 degree line are countries for which the gap is larger among orphans than nonorphans. Most of the dif-ferences are not statistically significantly different from zero: exceptions are typically from countries in Western Africa (Cameroon, the Central African Republic, The Gambia, Mali, Mauritania, and Senegal).

Disability

While there has been policy discussion about interventions to increase access to schooling for children with disabilities, there has been little sys-tematic empirical analysis on which to base this policy.[8] This is due large-ly to the lack of appropriate and comparable data. A review of household surveys for relevant variables yielded 14 data sets with the requisite infor-mation. These are DHS, MICS2, and IHS from 12 developing and 1 tran-sition country.

Defining disability is difficult—and controversial. The definitions of disability in the data sets used in this analysis are most closely consistent with a focus on impairment—such as missing a limb or having limited or

Figure 6.7   Differences in Enrollment of Children Ages 7–14, by Orphan Status and Gender, Conditional on Individual and Household Characteristics

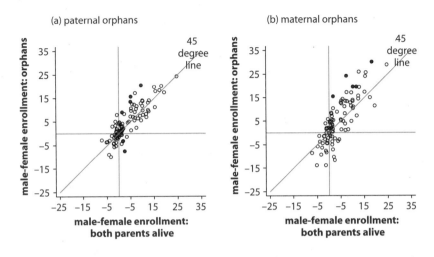

(a) paternal orphans

(b) maternal orphans

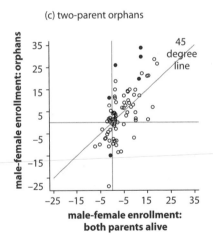

(c) two-parent orphans

Source: Ainsworth and Filmer 2006.

Note: Points show differences in predicted enrollment of males and females, of orphans and nonorphans after controlling for sex, age, economic status quintile, urban or rural residence, and geographic region. Solid points indicate that the male-female difference among orphans is statistically significantly different from that among nonorphans at the 5-percent level.

no sight. Across the surveys, however, there is substantial variation in definitions. For example, in the Cambodia Socio-Economic Survey the disability question includes a detailed list of potential cases—"amputation of one limb; amputation of more than one limb; unable to use one limb; unable to use more than one limb; paralyzed lower limbs only; paralyzed all four limbs"—whereas in Jamaica there is simply one category defined as a household member having a "physical or mental disability." Similarly, in Mongolia sight and hearing problems are described as seeing or hearing "with difficulty," whereas in other surveys they are typically characterized as "blind" and "deaf."

Despite these limitations, but keeping them in mind, the data are nevertheless revealing. Consistent with other similar surveys, the 14 surveys identify 1 to 2 percent of the population as having a disability. Results in Cambodia, which has two surveys with varying definitions of disability, suggest that the percentage is not always sensitive to the exact definition: different definitions can give similar prevalence rates, and vice versa. In addition, other aspects of the surveys, such as the training of enumerators or how the interviewees expect the survey to be used, might affect the overall estimated prevalence rates.

These surveys provide little evidence that youth with disabilities are generally more or less likely to live in rich or poor households. (Adults with disabilities, on the other hand, typically live in poorer households—although this is often because adults with disabilities have lower educational attainment, which in turn leads to lower economic status.) Given this finding, it is particularly worrisome that youth with disabilities are almost always substantially less likely to participate in schooling. Children with disabilities are less likely to start school, and in some countries they have lower transition rates resulting in reduced schooling attainment. The order of magnitude of the school participation disability deficit is typically larger than deficits associated with other characteristics, such as gender, residence, or economic status differentials (see figure 6.8).

This analysis suggests that disability is associated with long-run poverty: children with disabilities are less likely to acquire the human capital that will allow them to earn higher incomes. In all countries the schooling gap between children with and without a disability starts at grade 1, suggesting that efforts to boost enrollments of children with disabilities at the earliest grades are necessary to increase educational attainment for this population. An additional result that the disability deficit widens

Figure 6.8   Deficit in Current Enrollment Associated with Disability, Gender, Rural Residence, and Economic Status in Selected Countries

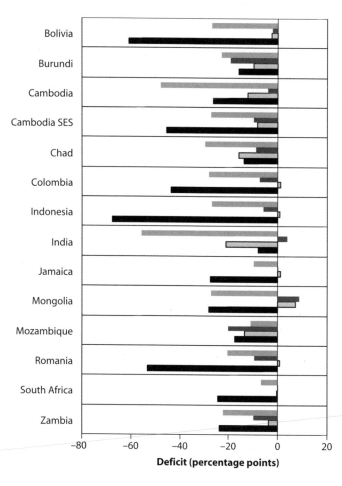

Deficit (percentage points)

■ With disability   ☐ Female   ■ Rural   ▨ Poorest-Richest quintile

Source: Filmer 2008.

Note: Deficits shown are the marginal effects of dummy variables for each characteristic in multivariate probit models. Maximum age is 14 in Burundi.

from grade to grade in countries that have achieved high enrollment among children without a disability suggests that special effort may be needed in all countries to keep youth with disabilities in school, once they have started attending.

Conclusion

Gaps in educational attainment associated with poverty are systematically large in poor countries. When universal completion is not achieved, poverty is usually one of the strongest correlates of the shortfall. But the pattern by which poverty manifests itself varies substantially. In some countries most of the difference between rich and poor starts at initial enrollment and remains fairly constant over the basic education cycle; in other countries initial gaps grow progressively over the basic education cycle; while in still others initial gaps are small and really express themselves only in the transition to secondary schooling. There are many other sources of education shortfalls within countries. Being female is sometimes associated with lower educational attainment—and when it is, the shortfall is largest among the poor. Likewise, orphanhood is sometimes associated with education deficits, although there is substantial heterogeneity across countries in the magnitude of that deficit. There is little evidence that the enrollment deficit among orphans is typically larger for girls (in the 7- to 14-year-old age range). Finally, although disability measured in household surveys identifies only a small share of the population as disabled, the education deficit for that population is large. Low educational attainment among people with a disability is associated with long-run poverty—suggesting a vicious circle.

Notes

1. This article draws from, and expands upon and updates, the discussion in Filmer (2006a). The primary completion rate—favored by the World Bank for monitoring progress toward reaching the Millennium Development Goals—is typically measured by its proxy: the ratio of the number of nonrepeaters in the terminal grade of primary school to the number of children of the official age of the terminal year of primary school.
2. See World Bank 2008.
3. See, for example, World Bank (2005).
4. This approach is described and defended—and applied to the analysis of education inequalities in India—in Filmer and Pritchett (2001). When this index

is not available, per capita household consumption is used to derive population quintiles.

5. This section and the following one on the pattern of educational attainment are based on Filmer and Pritchett (1999), with data updates from http://econ.worldbank.org/projects/edattain.

6. This discussion is based on Filmer (2006b) and data updates from http://econ.worldbank.org/projects/edattain.

7. This section is based on Ainsworth and Filmer (2006).

8. This section is based on Filmer 2008.

References

Ainsworth, Martha, and Deon Filmer. 2006. "Children's Schooling: AIDS, Orphanhood, Poverty, and Gender." *World Development* 34 (6): 1099–1128.

Filmer, Deon. 2008. "Disability, Poverty, and Schooling in Developing Countries: Results from 14 Household Surveys." *World Bank Economic Review* 22 (1): 141–163.

———. 2006a. "Education Inequalities around the World." In *Commonwealth Education Partnerships 2007.* Cambridge, U.K.: Nexus Strategic Partnerships for the Commonwealth Secretariat.

———. 2006b. "Gender and Wealth Disparities in Schooling: Evidence from 44 Countries." *International Journal of Educational Research* 43 (6): 351–369.

Filmer, Deon, and Lant Pritchett. 1999. "The Effect of Household Wealth on Educational Attainment: Evidence from 35 Countries." *Population and Development Review* 25 (1): 85–120.

———. 2001. "Estimating Wealth Effects without Expenditure Data—or Tears: With an Application to Educational Enrollments in States of India." *Demography* 38 (1): 115–132

World Bank. 2005. World Development Report 2006: *Equity and Development.* Washington, DC: World Bank.

———. 2008. *World Development Indicators 2008.* Washington, DC

CHAPTER 7

The Double Disadvantage of Gender and Social Exclusion in Education

Marlaine E. Lockheed[1]

Girls' education is a human right, provides economic and social benefits, and is an international objective (Birdsall, Levine, and Ibrahim 2005). Most countries have responded to this objective. Since 1960, primary school enrollment rates in the developing world have risen steeply for both boys and girls, with girls' participation converging with that of boys'.

Yet, the most recent estimate finds that about 72 million school-age children were still not in school in 2005 (down from about 98 million in 1999), and a majority of them were girls (UNESCO 2007). Of the 41 million school-age girls not enrolled, about 70 percent came from "socially excluded groups" (Lewis and Lockheed 2006).

This chapter presents evidence regarding the education of socially excluded girls in developing countries, reviews some research about education programs that work in mitigating the effects of social exclusion, and offers some policy recommendations and unanswered research questions. It draws heavily from work coauthored with Maureen Lewis (Lewis and Lockheed 2006, 2007, 2008).

Socially Excluded Groups

Some population subgroups are sidelined in their own countries, prevented by discrimination and indifference from receiving the social rights and protection meant for all citizens. These socially excluded groups include ethnic minorities, isolated clans, and groups in which a minority language predominates. Such population subgroups are not simply different, however; their difference is accorded lower esteem by the majority population. Several factors account for such lower esteem. Jacob Meerman (2005) defines socially excluded groups as cultural subgroups that are marginalized because of one or more of the following phenomena:

- Stigmatization resulting from trauma at the hands of the majority population—for example, a history of slavery (as experienced by blacks in Brazil, Cuba, and the United States) or dispossession of a homeland (as experienced by native peoples of Canada or the United States)
- Ethnic differences, including differences in race, language, and religion—for example, Hill Tribes in the Lao People's Democratic Republic or indigenous groups in Latin America
- Low status, whereby excluded groups are subordinated in the social hierarchy below the majority population, such as the Roma in Europe or lower caste groups in India or Nepal
- Involuntary minority status (in contrast to immigrant groups that are voluntary minorities)

Regardless of what creates the exclusion, the education consequences for the excluded—and excluded girls in particular—are real. They range from the merely disagreeable (teachers ignoring students in class) to the dire (destruction of schools and violence against teachers and communities). Thus, discrimination by the majority population effectively prevents the socially excluded from participating in education. Compounding the problem for girls, socially excluded groups are often *less likely* to send their daughters to school and *more likely* to allow them to drop out early, compared with their sons. Such household behavior can arise for both economic and cultural reasons, and mitigating their effects requires a two-pronged approach.

Some countries have few socially excluded groups, while others may have dozens if not hundreds of groups differentiated by ethnicity, geography, language, and culture. Countries that are ethnically and linguistically heterogeneous are particularly at risk. They have more difficulty reaching universal education—and more difficulty in bringing girls into school—than do more homogeneous countries at similar levels of development.

Social Exclusion and Education

In research for our book (Lewis and Lockheed 2007), we carried out regressions testing the association between girls' school participation and degree of country heterogeneity (also referred to as ethnolinguistic fractionalization) across 120 countries, using an index based on the work of ethnologists and anthropologists as reported by Alesina and others (2003). We focused on three main schooling variables: the female primary school completion rate (PCR), the *difference* between male and female PCRs, and a learning score created by Luis Crouch and Tazeen Fasih (2004), which is based on country-level performance on international tests of math, science, and reading. We found that countries with multiple ethnic and language groups have lower PCRs for girls, a larger gap between male and female PCRs, and lower overall achievement (see table 7.1).

Since heterogeneous countries are also more likely to be poor, we included various indicators of development in our estimates and found few differences in the importance of heterogeneity and girls' education. That said, we recognize the shortcomings of cross-country regression analysis. But consider two countries that are equally poor, where 82 percent of the population lives on less than $2 per day. In one, Bangladesh, a

Table 7.1 Elasticities of Primary Completion Rates and Learning and Ethnolinguistic Fractionalization

Coefficient	Log (female PCR)	Log (male PCR) – log (female PCR)	Log (learning score)
Ethnolinguistic fractionalization, log	−0.22[a]	0.09[a]	−0.17[a]
	[−4.27]	[3.99]	[−3.65]
Constant	4.06[a]	0.17[a]	5.74[a]
	[62.8]	[6.46]	[101]
Observations	118	118	55
R^2	0.14	0.12	0.20

Source: Lewis and Lockheed 2007.

Note: Figures in brackets are t-statistics. PCR = primary school completion rate.

a. Significant at the 1 percent level.

country with few ethnic and linguistic differences, 86 percent of primary school-age girls attend school. In the other, nearby Nepal, a country with many ethnic and linguistic subgroups, only 66 percent of primary school-age girls are in school. Greater heterogeneity seems to matter.

We also see that heterogeneity operates within countries. Specifically, within any given country, girls from excluded groups are less likely to enroll in school, complete fewer years of schooling, and are less likely to complete primary school or attend secondary school. Following are some examples from published reports:

- In Nigeria, minority Hausa-speaking girls have a 35 percent lower probability of attending school, compared with majority Yoruba-speaking boys (UIS 2005).
- In India, 37 percent of girls ages 7–14 belonging to scheduled castes or scheduled tribes do not attend school, compared with 26 percent of boys the same age from the same groups (Census of India 2001). About 35 percent of 15-year-old tribal girls are in school, compared with about 60 percent of tribal boys of the same age (Wu and others 2007).
- In Sri Lanka, minority Tamil girls ages 9–11 were 10 percent less likely to be in school than majority Sinhalese boys (Arunatilake 2006).
- In Lao PDR, Hill Tribe girls living in rural communities complete fewer than two years of school, whereas majority Lao-Tai girls living in urban communities complete eight years of school (King and van der Walle 2007).
- In Pakistan, only 10 percent of Balochi-Pathan rural girls complete primary school, compared with 40 percent of comparable boys, 55 percent of urban Punjabi girls, and 65 percent of urban Punjabi boys (Lloyd, Mete, and Grant 2007).
- In Guatemala, only 26 percent of indigenous, non-Spanish-speaking girls complete primary school, compared with 45 percent of indigenous boys and 62 percent of Spanish-speaking girls (Hallman and Peracca 2007).
- In the Slovak Republic, only 9 percent of minority girls—but 54 percent of Slovak girls—attend secondary school (Lewis and Lockheed 2006).

These cases give an idea about the extent and degree of the problem of girls' exclusion, but such concrete data are available for relatively few countries. Analyses that disaggregate education indicators by gender *and* exclusion remain to be carried out on the dozens of data sets already available from highly heterogeneous countries. And new data need to be gathered to expand our knowledge about other similar countries.

Once in school, all available evidence suggests that girls from excluded groups perform as well or even better than boys at the primary level. Most studies do not disaggregate achievement results, but findings from a handful of country studies are encouraging with respect to girls' achievement:

- A study by Santiago Cueto and Walter Secada (2004) of 29 schools located in Spanish-, Aymara-, and Quechua-speaking communities in Peru found that grade 5 reading and math scores of rural Quechua girls were no different from those of rural Quechua boys. But overall, Quechua children's achievement was substantially lower than that of nonindigenous children.
- A study by Adela Garcia Aracil and Donald Winkler (2004) found that indigenous girls in Ecuador scored higher than indigenous boys on grade 5 math tests, with scores nearly as high as those of nonindigenous children.
- Research reported by Neville Postlewaite for a national sample of schools in Lao PDR found that, while majority Tai Kedai children outperformed Hmong Emien and Mon Khmer children on tests of reading and math, there were no gender differences within any of the three groups (Postlewaite, pers. comm. 2007).

When girls encounter constraints in their access to learning, their performance can lag. Such constraints occur when girls are kept home from school and thus receive fewer hours of instruction; when their teachers discriminate against them; or when negative stereotypes and expectations are activated in the classroom, and girls' motivation is reduced.

Creative Ways of Reaching and Teaching Excluded Girls

Over the past decade, much has been learned about how to reach poor children and those from excluded groups. Most of this experience has come from developed and middle-income developing countries. Programs have been designed that raise enrollments, sustain attendance, and equalize learning outcomes of excluded children. But little is known about how to reach excluded girls in particular.

What we can infer, however, is that getting and keeping excluded girls in school entails both different approaches and higher costs. Cultural variations, linguistic differences, and the special needs of girls drive up costs, because they require new methods tailored to each group. Investment on two fronts—expanding school opportunities and boosting the demand for education—is essential for enrolling and retaining excluded children in general and girls in particular. But hard evidence about the effects of these programs for excluded girls is limited, and excellent work by multilateral agencies and nongovernmental organizations is rarely empirically evaluated. Many questions remain.

Improving and Diversifying the Supply of Education

There are three key areas for improving and diversifying the supply of education (Lewis and Lockheed 2006):

- *Altering education policies and addressing discrimination.* Policies that appear fair on the surface may be subtly biased against girls from excluded groups. For example, policies that require school to be taught in a majority language may have greater effects on girls than on boys, because girls from excluded groups often have fewer opportunities than boys to experience the majority language outside their home. Similarly, policies that require either single-sex schools or coeducation may limit girls' opportunities, according to cultural conditions. Discrimination that is promoted in school textbooks—what Stephen Heyneman (2003) discusses under the rubric of "social cohesion"—also must be addressed. Few, if any, studies have examined how girls from excluded groups are treated in textbooks, but the treatment of minorities in some textbooks reinforces negative stereotypes.
- *Expanding schooling options.* Parental concerns for the physical safety of daughters may mean that nearby community schools and informal alternative schools are better able to attract and retain girls from excluded groups than are formal schools located at a distance. For example, in Rajasthan, India, community schools employed paraprofessional teachers, allowed the community to select and supervise teachers, and hired part-time workers to escort girls from excluded groups to school. A World Bank (1999) study found that children in these schools had higher enrollment, attendance, and test scores compared with students in public schools. Preschools can help excluded children more easily transition to formal schools. In Bolivia, Brazil, India, and Turkey, preschool programs that involved both mothers and children from excluded groups have been effective in reducing children's subsequent primary school dropout rates and in boosting their achievement

(Behrman, Cheng, and Todd 2000; Kagitcibasi 1996; Kaul, Ramachandran, and Upadhyaya 1993; Paes de Barros and Mendonca 1999). Compensatory programs also help. Brazil, India, and Spain all have offered targeted, compensatory in-school or after-school programs designed to bolster the performance of disadvantaged students. Evaluations find that these programs help children of excluded groups stay in school and raise their achievement. For example, in a randomized evaluation of a remedial education program in India, where young women were hired to tutor children who were lagging behind, Abhijit Banerjee and his colleagues (2005) found that the largest achievement gains were recorded for the most economically disadvantaged children. Radio, television, and computers can also expand opportunities for girls, particularly for girls who are secluded at home after primary school.

• *Improving the quality and relevance of schools and classrooms.* School quality matters more for excluded girls than for boys or children from mainstream families. Studies by Elizabeth King and Dominique van de Walle (2007) in Laos PDR, and by Cynthia Lloyd and her colleagues (2003) in Egypt, found that compared with boys, girls were less likely to enroll in and more likely to drop out from poor quality schools. Poor quality schools include buildings with leaking roofs, shattered walls, and dysfunctional sanitary facilities, as well as schools whose teachers are absent and where textbooks and teaching materials never arrive. Weak student performance is a good indicator of poor school quality, and directing quality improvement programs at poorly performing schools benefits excluded children. An example comes from Chile. There, three education programs in the 1990s provided additional support to improve the quality of the lowest performing schools. Patrick McEwan's recent analysis of grade 8 achievement of nearly 200,000 students in Chile found that these programs not only boosted learning, but substantially reduced the gaps in learning achievement between indigenous and nonindigenous students—by 30 percent (McEwan 2006). Poor quality can also mean schools that are not adapted to local conditions or communities. An essential adaptation accommodates linguistic heterogeneity through bilingual education. UNESCO's review of the literature has found that introducing reading, writing, and thinking skills in the child's mother tongue is particularly beneficial for excluded girls' school enrollment and retention (Benson 2005).

Creating Incentives for Households to Send Girls to School

The second line of attack—boosting demand for education—involves creating incentives for households to send girls to school. Evidence regarding incentives is scant, and this line of attack needs more focused evaluation.

- *Conditional cash transfers* (CCTs) extend resources to households to defray some of the costs of sending their children to school, tying social assistance payments to desirable behaviors. Although challenging to administer in many settings, CCTs offer incentives for families to send children to school. Programs in Bangladesh, Ecuador, and Mexico, among others, have been successful, although their specific impact on excluded groups has not been assessed. The experience of Progressa in Mexico suggests that without careful targeting, resources spent on CCTs may not have the desired results (de Janvry and Sadoulet 2006). Specifically, the program benefited indigenous boys more than indigenous girls. A CCT program in Ecuador boosted school enrollment overall by 3.7 percentage points, but did not differentially benefit girls or minority students (Schady and Araujo 2006).
- *Scholarships and stipends* also offset the cost of schooling. Secondary school scholarship programs offer girls financing and encouragement to stay in school. They compensate families for the direct and indirect costs of education. They have been highly effective in several countries, notably Bangladesh, where scholarships increased girls' enrollment to twice that of the national average. Stipend programs also compensate parents for the cost of schooling, but they are tied to such school inputs as uniforms, books, materials, and transportation. Even the opportunity to earn a scholarship has been found to boost student achievement. In Kenya, Kremer, Miguel, and Thornton (2004) carried out a randomized evaluation of the impact of girls' scholarship incentives (that is, the opportunity to receive a scholarship) on girls' learning achievement. The experiment, involving 127 schools, found that both boys and girls in schools with girls' scholarship programs achieved higher scores than those in control schools.
- Various types of *school feeding programs* show an association with higher enrollment and attendance. In Kenya, meals raised attendance in program schools by 30 percent, relative to schools without a free lunch, and test scores rose nearly half a standard deviation. But a careful analy-

sis of this program showed that most benefits accrued to boys rather than to girls and had little impact on reducing the gender gap (Vermeersch and Kremer 2004).

Practical Actions to Promote Education for Excluded Girls

What are some practical actions to promote education for excluded girls?

Middle-income countries like Chile, Malaysia, and Mexico have pioneered means of reaching the excluded, and we have learned from these experiences. But low-income countries simply cannot afford the extra efforts that are required to reach excluded groups and the out-of-school girls in those communities. External support will be required to finance needed initiatives, evaluate their impact on excluded girls, and monitor progress.

- **The UNESCO Institute for Statistics should report school participation and achievement data disaggregated by gender and exclusion.** Disaggregation of school enrollment by gender was essential in monitoring progress toward gender equity, and the same will be the case for monitoring improvement in education for excluded girls.
- **Bilateral, multilateral, and private donors should target their support to programs that have demonstrated positive effects for excluded girls.** A trust fund could be established to provide the financial basis for expanding successful efforts of donors and government in reaching, retaining, and teaching excluded girls.
- In implementing new programs, a **Girls' Education Evaluation Fund** could help expand the knowledge base about what works, particularly in Africa, where evidence is slim and more than 40 percent of excluded girls reside.

Many issues about excluded girls remain unresolved and many questions remain unanswered. Following are a few questions that deserve further investigation:

- Exactly how large is the problem? That is, how many out-of-school girls are members of excluded groups?
- Under what conditions are various programs effective in bringing excluded girls into school? Keeping them in school? Teaching them?

- What would it cost to implement these programs?
- And perhaps most important, how can countries overcome their own histories of exclusion to build a culture of equal opportunity and resource sharing, creating inclusion from the ashes of exclusion?

Note

1. The author is a Visiting Fellow at the Center for Global Development and lecturer at Princeton University's Woodrow Wilson School of Public and International Affairs. This paper was presented at the World Bank's Global Symposium on Education: A Critical Path to Gender Equality and Women's Empowerment, October 2–3, 2007. This paper draws heavily from *Inexcusable Absence: Why 60 Million Girls Still Aren't in School and What to Do About It* by Maureen Lewis and Marlaine Lockheed (2006) and *Exclusion, Gender and Education: Case Studies from the Developing World*, also by Lewis and Lockheed (2007).

References

Alesina A., A. Devleeschauwer, W. Easterly, S. Kurlat, and R. Wacziarg. 2003. "Fractionalization." *Journal of Economic Growth* 8 (2): 155–194.

Arunatilake, N. 2006. "Education Participation in Sri Lanka–Why All Are Not in School." *International Journal of Educational Research* 445 (3): 137–151.

Banerjee, A., S. Cole, E. Duflo, and L. Linden. 2005. "Remedying Education: Evidence from Two Randomized Experiments in India." Working Paper 109. Bureau for Research in Economic Analysis of Development, Harvard University, Cambridge, MA.

Benson, C. 2005. *Mother Tongue-Based Teaching and Education for Girls.* Bangkok: United Nations Educational, Scientific, and Cultural Organization.

Behrman, J. R., Y. Cheng, and P. Todd. 2000. "Evaluating Preschool Programs When Length of Exposure to the Program Varies: A Nonparametric Approach." PPIER Working Paper 01-034, Pennsylvania Institute for Economic Research, University of Pennsylvania, Department of Economics, Philadelphia, PA.

Birdsall, N., R. Levine, and A. Ibrahim, eds. 2005. *Towards Universal Primary Education: Investments, Incentives and Institutions.* Sterling, VA: Stylus Publishing.

Census of India. 2001. Office of the Registrar General and Census Commissioner, India.

Organizations and governments have interpreted gender, education, development, child rights, empowerment, and equality differently. A major reason for this is that their interpretations are buttressed by differing frameworks to research and gender analysis.

Gender inequality and other disparities continue to affect many developing countries through deepening poverty, disease (pandemics), civil conflict, natural disasters, social discrimination, and weak governance. A case in point is Central and Eastern European countries and the Commonwealth of Independent States, where high enrollment statistics hide wider regional, ethnic, and gender variations. For instance, inequities in education access remain for children from ethnic minority backgrounds, especially Roma. Children from poor and rural areas, as well as children with disabilities, face a particular challenge in gaining access to quality education. The Philippines is noting a continuation of the decline in participation and cohort survival rates, as a result of the depressed economy, low population growth, and underinvestment in education.

These contrasting frameworks will be reviewed to illustrate how they are being used in countries to grapple with the challenges of making schools gender friendly. This chapter will show how lessons and good practices from schools on the path toward being gender friendly are being taken upstream through sectorwide approaches (SWAps); education sector plans; and partnerships like EFA, Fast-Track Initiative (FTI), and the United Nations Girls' Education Initiative (UNGEI). The chapter demonstrates that the concept of gender-friendly schools and learning spaces is understood in several ways, depending on the framework used for gender analysis.

Bringing Girls and Women into Schools and Learning Spaces through WID

The WID approach views schools as the vehicle through which girls can gain access to education. The bottom line is the expansion of schooling to ensure that girls and women are educated so that they contribute more effectively to economic development and poverty reduction. This framework, with its focus on access, generates clear policy directives on issues such as employment of more women teachers, counting the numbers of girls and women in and out of school, overcoming barriers to girls' education, and realizing the benefits of schooling (Delors 1996; King and Hill 1991; World Bank 1995). This is in line with the gender parity goals, which focus on achieving equal participation of girls and boys in schools, determined by their proportion in the relevant age groups in the population (Subrahmanian 2005). That is why in education, gender parity is viewed as the path toward gender equality.

During the last decade, countries with low enrollment and wide gender gaps (mainly in South Asia and Sub-Saharan Africa) showed a much higher rate of progress in terms of average annual rate of increase (AARI) in enrollment than countries already on track for achieving the access and parity goals (UNICEF 2005a). However, despite impressive performance in their AARI in enrollment, many off-track countries have failed to achieve the gender parity target set for 2005. They also need to do much better to get on a viable trajectory for achieving universal access and completion by 2015 (UNICEF Thematic Report 2006). For many of the on-track countries, closing the final gap in access and parity may be more challenging than envisaged. Moreover, gains in access and parity were often achieved in the face of persistent barriers as well as formidable new challenges and threats. All of this highlights the complex dynamics of factors affecting progress toward the MDGs in different categories of countries.

Within this framework, one intervention to tackle access and parity is boarding facilities that allow girls in remote and sparsely populated areas to attend school. Staying in a hostel may provide a girl with time, space, and resources for homework. Girls would also have the time to interact with friends, which they may otherwise be denied. However, boarding schools must be safe and secure, comfortable, and conducive, with good facilities and adequate food and supervision.

Countries in Sub-Saharan Africa—like Kenya, Malawi, Tanzania, and Uganda—have rapidly increased access to primary education through several interventions: (1) promoting policy development and implementation of girls' education; and (2) targeting the excluded and most vulnerable children, especially girls and overage children, through alternative forms of education. WID does provide clear policy directives, unlike GAD, which highlights the complexities surrounding the changing institutions of the school and education at large.

School and Society as Gendered Power Structures

Education within the GAD framework aims at addressing school insecurity and violence, sexual division of labor, facilities and infrastructure, nutrition, health, teaching methods, the curriculum content, and school governance. The ongoing work in gender-friendly schools to strengthen the structures, processes, and outcomes of education is being used upstream to inform gender-sensitive policy in areas such as gender mainstreaming, gender budgeting, and gender audits. By 2001 the United Nations Children Fund (UNICEF) support of girls' education programs was rapidly gaining momentum, especially after the EFA Dakar conference in 2000, during which UNICEF was appointed to lead the UNGEI. The gender reviews and the girls' education programs from countries in 2002–2003 made it evident that girls' education from a gender perspective benefited boys, too. However, some stakeholders still believed that girls' education marginalized boys and took away from their equal treatment in schools. These perceptions highlighted the important role of the UNGEI in advocating for girls' education and demonstrating that the framework used was GAD rather than WID.

Unlike WID, GAD goes beyond access to examine the quality of education once girls are included. This vision of quality education for girls is not limited to the formal school system. It also extends to the provision of complementary basic education programs that provide first- and second-chance opportunities to girls who would otherwise be excluded. Such chances enable girls who need to work during regular school hours and teenage mothers to attend school. They are able to play and enjoy their childhood, free from sexual exploitation, harassment, and violent abuse in the family, school, and community.

In contrast to WID, which focuses on access and equal opportunity to education for girls only, GAD examines the impact of gender on the education of both girls and boys. In countries like Malawi, Swaziland, and Zambia, where the impact of the HIV and AIDS pandemic is acute, prevalence rates are considerably higher among adolescent girls than boys. School environments are unsafe and insecure for girls. Their predicament is evident in the classrooms, where male discourse dominates, sexual harassment of girls is prevalent, irrelevant and outdated curricula portray girls and women in subservient roles, and policies unfairly discriminate against them. The situation hardly represents quality and greatly undermines girls' rights in multiple domains. HIV and AIDS and the rising number of orphans in the countries affect the quality of learning among children, particularly girls who are confronted with responsibilities and prejudices that take them away from learning.

In countries like Burundi, Kenya, Madagascar, and Swaziland, dropout rates by gender at first and final grades demonstrate that girls are more likely to drop out of school than boys. But in Angola, a country that is just coming out of war, the dropout rate of boys is higher than that of girls in the final grade. In some countries like Djibouti, Sudan, and Yemen, the focus is not only on accelerating progress to reach the MDGs, but also on quality improvements and the related goal of keeping children, especially girls, in school (UNESCO 2005; UNICEF 2005a).

Quality cannot be defined or measured only by traditional, narrow means, such as examination results. Some of the factors shaping educational experience are school based, but others relate to the family, community, social, and cultural aspects of the child's environment. This environment must be safe, healthy, gender responsive, and conducive to learning. It is only when education is examined in relation to social, political, cultural, and economic contexts that we can understand education quality as multifaceted and made up of multiple, interlinking dimensions. Curricula—especially in disciplines such as the social sciences, literacy, and life skills—should therefore challenge the status quo of inequitable gender relations. All subjects should be equally open to girls, who should feel comfortable and confident about making choices for, or against, traditionally male or traditionally female subjects. Especially for informal adolescent education programs, content should be demand driven and informed by the views and aspirations of the learners.

The teaching materials, as well as the supporting resources, should reflect the possibilities for boys and girls to take part in a variety of social roles and pursue different careers. Quality educational content for girls must also include the information and skills that girls need to make informed decisions about their sexual and reproductive health. Training in life skills should be comprehensive and well designed, ensuring that school grounds, classrooms, and corridors are places where girls feel physically safe and psychologically at ease (Pattman and Chege 2004). Girl-friendly schools must have separate, well maintained, and equipped restrooms for girls and boys. If physical education is offered, there should be changing facilities that are private and clean. Research has shown that in schools without appropriate facilities for adolescent girls, many girls stay home during their menstrual periods and miss classes. This affects their performance. Developing activities to help both teachers and health workers be more sensitive to the needs of girls who have been victims of rape and sexual abuse is also an important collaborative strategy that can make a difference.

Within the GAD approach, implementation of policies against discrimination, harassment, and abuse by pupils or staff is a prerequisite of a quality learning environment for girls (UNAIDS 2005). Girl-friendly policies should be in place to ensure that, if girls become pregnant, they are able to continue their education without stigma, discrimination, or other adverse effects. Equally important is the right to education for girls living with HIV and AIDS or participation in community or home-based care activities for others affected by HIV and AIDS. Comprehensive and well-implemented gender and education policies not only draw attention to discriminatory practices, but also provide recourse against them.

The gender make-up of the teaching and nonteaching staff of the school should be conducive to girls. Women teachers and head teachers, who are well respected and whose gender needs are well met, can be inspirational role models for female students. With relevant training, support, and professional recognition, female teachers can also provide information, guidance, and advice to girls on subjects such as sexuality and reproductive health. They may also conduct girls-only science and math classes to promote the active participation of girls in these traditionally male-dominated subjects.

Evidenced-based information demonstrates that gender is an effective entry point to address qualitative matters related to gender violence in schools, the impact of HIV and AIDS, and the feminization of poverty on children in school systems (Abramovay and das Graces 2005; Pinheiro 2006; UNICEF 2003). It is vital for schools to address the safety and security of adolescent girls and the feminine hygiene of girls from poor families to retain them in school (Salem-Pickertz 2005). School environments can be hostile to children because children feel insecure and unsafe, teachers are unqualified, children are taught in overcrowded classrooms, and student performance is poor. Unsafe and insecure schools lead to a breakdown in trust, which can have far-reaching effects on children, especially girls. This breakdown in trust and hostile school environments are blamed on WID and GAD approaches by the poststructuralists, who argue that power relations in institutions like schools and methodologies used in research silence the marginalized and vulnerable, especially girls and ethnic minorities.

The Poststructuralist Challenge to Gender, Sexuality, Education, and Development

The WID and GAD approaches emerged from the development paradigm. In contrast, poststructuralism arose out of a critique of a range of development practices and methodologies. Researchers like Mohanty (1988) and Pattman and Chege (2003) made observations on the challenges around the universalization of terms like *third-world women* and *development* and of the power relations camouflaged by the development assistance rhetoric. A noticeable aspect of poststructuralism is the critique of schooling as an institution that marginalizes and diminishes the power of local indigenous knowledge. Another unique component of this framework is its questioning of methodologies, the process by which research participants—including school girls, boys, teachers, and parents—become gendered in relation to stereotypes that exclude girls and women from conventional sources of data collection. Linked to this is the framework's focus on identities and how gender includes shifting processes of identification within the fixed structures noted by GAD analysts (Unterhalter 2005). Time and again, research in developing countries objectifies the identities of girls and women, and interventions have a problematic understanding of the participation of children and youth, particularly girls and women.

The complexities of the threats and risks posed by the HIV and AIDS pandemic have generated work that takes into account the gendered and sexualized identities of learners and teachers (Akunga 2004; Chilisa et al. 2005; Pattman and Chege 2003). A UNICEF-commissioned six-country study illustrated how girls and boys construct their identities and negotiate, adapt to, and resist common articulations of masculinity and femininity. The study also showed why it is wrong to constantly associate gender with girls and women. Instead, girls and boys were given space to challenge such constructs and reclaim their power and right to be heard as experts about their own gendered and sexual lives. An important output of the study was the development of life-skills manuals on gender, sexuality, and HIV and AIDS to be used in development of capacities of both young people in school and teachers (Pattman and Chege 2004). This framework is slowly but surely influencing curriculum content and the focus of what is being published. The analysis of identities is gaining momentum in social mobilization and participation of subordinated identities such as girls, ethnic minorities, and languages of instruction.

Transformative Action through Rights to Education and Gender Equality

For work in human rights, gender equality, and education, the global compacts (Universal Declaration of Human Rights, Convention on the Rights of the Child, Beijing Declaration, and the EFA Dakar declaration) are the generally acknowledged context. At the same time, gender equality is understood differently by each of these frameworks. In the education sphere, priority is given to achieving gender justice as reflected in the MDGs and EFA goals. A consideration of gender equality in education needs to be understood as the *right to education* (access and participation) together with the *rights within education* (gender-sensitive education environments, processes, and outcomes) and *through education* (relevant education outcomes that connect quality education with the wider process of gender justice in society; Subrahmanian 2005). The operation of rights is viewed as circular with rights in each of these three dimensions linking positively to other rights. As these rights are indivisible, they form a substantial component of a program of action that would promote both gender parity and gender equality.

The child-friendly schools (CFS) approach addresses the concerns raised in all three frameworks. In the early 1990s UNICEF began to support CFS initiatives in countries to promote children's rights through a holistic and comprehensive approach to quality education (UNICEF 2005b, 2006) For the last decade UNICEF has been supporting around 50 countries to develop CFS because they foster girl-friendly environments. It is through these CFS that the gem of gender-friendly schools began to take shape. CFS are also gender friendly because the holistic approach to quality facilitated the school and education sector to tackle the above-mentioned rights to gender equality. Within the context of the right to education, the CFS approach seeks out those who are excluded because of gender and other disparities. Inclusion of girls and boys who are out of school is vital in South Asia and the postconflict countries of Sub-Saharan Africa, where huge numbers of girls are out of school. The barriers to the inclusion of girls in schooling are rooted in discrimination, stereotypes, social norms that devalue women, and, of course, poverty.

The right to education directly deals with the rights of girls and women to gender-friendly schools by tackling discrimination, stigma, stereotypes, curriculum content, learning-teaching methods, gender violence, sexual harassment, community disengagement, and school governance. Quality content for girls must reflect the Convention on the Rights of the Child, which articulates children's right to education content that develops all the child's talents and abilities to the fullest potential. Quality content respects human rights and fundamental freedoms; respects the child's family, language, and cultural identity; and promotes gender equality, peace and tolerance, and respect for the natural environment.

In these countries, CFS have a multifaceted approach to education that demands macro-level policy change from governments and education authorities, plus a micro-level change from the family, the school, and the community. This vision of quality education for girls is not limited to the formal school system. The provision of complementary schooling is a very important means of providing first- and second-chance opportunities to girls who would otherwise be excluded. This could enable school attendance by girls who need to work during regular school hours or teenage mothers.

Violence in school can take many forms, including corporal punishment, verbally abusive comments, gender violence, bullying (peer violence), and gang-related brutality. As the UNICEF study demonstrated, "Positive, nonviolent ways of discipline and child-rearing are being promoted and applied in all regions and cultures" (Hart et al. 2005, 121). Some of these forms of violence are perpetrated by teachers and other school personnel, and sometimes children and young people themselves are the perpetrators. The physical location of a restroom, a staircase, or a playing field is not in itself necessarily dangerous. Rather, it is the social environment of the school that turns these physical spaces into sites of violence for girls. In studies where children have been asked to "map" (through photography, transect maps, and various other tools) the danger zones or safety zones of their schools and playgrounds (Leach et al. 2003; Leach and Machakanja 2000; Pattman and Chege 2003; Pinheiro 2006; UNICEF 2003), girls have been very adept at representing where they feel safe and not so safe. In these studies as well as in others where the teachers or researchers have organized some sort of safety audit or walkabout with children, girls have said that they did not want to walk past places where groups of boys congregate (Pattman and Chege 2003; Pinheiro 2006).

Restrooms come up repeatedly in the literature as a particularly dangerous area of schools for girls. Most sexual abuse, for example, of very young children in daycare centers, takes place in restrooms (Finklehor and Williams 1988). There are numerous studies that refer to restrooms as danger zones in schools (Mitchell and Moletsane 2004). Other studies found that when teachers supervised the restrooms that were located a great distance from the school, the incidence of gender violence decreased (Brookes and Higson-Smith 2004).

Discrimination, stigmatization, gender stereotyping, bullying, peer violence, and gang behaviors like extortion are used to exclude certain children from spaces within and around schools. A seven-country study of violence in schools in the Middle Eastern and North African region found many shortcomings in the physical environments of schools, ranging from damaged spaces and furniture to a lack of basic hygiene (Payet 2005). These physical factors along with other social factors had a negative impact on girls as well as teachers' capability and motivation to attend to a productive teaching-learning process. Chege's (2006) study of Kenya student teachers' memories of childhood violence illustrates how teachers' values and attitudes toward teaching are influenced by their childhood experiences and how effective teacher education should incorporate these memories into the pedagogy.

CFS is being used to address issues of quality by almost all countries in East Asia and the Pacific, where enrollment rates stand at more than 95 percent but low quality is seen as a key factor in persistent dropout and repetition rates. In countries like China and Rwanda, UNICEF focused on advocating for and mainstreaming CFS as a comprehensive model for quality education. In these gender-sensitive CFS, girls' participation in the classroom and school is facilitated. Quality is a means of attracting girls and boys to school, keeping them through to completion, and promoting improved learning achievement.

Transforming schools from being unsafe and insecure to being gender-friendly, protective environments within which children can learn and have access to quality education is desirable. An unsafe and insecure school damages the psyche of both girls and boys. It interferes with learning, and more than anything, it erodes the potential that schools have to make a positive impact on society at large. Although girls may be exposed to danger on the way to and from school, much more disturbing is the recognition that, when they are at school, they may encounter a lack of teachers; endure inadequate water and sanitation; and suffer from hunger, ill health, and violence.

Unsafe and insecure learning environments negatively impact the participation of girls in schools and classrooms. Yet for schools to provide girls with the quality education they require, education systems must ensure girls participate in all aspects of school life. Participation—hearing the voices of children—should not be separated from taking action (Hart et al. 2005). It may not always be possible to involve children directly in taking action, but opportunities abound for girls to participate in class-room, extracurricular, and other school activities. For instance, it is impor-tant that children and youth participate in researching insecurity and lack of safety in schools and developing child-focused interventions for addressing hostile environments in and around schools (Wilson and Lipsey 2005). What is emphasized as a principle is that the code of con-duct should not simply "hear" the voices of children for the purpose of research. A good example of approaches that draw on children's voices in program development and policy making can be seen in a recent publica-tion by the Population Council (Chung, Hallman, and Bray 2005) on their work with very young adolescents (10–14-year-olds).

One example that stands out for its creativity, affordability, and imme-diate impact is the girl-friendly school initiative in rural districts in The Gambia (Mitchell and Moletsane 2004). There a select number of schools have developed a school-based visual data scheme for charting the atten-dance of children. On the wall of the office of the head teacher are large and inexpensive flip charts providing a visual map of who is at school and who is not on a monthly basis. The charts offer a straightforward visual analysis of attendance based on the village that children come from, their age, sex, grade, and distance from the school. Having to travel a long dis-tance to school is often a security risk, particularly for girls. On another chart is a simple bar graph of enrollments of boys and girls in the school over the last five years. The fact that schools have actually collected such data themselves is significant. They have developed a scheme that makes the data accessible to parent-community groups that are involved in the governance of the school and to all the teachers in the school, offering an example of shared responsibility for school management. Clearly a simi-lar approach could be effective for schools to record other types of data related to safety and security. Gender equity is integral to gender equali-ty because it utilizes specific measures to redress specific inequalities that constrain girls' full participation and achievement in schools. Gender equity measures need to be both gender sensitive and transformative of gender relations by tackling internal and external barriers. The internal barriers include low self-esteem of girls because of the dominant mas-culinities and femininities in the family, school, and community.

Rights through education focuses on evidence of inequalities that continue to face girls and women in employment, work, the family, the political and other public arenas. Gendered performance patterns compel the use of rights through education as relevant indicators of gender equality. As girls transition or fail to transition from primary to postprimary education, gender-sensitive CFS will ensure that the outcomes of education for girls are of good quality and will transition to postprimary education.

UNGEI, anchored by UNICEF, provides advocacy and technical support for gender parity and equality in designing, financing, and implementing national education plans. Through UNGEI, major partners in girls' education and gender equality are better able to marshal the influence and resources of a range of partners to support gender parity and equality at macro levels in national education plans and priorities at micro levels in schools.

Concluding Remarks

A multidimensional and comprehensive approach is required for addressing gender equality and quality in education. To ensure that formal education in institutions like schools, colleges, and universities supports gender equality, enabling factors need to be pinpointed and taken into account. Gender equity, too, is vital for evaluating the outcomes and impact of measures used to achieve gender equality in gender-sensitive, child-friendly schools. Equality of treatment and opportunity through a gender lens demands that schools and education systems pay close attention to the behaviors and attitudes of boys and impose gendered expectations of males within both the classroom and schoolyard. Studies in the Caribbean, South Africa, and the United Kingdom have demonstrated that boys' performance in school is unduly affected by dominant constructions of male identity and masculinity (Jha and Kelleher 2006). Therefore, schools are not gender friendly when they discriminate against both girls and boys. Discrimination against boys involves the constant reinforcement of those dominant masculinities that encourage boys to underperform and perceive girls as socially inferior and weaker. In turn, the girls buy into this masculine construction of femininity as powerless and voiceless and of masculinity as all powerful. As a consequence, boys and men in schools behave in ways that limit the full participation of girls and women in structures and processes of schooling.

Note

1. Material in this chapter was originally presented at the World Bank's Global Symposium "Education: A Critical Path to Gender Equality and Empowerment" October 2–3, 2003 in Washington, D.C. All views expressed are those of the author and should not be attributed to UNICEF.

References

Abramovay, M., and Rua M. das Graces. 2005. *Violence in Schools.* Brazil: United Nations Educational, Scientific, and Cultural Organization.

Akunga, A. 2004. *The Voices of Young Kenyans. Gender, Sexuality and HIV/AIDS in Education.* Africa: Young Voices Series No. 2. Nairobi, Kenya: UNICEF Eastern and Southern Africa Regional Office.

Brookes, H., and C. Higson-Smith. 2004. "Responses to Gender-Based Violence in Schools." In *Sexual Abuse of Young Children in Southern Africa*, eds. L. Richter, A. Dawes, and C. Higson-Smith. Cape Town, South Africa: HSRC Press.

Chege, F. 2006. "Memories of Childhood Violence: Life Cycle Reflections of African Student Teachers." Submission to the United Nations Secretary-General's Study on Violence Against Children. Nairobi, Kenya: UNICEF Eastern and Southern Africa Regional Office.

Chilisa, B., M. W. Dube., N. Tsheko, B. Mazile. 2005. *Voices and Identities of Botswana's School Children: Gender, Sexuality, HIV/AIDS and Life Skills Education.* Nairobi, Kenya: UNICEF Eastern and Southern Africa Regional Office.

Chung, E., K. Hallman, and M. Bray. 2005. *Generating the Evidence Base for HIV/AIDS Policies and Programs for Very Young Adolescents.* New York: Population Council.

Colclough, C., S. Al-Sumarrai, P. Rose, M. Tembon. 2003. *Achieving Schooling for All in Africa: Costs, Commitment and Gender.* Ashgate, U.K.: Aldershot.

Delors, J. 1996. *Learning the Treasure Within.* Paris: UNESCO.

Dunne M., and F. Leach. 2003. "Institutional Sexism: Context and Texts in Botswana and Ghana." Paper presented at the 7th Oxford International Conference on Educational Development, September 9–11 2003.

Finklehor, D., and L. Williams. 1988. *Nursery Crimes: Sexual Abuse in Day Care.* London: Sage.

Hart, N. S., J. Durrant, P. Newell, and C. F. Power. 2005. *Eliminating Corporal Punishment: The Way Forward to Constructive Child Discipline.* Paris: United Nations Educational, Scientific, and Cultural Organization.

Jha, J., and F. Kelleher. 2006. *Boys' Underachievement in Education*. London: Commonwealth Secretariat and Commonwealth of Learning.

King, E. M., and M. A. Hill, eds. 1991. *Women's Education in Developing Countries: Barriers, Benefits and Policies*. Washington, DC: World Bank.

Leach F., V. Fiscian, E. Kadzamira, E. Lemani, and P. Machakanja 2003. *An Investigative Study of the Abuse of Girls in African Schools*. Education Research Report No.54. London: Education Department, University of Sussex.

Leach, F., 2000 with P. Machakanja. 2000. *Preliminary Investigation of the Abuse of Girls in Zimbabwean Junior Secondary Schools*. Department of International Development Education Research Report No. 39. London.

Mitchell, C., and R. Moletsane. 2004. "School-Based Initiatives in Response to Violence and HIV and AIDS." Paper presented to the annual conference of the American Educational Research Association, San Diego, CA, April 12–16.

Mohanty, C. 1988. "Under Western Eyes: Feminist Scholarship and Colonial Discourse." *Feminist Review* 30: 61–88.

Pattman, R., and F. Chege. 2003. *Finding Our Voices: Gender and Sexual Identities and HIV/AIDS in Education*. Nairobi, Kenya: UNICEF Eastern and Southern Africa Regional Office.

———. 2004. *Life Skills Education with a Focus on HIV/AIDS Manual*. Nairobi, Kenya: UNICEF Eastern and Southern Africa Regional Office.

Payet, J. 2005. La realite de certaines etablisseements a Tunis. Pur une ecole du dialogue et du respect. Paper presented at the CNIPRE Conference, UNICEF, Tunis, April 14–16.

Pinheiro, S. P. 2006. *World Report on Violence Against Children, United Nations Secretary-General's Study on Violence Against Children*. Geneva: United Nations.

Salem-Pickertz, Josi. 2005. *Violence in Schools in the Middle East and North Africa—Features, Causes, Intervention and Prevention*. Amman, Jordan: UNICEF Middle East and North Africa Regional Office.

Subrahmanian R. 2005. "Gender Equality in Education: Definitions and Measurements." *International Journal of Educational Development* 25: 395–407.

UNAIDS (Joint United Nations Programme on HIV/AIDS). 2005. *Facing the Future Together: Report of the United Nations Secretary-General's Task Force on Women, Girls and HIV/AIDS in Southern Africa*. Johannesburg, South Africa: UNAIDS.

UNESCO (United Nations Educational, Scientific, and Cultural Organization). 2005. *Education for All Global Monitoring Report 2006*. Paris: UNESCO.

UNICEF (United Nations Children's Fund). 2003. *Violence against Children in Schools and Families in Maldives with Focus on Sexual Abuse.* Geneva: UNICEF and the Unit on the Rights of Children.

———. 2005a. *The Voices of Child Friendly Schools.* New York: UNICEF.

———. 2005b. *Gender Achievements and Prospects in Education.* The GAP Report, Part One. New York: UNICEF.

UNICEF. 2006. *Child Friendly Schools and Care and Support in Schools.* UNICEF Eastern and Southern Africa Region Office (ESARD) Volume 6, No. 1, March 2006.

United Nations. 1995. *Fourth World Conference on Women Beijing Declaration.* New York: United Nations.

Unterhalter, E. 2005. "Fragmented Frameworks? Researching Women, Gender, Education and Development." In *Beyond Access: Transforming Policy and Practice for Gender Equality in Education,* eds. S. Aikman and E. Unterhalter. Oxford: Oxfam.

Wilson, S. J., and M. W. Lipsey. 2005. *The Effectiveness of School-Based Violence Prevention Programs for Reducing Disruptive and Aggressive Behavior.* Nashville, TN: Center for Evaluation Research and Methodology, Vanderbilt University.

World Bank. 1995. *Priorities and Strategies in Education.* Washington DC: World Bank.

CHAPTER 9

Combating Gender-Based Violence in Benin[1]

Michele Akpo

Gender-based violence (GBV) in Benin affects girls and women from all walks of life because it is a culturally accepted practice. The worst form of GBV in schools is sexual harassment and abuse. The school community commonly overlooks such violence even though it endangers the girls and engenders poor physical and psychological health and even death. For a long time, the issue of GBV was taboo to discuss. Only recently have women's groups and other women-led nongovernmental organizations (NGOs) started to talk about this issue openly and make the legislature address it through the enactment of new laws. Although Benin has made significant efforts to provide equitable access to education to all Beninese children, GBV remains one of the many obstacles to the promotion of girls' education. It is imperative that recently passed laws—mainly the Family Code, which guarantees legal rights for women, and the Law on Sexual Harassment in Schools and in the Workplace—

As the author notes elsewhere, there are disagreements about the prevalence of the abuse of girls in Benin, in part due to a lack of formal documentation. This chapter is based on her personal observations and the results of focus group discussions.

Box 9.1

A Developing Democracy

Benin, located on the west coast of Africa, has a population of 6.7 million and a projected annual population growth of 3.2 percent, according to the Benin 10-year plan. Benin is known for its rich history and culture, and its people are known throughout West Africa for their warmth and hospitality. The country enjoys a relative peace and is considered the leader in democracy in the region. But it still faces significant development problems, such as poor roads and infrastructure, insufficient access to clean water, and poor health conditions. According to the United Nations Development Programme *Human Development Report 2002,* Benin is ranked 161st, one of the world's least developed and poorest countries. Since 1991, after almost 17 years of a Marxist regime, Benin has established a vibrant democratic state on the path to free-market economic reform.

be disseminated, implemented, and enforced to reduce the prevalence of this social ill.

Under the Marxist government in the late 1980s, the quality of education was seriously eroded. By 1989 the Beninese education system was in a state of collapse. Various stakeholders were motivated to hold a National Conference on Education (*Etats Généraux de l'Education*) in 1990, which adopted a national policy and strategy to improve education.

Beginning in 1991, the government of Benin introduced significant changes to the education system, emphasizing access and equity. The donor community has supported this primary education reform. Its involvement and support has resulted in a significant increase in access to education for all Beninese children. The gross enrollment rate for both boys and girls increased from 41 percent in 1990 to 96 percent in 2005. Girls' enrollment increased from 36 percent to 85 percent in 2005 (Benin 10-year plan). Gender balance and geographic equity have shown major improvements; however, severe constraints and challenges remain to reach the goal of universal education at all levels by 2015. For example, only 47 percent of girls who enter primary school in urban areas and 14 percent in rural areas are able to transition to secondary school, compared with 70 percent of boys in urban areas and 39 percent in rural areas.

Various constraints and obstacles undermine efforts to provide equitable education to all children. Some of these constraints, such as poverty and cultural barriers, are being discussed openly and being alleviated through various interventions. However, GBV—which is very often manifested in verbal, physical, and sexual harassment and abuse in schools—is overlooked by the school community. Discussing GBV is still taboo, and GBV remains a societal problem in Benin. Until recently, victims rarely came forward to speak out about this social problem. Sexual harassment and abuse of girls discourage parents from sending their daughters to school because the girls will end up dropping out anyway with unwanted or early pregnancies that seriously compromise the family's honor. Sexual harassment and abuse are two of the many constraints that undermine efforts to reach significant achievement rates for girls in schools, making it very difficult for girls to succeed in schools and be productive. This chapter discusses the impact of GBV on the well-being of the children and the family and its implications for the socioeconomic development of the community and the nation. It also suggests ways to overcome that social plague that undermines efforts to promote girls' education.

Benin and Millennium Development Goal 3

The third Millennium Development Goal (MDG) states, "Eliminate gender disparity in primary and secondary education, preferably by 2005, and in all levels of education no later than 2015." During the past decade, Benin has made significant strides to eliminate gender disparity in primary and secondary schools (Benin Sector year). In 2002 the ratio of girls' to boys' gross enrollment rates for primary and secondary education was 0.66:1, meaning that for every three boys in school, there were approximately two girls. In 2004 this ratio increased to 0.75:1. In 2002 the literacy rate for women ages 15–24 was estimated at 33.2 percent compared with 59.2 percent for men. For women's participation in development, the composite "women participation indicator" increased by 13 percent from 0.315 in 2001 to 0.356 in 2004. Despite this progress, only 7.2 percent of members of the parliament are women, resulting in weak female participation in decision making and the political process.

Based on the above data, it is obvious that Benin will not reach MDG 3 unless adequate actions are taken to overcome obstacles that girls face in becoming productive women and citizens in the future.

GBV in Benin—A Culturally Accepted Practice with Major Health and Human Rights Implications

Defining Gender-Based Violence

Although GBV can affect boys, girls, men, and women, girls and women are the most affected in Benin because of socially constructed gender roles (Wible 2004). It is usually manifested in various types of abuse and traditional practices: early child marriage, levirate, widowhood practices, rape, kidnapping, genital mutilation, sexual harassment and abuse in schools and at the workplace, and psychological abuse—all of which expose girls and women to serious reproductive health issues and to sexually transmitted diseases, including HIV/AIDS. As stated by Thoroya Ahmed Obaid, United Nations Population Fund executive director, at the UN Security Council open debate on Resolution 1325 on October 28, 2004, "If women and girls and communities as a whole are threatened by gender-based violence, then there is no real chance for peace and security." It is not an exaggeration to add that a nation can never aspire to higher levels of development if a major portion of its population is denied rights. Yet, schools—where the future is shaped—have become the place where such wrongdoings prevail.

GBV in Benin Schools: Myth or Reality?

Even though the constitution of Benin establishes equality between women and men, social and cultural norms value women less than men, thus creating a sense of insecurity in girls and women. To maintain male

Box 9.2

Defining Violence

As defined in the Declaration on the Elimination of Violence Against Women, a UN General Assembly resolution passed in 1993, gender-based violence is not limited to physical or sexual violence. GBV also includes equally insidious forms of violence against girls such as economically coerced sex, sexual harassment, demeaning language that undermines self-esteem, and even assigning girls to perform domestic tasks at school while others study. GBV is thus a broadly-defined term encompassing an array of behaviors that cause physical, sexual, or psychological harm to women or girls.

dominance over women, men frequently oppress women despite the fact that women are approximately 52 percent of the population. Women have very low status, and traditional beliefs confine them in their roles as mothers and wives. Women's low status is reflected in physical abuse, limited access to education, and limited access to health care, including family planning. GBV is culturally accepted because of ignorance of the laws that protect girls' and women's rights and the denial of those rights. Women also lack the means to self-determination because of feminization of poverty in Benin. The majority of Beninese women (54 percent) are employed in the agriculture sector. But they do not have access to land, which means they work primarily on family farms.

Like many girls in Africa, Beninese girls suffer from various types of abuse in schools.[1] In Benin there are no quantitative data to prove that GBV exists in schools or in the society in general because very few victims have come forward to talk about it. However, information was gathered during focus group discussions of research on sexual harassment in Benin schools conducted by the Academy for Educational Development in 2004. The results indicated that "sexual harassment has become deeply embedded in the Beninese schools." Several girls indicated that they "witnessed or experienced" such problems in school. During project implementation in various parts of the country, parents confirmed that GBV exists in schools, even though most parents or girls have never brought the issue to law enforcement authorities because of fear of disgracing the family. The absence of hard evidence makes some people doubt the existence of GBV in schools.

Cultural barriers, traditional beliefs, and economic hardships make parents reluctant to send their daughters to school. And when it becomes obvious that the school does not always provide a safe environment for girls, parents become even more reluctant.

Sexual harassment and abuse. The most serious GBV in Beninese schools is sexual harassment and abuse by male teachers. This is a persistent problem that undermines efforts to promote girls' education. Evidence shows that it has a significantly negative impact on girls' attainment and completion of schooling. Teachers are supposed to protect students at schools, but some fail to. It is not uncommon in Beninese schools for teachers to have intimate relationships with girl students. Teachers who perpetrate such crimes offer girls better grades or punish girls who do not acquiesce by giving them bad marks and failing grades or threatening to force the girl to repeat the class. Girls who

Box 9.3

Recommendations from Girls to Schools and Teachers to Prevent Problems the Girls Face

- Teachers should focus on their work as teachers rather than pursuing their students for sex.
- School authorities should not grope or "bother" students in their offices.
- Students must not seduce teachers or "negotiate" grades with sex.
- Teachers must avoid pressuring their students after their advances have been refused.

cannot discuss these issues with parents accept teachers' advances. Often this results in dropout, unwanted pregnancy, and unsafe abortions, which can lead to psychological and physical problems in the future, or even death. Parents report that complaints to school administrations about these practices do not deter teachers from abusing girls—nor do school administrations take this issue seriously. The strongest punishment for an abusive teacher is redeployment to another school, where he can easily start over.

Poverty and the "sugar daddy" phenomenon. Poverty is another major factor in teacher-student relationships. Some girls enter into intimate relationships with teachers for monetary compensation. When a girl cannot afford to eat, dress properly, or have all the material goods that other girls have, she becomes vulnerable and accepts teachers' advances.

Impacts and Implications of GBV at School

- *Poor performance.* In cases where the girl does not accept the teacher's advances, she fears every day to go to school to face that teacher pressuring her. Fear can make girls stop believing in their potential to succeed and often results in a poor performance in school.
- *Poor achievement.* When a girl is coerced into sex for good grades, she may later find herself in difficult circumstances in other classes because she did not acquire the required skills to perform at her grade level. She therefore fails altogether and ends up dropping out. It is clear that poor

performance and achievement lead to high girl dropout rates, thus maintaining a disparity between girls and boys.

- *Low self-esteem.* Girls in general fear that their male peers will consider them not capable of doing as well as their male counterparts in school. Girls who find themselves in sexual relationships with their teachers become pariahs in their classroom, and their male peers do not hesitate to bully them and to act violently against these girls. Girls are thus very isolated in their classes and end up dropping out.
- *Health issues (physical and psychological).* Sexual relationships often lead girls to early pregnancies, unwanted pregnancies, unsafe abortions, death, and exposure to HIV/AIDS and other sexually transmitted diseases.
- *Loss in national productivity.* Economic empowerment comes from education, and uneducated women cannot contribute significantly to economic development of a country. Moreover, when a woman is educated, she knows her rights and duties as a citizen, considers getting married only when she is self-sufficient, and has a smaller family later on, thus contributing to her family's well-being. And obviously, she will be more likely to place her children in school and ensure that they succeed in school.

Policy Frameworks to Address GBV in Schools

In 1988 the Benin Ministry of Education enacted a policy to address sexual relationships between teachers and girls as well as between students. The policy included a provision for strong punishment if teachers attempted to coerce girls to have abortions; however, it did not have any provision for teachers who abused or raped students. The policy also included a provision to punish girls who "provoke teachers." For example, the policy required girls to have short hair like boys. Through these provisions, the policy attempted to provide and preserve safety in schools for girls; however, it has proven ineffective because of the lack of enforcement.

The Persons and Family Code of Benin was passed in 2004. The law raises the minimum age for marriage, addresses women's rights in the home and in society, and outlaws polygamy. To a large extent implementation of this law will progressively eliminate violence against girls and women in Beninese schools and society in general. It is therefore essential that it is implemented and enforced.

In June 2006 a landmark sexual harassment law was passed that pre-scribes strong sanctions to deter sexual harassment and violence, not only in schools but also in the workplace. This is significant proof that Beninese legislators are taking sexual harassment seriously in order to provide a safe environment for girls and women in the home, in school, and in the work-place. But again, it needs to be implemented and enforced to attain the expected results.

Why GBV in Schools Persists and Ways to Overcome It to Promote Girls' Education

There is a significant gap between the recent laws and their implementa-tion and enforcement. It is obvious that there is lack of knowledge about the laws that protect girls' and women's rights in society. Generally, peo-ple do not know what their rights are and what consequences follow a breach. This raises the issue of victims not knowing that they are victims. It is therefore imperative to raise awareness of rights and responsibilities among the population to induce a change of attitude as well as help ensure that laws are implemented and constantly enforced.

There are no official channels through which victims of abuse can report perpetrators and get help. In the case of rape, a victim would often rather keep silent than bring humiliation and dishonor to her family. Victims will start coming forward and speaking out when they know that they will not become pariahs in their communities and that they will get all the support needed to overcome the psychological and health conse-quences. The establishment of these victims' support channels will help victims come forward, facilitating the enforcement of the law.

The Beninese judiciary system is very weak and lacks adequate person-nel. Although victims can go to the police to file complaints, police are not well equipped to handle their complaints. The police need both addi-tional capacity and training. The ongoing reform of the Beninese justice system will address some these issues.

Education and enlisting male leaders as anti-GBV champions through aggressive awareness and behavior-change campaigns will ensure a pro-gressive elimination of this social problem.

Even though GBV is a societal issue in Benin, it is known to vary from one tribe to another, from urban to rural, from south to north, from east to west, and from one sector activity to another. A thorough sociological and cross-cultural study will explain these phenomena. In the meantime, it is imperative that Benin adopt a systemic approach as a response to GBV in schools and in Beninese society in general to create a positive change of attitude. This will require the establishment of institutional mechanisms to support victims, prevent the occurrence of GBV, and encourage the consistent enforcement of the law.

The donor community and other developed countries are helping Benin address this issue through bilateral agreements. It is hoped that by taking baby steps toward the elimination of this social ill, Benin is ineluctably working toward one of its main challenges to development. In the existing Benin political environment, socioeconomic development issues are addressed through a decentralization process that empowers local elected officials. Engaging them at the community level will ensure that girls' and women's issues become an important item on the council's agenda, thus providing good support to eliminate this phenomenon in a sustainable way.

Note

1. Information contained herein was gathered during life experience and through the implementation of various projects' interventions that seek to promote girls' education in Benin.

References

UNDP. 2003. *Benin Sector Report on Millenium Development Goals* (in French, Extrait du Rapport départemental sur les OMD au Bénin, OMD-DSRP et OCS/MDEF. 52). New York.

Wible, Brent. 2004. *Making Schools Safe for Girls: Combating Gender-Based Violence in Benin.* Washington, DC: Academy for Educational Development.

CHAPTER 10

Addressing Gender Disparities in Education in Contexts of Crisis, Postcrisis, and State Fragility

Jackie Kirk

Of the 43 million children living in crisis-affected countries who are not in school, well over half are girls (International Save the Children Alliance 2006). Crisis situations create challenges for girls to gain access to education. But crises can also create some windows of opportunity for improving education access and quality for girls and women, as well as for education to contribute to enhanced gender equality. There are no simple relationships between crisis, gender, and education. Nevertheless, as girls are disproportionately marginalized from education in such contexts, addressing the interconnected gender- and crisis-related barriers to quality, relevant education is an important rights issue. It is also critical to the achievement of Education for All (EFA) targets.

In recent years the field of education in emergencies has evolved as a specific area of policy and practice, and increasingly of academic teaching, research, and writing. The term *education in emergencies* is often used as shorthand for education in a range of crisis and postcrisis situations. The term refers to a comprehensive set of responses to the cognitive, social, and emotional needs of children following the immediate and long-term impacts of natural and man-made disasters. It reflects a realization of the challenges to EFA and the Millennium Development Goals (MDGs) posed by crisis situations. It embodies a greater understanding of—and commitment to—the role of education in humanitarian response as well as deeper understandings of education's role in processes of peacebuilding and reconstruction. Education in emergencies encompasses formal and nonformal learning activities for internally displaced persons (IDPs), refugees, returnees, host communities, and communities that are affected by emergencies but are not displaced. It spans interventions during acute and chronic crisis situations, as well as in communities during early reconstruction periods. The relationships between education and state fragility have also started to be mapped (for example, Kirk 2007; Rose and Greeley 2006).

Education in emergencies is premised on a commitment to fulfilling the right to education of *all* children. There is also the belief that education is a particularly critical intervention for children and youth in crisis situations, offering multiple benefits to them and their families, including protection from harm (Nicolai and Triplehorn 2003). It is important to acknowledge that women and girls experience crises differently from men and boys. Crises affect girls' education opportunities in particular ways. School-going girls are often forced to drop out, and those excluded in precrisis times may have even less chance of access. In times of conflict and crisis, when resources are scarce and families are intent on survival, education discrimination in favor of boys can be even stronger. Girls who are further marginalized by factors such as disability, ethnicity, and location are even more likely to miss out on education. For women and girls, sexual and gender-based violence (GBV) is a particular risk. As discussed in the following section, this risk affects both access to and quality of education, with particular repercussions for adolescent girls. At the same time, as mentioned above, new and improved learning opportunities for girls may be created in a crisis or postcrisis situation. The involvement of new education actors (nongovernmental organizations [NGOs] and community-based organizations, for example), additional funding, as well as shifts in gender roles and relations create opportunities. These issues have serious implications for the ways in which education in emergencies is designed and implemented. Education interventions should be both preventive and responsive, and also build on any new opportunities that are created for gender equality.

This chapter presents some of the prevailing gender inequalities in education programming during emergencies. The chapter discusses some of the concrete global policy developments that may support increased attention to gender equality and GBV. These developments include the Minimum Standards for Education in Emergencies, Chronic Crises, and Early Reconstruction developed by the Inter-Agency Network for Education in Emergencies (INEE), and the Education Cluster within the UN humanitarian reform processes. The chapter ends with concrete programming strategies to promote gender equality in and through education in contexts of crisis, postcrisis, and state fragility.

Challenges and Opportunities: Gender Issues in Education in Emergencies and Fragile States

Worldwide, approximately half the primary school–age children who are not in school live in conflict-affected and fragile states. Thousands more children who live in areas affected by natural disasters have no access to schooling. The situation is particularly dire for refugees and IDPs, whose access to education, particularly postprimary, is extremely limited. Only 3 percent of the estimated 7 million child refugees ages 12–17 have access to education (RET 2008). Ensuring access to education in emergencies is an important strategy in the protection of children's rights—not only the right to education, but also the right to protection from abuse and exploitation. Access to education in emergencies has immediate protection benefits for girls and boys. It also provides longer-term benefits for the promotion of the rights and responsibilities of children, especially with regard to participation and active citizenship.

Table 10.1 highlights the limited progress on the education MDGs in what Save the Children has identified as conflict-affected fragile states (CAFS). The table shows how the CAFS compare to other low-income countries (LICs) that are not CAFS and other developing countries (Bird, Dolan, and Nicolai 2006).

Access to Education for Girls

Table 10.1 highlights the immense challenges to ensuring access to education in CAFS, as well as the extent of the gender gaps in enrollment. But the statistics do not show the prevalent patterns of increasing gender

Table 10.1   Conflict-Affected Fragile States and Education

	CAFS	LICs (non-CAFS)	Other developing countries
Out-of-school, primary school–age children	43 million	32 million	95 million
MDG2: Net primary education enrollment (percent)	67.8	71.2	83.2
MDG3: Primary education female: male enrollment ratio	0.87	0.91	0.95

Source: Bird, Dolan, and Nicolai 2006.

disparity at upper primary and secondary levels. In contexts of crisis, post-crisis, and state fragility, gender issues in education may look similar to issues in development contexts. Access to education for girls is limited by factors such as accessibility of schools, girls' workloads, sibling care, early marriage, and motherhood. Yet there are other specific issues and aspects of these limitations for girls that are of particular concern in unstable contexts. These include, for example, safety and security issues, which can be of great concern to parents. The journey to and from school may place girls at considerable risk of attack and sexual violence, especially in areas in which fighting forces are present. Early marriage and motherhood tend to mean the end of schooling opportunities for girls, and the rates of early marriage and teen pregnancy tend to be particularly high in insecure environments. This may be the result of high levels of GBV, as well as to parents' desire to secure early marriage for their daughters for both protection for them and economic survival. Feelings of insecurity and uncertainty, frustration with the current situation, lack of access to education and other opportunities, and a sense of futility among youth may also fuel risk-taking behaviors such as early sexual activity as well as aggressive and violent attitudes toward women and girls by men and boys (UNESCO and UNHCR 2007).

Although conflict can bring with it some positive changes in gender roles and expectations, conflict both exacerbates inequities in education for women and girls and increases vulnerabilities (World Vision 2001). Gender roles and stereotypes are often reinforced by the need to protect women and girls and by the additional time and energy spent in traditional roles such as collecting water. In southern Sudan, the work of women and girls has doubled or trebled, and yet the situation has left boys with no new or heavier work. There is very little time or energy left for girls to attend school, yet schooling for boys is planned to give them something to do (Obura 2001). Conflict and its aftermath can also be a time when gender roles have to change. The practical and economic imperatives of survival and reconstruction take priority over education, especially for girls and women who may be forced into new roles such as petty trading to generate income.

Other issues for girls in crisis include limited access to school places (when schools are destroyed or just fail to operate as usual). Education for all children suffers. But because of their different social positions—possibilities for movement outside of the home or community and income-generation activities to pay school fees and other costs—boys are often more able to seek out opportunities for learning than girls. Protection risks may also inhibit women teachers' mobility and access to school and professional development opportunities. In some contexts, the lack of women teachers also creates a barrier to girls' access to education, particularly older girls in upper primary and secondary classes (Kirk 2006b).

Quality in Education for Girls

There are many issues related to the quality of education for girls and young women that, although similar to issues in other development contexts, may have particular dimensions in contexts of crisis, postcrisis, and state fragility. These include safety and security, the relevance of the curriculum and learning content, and the quality of instruction.

Recent research indicates the sad reality that, in many contexts, GBV is inextricably linked with education. Girls may be at risk of sexual attack, harassment, and abuse on the way to and from school. Teachers or male students may perpetrate violence within the school buildings and grounds. Furthermore, girls who have no other way to raise the necessary money for school fees, books, uniforms, and other "hidden costs" may agree to transactional sex. In conflict contexts, there are additional layers of complexity to examine. The vulnerability of girls to sexual violence may be increased because of the presence of high numbers of security and fighting forces in any location and forced or "voluntary" recruitment into the fighting forces. In addition, security and survival imperatives may pressure families to ensure protection through early marriage. Furthermore, sexual violence—rape in particular—has become a weapon of war widely used as part of the struggle for power and domination of one ethnic or religious group over another. Through all these scenarios runs a common theme of aggressive masculinities, the socialization of men and boys to assert their masculinity through physical and sexual domination of women and girls. In such contexts, violent and asymmetrical power relations between men and women and between young boys and girls are normalized. Men and boys may learn to constitute their identities as fighters and defenders of the family honor—but as teachers and male students, also through the sexual abuse and exploitation of women and girls (Enloe 1989, 2000; Kirk, forthcoming–a; Whitworth 2004).

The relevance and appropriateness of curricula is also an important issue. It is common for curricula to be more focused on the experiences of boys, not to reflect the specific experiences of girls and women, and not to explicitly challenge gender stereotypes or to promote gender equality. International Rescue Committee (IRC) reviews of sample learning materials used in refugee camp programs in Ethiopia and Sierra Leone revealed startling disparities between the portrayal of women and men and of boys and girls. There was very little presence of women and girls—and then only in roles of servitude, assistance, and vulnerability (Kirk 2004a, 2004b). Various possible factors contribute to crisis-affected contexts, including the lack of a coherent, unified curriculum and the fact that curriculum is often itself a factor in conflict. For example, this has been the case in southern Sudan for many years and even since the signing of the Comprehensive Peace Agreements. In the absence of a full southern Sudanese curriculum, schools make do with a combination of materials from neighboring countries. With such scarcity of resources, gender responsiveness is not a priority. Especially in the case of ethnic or religious conflicts, the importance of curriculum may be reflected in the peace agreement texts. However, even in conflict contexts in which the rights of women and girls have been violated, gender issues in curriculum are not necessarily discussed. Curriculum may be used to reinforce traditional notions of family honor dependent on women's and girls' behavior (Saigol 1995, 2000).

An additional, important point relating to the relevance and responsiveness of girls' education is the quality of instruction provided in schools and learning spaces. In many crisis-affected contexts, communities rely on inexperienced and underqualified teachers. Although NGOs and other partners may support communities with rapid teacher training and ongoing supervision, the teachers may be struggling with basic teaching methods. Gender equality in the classroom is not prioritized. Training tends to focus on basic teaching and classroom management skills. Gender training may be considered only later in the teachers' careers.

Furthermore, factors such as few female school graduates, safety and security concerns, and increased household chores and income-generation responsibilities mean that in many situations, the teaching profession is dominated by men. Although this may not necessarily create a specific barrier for girls, the lack of female role models and confidantes in the school creates learning environments in which girls may not feel particularly supported, encouraged, or represented. It also means that the activities in the school inevitably reflect the experiences of the boys and men who dominate.

Opportunities in Education for Girls

Graça Machel (2001, p. 31) stresses the importance of education for all children in times of conflict: "Education gives shape and structure to children's lives. When everything around is chaos, schools can be a haven of security that is vital to the well-being of war-affected children and their communities." However, she also points out that this is especially important for girls: "Education, especially literacy and numeracy, is precisely what girls need during and after armed conflict. Education can help prepare adolescent girls for the new roles and responsibilities that they are often obliged to take on in conflict situations" (Machel 2001, p. 32). Machel's statement adds extra weight to the EFA and MDG imperatives and should encourage different actors at international, national, and local levels to increase efforts to ensure quality and relevant education for girls affected by conflict.

While highlighting many of the education challenges for girls and young women affected by crises, it is also important to highlight how, in certain circumstances, crises can create new opportunities for girls to access education. Crises can sometimes create windows of opportunity for education and particularly for improvements in access and quality. One example of this is in the earthquake-affected areas of Pakistan, where access to education for girls in the remote, mountainous, and conservative communities was very limited. After the earthquake, however, girls who moved with their families to IDP camps in the valleys were able to attend school for the first time. Factors that allowed this included the accessibility of NGO-supported schools with women teachers within a safe, walking distance from the students' homes, the reduction in household chores and other tasks for girls in the IDP camps, and the increased parental confidence in the quality of education assured by NGOs (Kirk, forthcoming–b). Although in general the conflict in Nepal has had a devastating impact on education, there is also some evidence of a positive impact on girls' education opportunities. For example, in a region affected by Maoist insurgency, parents have sent their sons away to school in Katmandu to avoid the politicization of schools and campuses, but girls have stayed and entered the local schools (Manchanda 2001). Afghan refugee girls and women teachers in Pakistan have also been able to access education opportunities that were denied to girls and women inside Afghanistan. Programs such as the IRC's Female Education Program, running since 1992, continue to contribute to human resource development for Afghanistan (Qahir, forthcoming). Although there are no specific tracer data available, individual stories provide evidence that graduates of the refugee schools are now filling important jobs in NGOs and government departments in Afghanistan.

Becoming a teacher may also be a transformative experience for women affected by crises (Kirk 2004c, 2004d). It can be a way for women to provide important income or supplies for themselves and for their families. This is a critical issue in conflict contexts. There are often high percentages of female-headed households because of the large numbers of men killed or displaced. Even in the absence of government salaries, small incentives paid by agencies and NGOs can make a significant impact on the well-being of teachers and their families. In addition to meeting the practical gender needs of women, becoming a teacher may also start to address women's strategic interests.[1] The personal and professional development that women can experience through being a teacher can be empowering in different ways. Being able to support one's family can have an important impact on the psychosocial well-being of women who have been affected by conflict. Teachers in Afghanistan, for example, have indicated that—instead of being alone, surrounded by their own problems, and constantly reliving the trauma and loss of the conflict—the opportunity to teach gives them something else to think about. Especially if there are no other opportunities for them to continue their own education, teaching is often considered a good way to extend their knowledge.

Teaching also benefits women psychosocially because they feel a sense of contributing to their community, knowing that they are doing their best, and contributing positively to the future. In some contexts it is harder for women to be active in the public realm than men, but teaching can be a culturally acceptable way to do so and a means to gaining status and respect in a community. In Afghanistan, women teachers had returned from Pakistan to find that the girls in their villages had no opportunities to go to school at all. Being able to do something for these girls, and for their community, is clearly important to these women, even though they have no formal training as teachers (Kirk 2004c). In a refugee camp in Ethiopia, Kunama women teachers, who had fled with their community from Eritrea in 2001, were nominated by the community to teach. Although they had not yet completed secondary education, there were no more educated women in the camp. Still somewhat tentative in their professional identities as teachers, these women felt that it was important to share with the students what they had learned in Eritrea before they had had to flee. Six years later, women who have continued to teach and to develop their skills are now interested in formal teacher certification (Kirk and Winthrop 2007b).

Promising Policy Developments at the Global Level

Women, Girls, Peace, and Security

Unlike in previous eras, war and conflict of the late 20th century occurred within, rather than between, nations. Fighting happens within communities and involves ordinary civilians, spilling into homes, workplaces, and even schools. Although more men and boys are killed in conflict, ethnic hatred, oppression, and intolerance are played out on the bodies of women and girls. Fighting forces commonly use sexual violence as a weapon of war. Rape is now recognized as a specific war crime in the statutes of the International Criminal Court (art. 8). This recognition at the highest international policy levels is significant, but this may create little improvement in the lives of the many women and girls who experience such horrors (Kirk and Taylor 2007). It is also well documented that GBV does not necessarily abate with the signing of peace agreements. Many women and girls face a high risk of GBV during the early reconstruction period and beyond. Rape and sexual attacks continue and other forms of GBV occur, including harmful traditional practices, such as female genital mutilation, forced early marriage, honor killings, and domestic violence (IASC 2005).

At the same time, there is an increased recognition of the extent of sexual violence and exploitation of women and girls in conflict and a number of positive developments addressing the protection and partici-pation needs of women and girls. The landmark UN Security Council Resolution on Women, Peace, and Security (UNSCR 1325) (United Nations Security Council 2000) recognizes the need to protect women and girls from sexual violence. This inclusive language (that is, *women and girls*) is translated into policy documents of different agencies and organ-izations. However, as discussed by Kirk and Taylor (2004), there is less specific attention paid to the age-differentiated dimensions of sexual vio-lence and to the particular experiences of girls and young women. To adapt a phrase from Susan McKay (Karam 2001), a *womenandgirls* approach tends to dominate, and there is less attention given to the par-ticular experiences of sexual violence against young women and adoles-cent girls. Sexual violence in and around schools and related to education, for example, particularly affects girls rather than women.

Although not explicitly addressed in the UNSCR 1325 text, education clearly plays an important role in supporting the active and meaningful participation of women in peacebuilding. Furthermore, education for girls promotes their participation as active agents in peacebuilding and ensures a future generation of women who are able to participate in the highest levels of peace negotiations and of state reconstruction. With specific attention to the particular protection and participation of girls, UNSCR 1325 can provide a very useful policy framework with which to link gen-der equality in education in emergencies and fragile states to activists and interventions working in the area of women, peace, and security.

INEE Minimum Standards for Education in Emergencies, Chronic Crises, and Early Reconstruction

The Minimum Standards for Education in Emergencies, Chronic Crises, and Early Reconstruction, developed by the Inter-Agency Network for Education in Emergencies, represent a comprehensive picture of current practice and future priority directions. The standards were developed in a participatory way, drawing on existing good practice and field-based expe-rience with realistic targets (Kirk 2006a). Grounded in the rights of the child as well as in other relevant rights-based instruments, the standards were developed through a highly consultative process as a tool to guide policy and programming. They are also intended to ensure that the com-mitments made in human rights instruments, such as the Convention on the Rights of the Child and the EFA and MDG targets, are implemented in these challenging circumstances. Gender equality does not have a separate category, but it is a cross-cutting theme integrated across all categories of standards. This is considered essential to ensure that not only do girls have equal access to the benefits of education, but also that the content and processes of education in such circumstances meet the needs and priorities of girls as well as boys. Gender-specific rights instruments such as the Convention on the Elimination of All Forms of Discrimination against Women and the Beijing Platform for Action are not explicitly mentioned in the standards, but the standards reflect their priorities in terms of access to relevant and gender-responsive education.

The field of education in emergencies is premised on the recognition that children in contexts of emergency, chronic crisis, and early reconstruction have particular protection needs, some of which may be met through schooling, at least to a certain extent. Protection in this context encompasses both physical and psychosocial protection, and Standard 2 (Access and Learning Environment) insists that education providers ensure that "learning environments are secure, promote the protection and mental and emotional well-being of learners." Gender equality priorities relate to the need for ensuring equal access for girls to the protection benefits of education. At the same time, girls' vulnerabilities to sexual violence may even be heightened precisely because they come to school. In Guidance Note 4, Standard 2 (Protection and Well-Being, Access and Learning Environment) provides,

> Students, especially minorities and girls, often become targets for abuse, violence, recruitment or abduction when going to and from school. In these cases students' security can be improved by a combination of community information campaigns and by having adults from the community escort them ... In addition, education programmes should include monitoring of the level of harassment experienced by girls and women. (INEE 2004)

The standards provide a holistic framework for the integration of gender equality and protection concerns through all aspects of education in emergencies, chronic crises, and early reconstruction. For example, the Assessment Standard of the category Teaching and Learning pays particular attention to fair and nonexploitative assessment processes. A code of conduct for all teachers and other education personnel should address protection for students from sexual and other forms of exploitation and abuse. Such a code should include the teachers' responsibility to promote, among other things, a positive learning environment and the well-being of learners (Standard 2, Teachers and other Education Personnel). Although not specifically gendered, the standards recognize the need for education content appropriate to the particular circumstances of children affected by conflict and, in particular, education content and key messages that are life enhancing or even life saving. Standard 1 on Curricula in the category Teaching and Learning asserts, "Culturally, socially and linguistically relevant curricula are used to provide formal and nonformal education, appropriate to the particular emergency situation." Within this standard, we are also encouraged to consider relevant learning content related to peacebuilding, conflict resolution, and other similar skills. While the vulnerability of girls to sexual violence and exploitation is more widely acknowledged, it is important for educators to work with young people and their communities to identify and respond through curriculum content and other means to the gendered risks and protection needs of girls *and* boys. It may be, for example, that boys have heightened risks of abduction and conscription into fighting forces than girls. Although less documented and discussed, the vulnerability of boys to sexual abuse and exploitation is also a reality to be addressed in certain crisis-affected contexts.

Access to education, learning content, processes, and the interactions between teachers and students are important areas for attention to gender equality. The standards framework also highlights the complementarity of efforts in the areas of community participation, analysis, and education policy and coordination. Community participation, for example, should involve women as well as men (Community Participation, Standard 1, Guidance Note 1). Women in the community can play a special role in the schools (Community Participation, Standard 2, Guidance Note 2). From the needs assessment stage through monitoring and evaluation, analysis should be as comprehensive and in-depth as possible (including gender-desegregated data) (Analysis, Standard 1). At the same time, strong and relevant education policy is needed to protect the rights of vulnerable groups (Education Policy and Coordination, Standard 1). Good coordination and information sharing between different education stakeholders (Education Policy and Coordination, Standard 2) can help to ensure that girls and other vulnerable groups do not fall through the cracks and that there are accessible and appropriate learning opportunities available for all.

INEE Gender Task Team

The above section highlights the potential of the INEE Minimum Standards as a framework for gender-responsive education in emergencies, chronic crises, and early reconstruction contexts. After the second INEE Global Consultations in Cape Town in December 2004, IRC initiated the INEE Gender Task Team (GTT) to create additional attention, tools, and resources to ensure gender-responsive implementation and the fullest realization of the potential of the standards. The GTT consists of education specialists with an interest in and commitment to gender, who have identified technical gaps and prioritized group tasks (see www.ineesite.org). Since its establishment, GTT outputs include

- A gender and education in emergencies resource database
- A thematic series of Gender Strategies for Education in Emergencies tools that relate to specific INEE Minimum Standards on women teachers, GBV, and gender-responsive sanitation, health, and hygiene education[2]
- Updated *INEE Good Practice Guide on Women and Girls' Education*
- An education chapter in the *Gender Handbook for Humanitarian Action* of the Inter-Agency Standing Committee (IASC)
- Links with other key gender and education initiatives, such as the UN Girls' Education Initiative

Regular contact and communication between the GTT and the INEE Secretariat, as well as regular reports to the INEE Steering Committee and the INEE Working Group on Minimum Standards, facilitate enhanced attention to the integration of gender perspectives. For example, as the training materials for the Minimum Standards Training of Trainers and the INEE Minimum Standards Toolkit have been developed, piloted, and reviewed, the GTT has provided additional gender content and materials.

Gender Mainstreaming in the Education Cluster

The United Nations Secretary General's report, *Strengthening the Coordination of Emergency Humanitarian Assistance of the United Nations* (UN 2001), and the *Humanitarian Response Review* (UN 2005) highlighted serious gaps in the capacity of the humanitarian community to respond effectively to crises and made recommendations for addressing these gaps. The IASC subsequently established clusters for nine sectors and issues in which particular gaps had been identified: logistics; telecommunications; shelter; health; nutrition; water, sanitation, and hygiene; early recovery; camp coordination and camp management; and protection. Different UN agencies were nominated as the cluster leads for each. Although initially the IASC did not establish an Education Cluster, subsequent advocacy from education actors resulted in the formal endorsement of the cluster approach in education in November 2006.

According to IASC, the cluster approach aims to improve the predictability, timeliness, and effectiveness of humanitarian response and pave the way for recovery. The cluster approach should strengthen the collaborative response by enhancing partnerships and complementarity among the UN, the Red Cross Movement, and NGOs (IASC 2007). The cluster approach operates on two levels: global and field. Global-level cluster activities, for which funding was requested through a cluster appeal to donors in April 2007, include up-to-date assessments and reviews of the overall needs for human, financial, and institutional capacity, as well as actions to improve rosters, stockpiles, training, and systems development. There are links with other clusters, including preparedness and long-term planning, standards, best practice, advocacy, and resource mobilization (UN OCHA 2007). At the field level, the cluster approach is oriented to addressing the specific needs in a particular response effort, particularly through the mobilization and coordination of different humanitarian agencies.

A global Education Cluster aims to improve the coverage and quality of the response to a need for education in an emergency. Planned cluster activities include the preparation of tools and resource materials, needs assessment protocols, and rosters of experienced staff. These activities intend to address gaps in capacity, especially surge capacity, to ensure predictable, quality, and comprehensive education interventions that reach all children in an emergency situation. A preliminary gaps analysis was conducted, and priority projects were developed by the Education Cluster for inclusion in the cluster appeal document. Gender is identified by the Education Cluster as a key gap to be addressed through the cluster approach. The gap relates to human resource capacities, limited mechanisms for preparedness, response and coordination, the variety of approaches, lack of standardization, and specific technical gaps such as gender analysis. The Education Cluster is committed to increased attention to equity issues involving age, gender, and vulnerable groups and has referred explicitly to gender in three of its four cluster projects.

The IASC Sub–Working Group (SWG) on Gender in Humanitarian Assistance existed prior to the establishment of the clusters. The SWG is committed to integrating gender equality into the humanitarian response system, particularly through the rollout of the *IASC Gender Handbook* (to which the INEE GTT contributed an education chapter) and the *IASC GBV Guidelines*. The SWG also developed three projects to include in the cluster appeal to donors in April 2007: sex-disaggregated data collection and management, the integration of gender equality into all policy and program work of the clusters/sectors, and building capacity of field actors to understand and use the IASC Gender Handbook and IASC GBV Guidelines in all sector/cluster work.

Through the GTT Convener, INEE is represented on the IASC Gender SWG, as well as on other relevant "sub-sub-working groups." In these settings, INEE works to ensure that education is represented among the different sectors, that lessons from other sectors about gender main-streaming in humanitarian action can be applied to education, and that the strategies and lessons learned from education work can inform other sectors. This participation has facilitated the following accomplishments:

- Education chapter in the *IASC-OCHA Gender Mainstreaming in Humanitarian Action Handbook,* aligned with the INEE Minimum Standards[3]
- Education content included in the predeployment training and materials package for GenCAP advisors, including the INEE Minimum Standards (May 2007)
- Education content and tools integrated into the workshop session on Gender and Early Recovery (June 2007).
- Enhanced attention to education in the rollout and review of *IASC GBV Guidelines*

As the operating structures and processes of the Education Cluster are being defined and the specific projects further worked out, efforts are now being made to ensure a strong and integrated focus on gender equality. The role of the INEE GTT will therefore expand. With a new recruitment process, the team's mandate has expanded to support gender main-streaming within both the INEE and the Education Cluster, thereby leveraging the links already made and the interest and capacities of the individuals and agencies already involved. IRC will continue to play a lead role, convening the group and providing technical assistance to its work.

Implications: Learning for Peace and Equality

The above discussion has highlighted the need and the possibilities for systematic mainstreaming of gender equality concerns throughout education in emergencies and fragile states. It has presented the INEE Minimum Standards as a framework that highlights gender equality concerns across all aspects of education planning, content, methodology, and policy development and coordination. Drawing on this discussion, the following section presents three broad areas for particular programming attention: ensuring strategic protection; taking holistic perspectives on protection, water and sanitation, hygiene, and reproductive health; and building the capacity of women teachers and education leaders.

Ensure Strategic Protection for Girls in and through Education

The attention given to the protection of women and girls affected by crisis and to the imperative for girls to attend school is encouraging. From a critical gender and empowerment perspective, however, an exclusive focus on protection is somewhat problematic. There is a tendency to focus on solely the girls as somewhat problematically in need of attention and protection; thus the potential for protection strategies becomes limiting and restrictive. Furthermore, interventions developed to mitigate against sexual violence and reproductive health issues focus on the immediate and practical needs of either girls or women. Little attention is given to the strategic and long-term collective gender needs of both (Kirk and Winthrop, forthcoming). In general, there has been limited discussion of the ways in which women and girls can work together to promote gender equality and to change school and community cultures. More attention is required to learn how to successfully shift school cultures from ones in which girls require protection to ones in which girls and boys and male and female teachers are able to enjoy stimulating teaching and learning experiences. Girls can be active developers of strategies to increase their own and others' security and well-being.

Drawing on fieldwork in Guinea and Sierra Leone and assessments of a classroom assistant program initiated to protect girls from abuse and exploitation by teachers, Kirk and Winthrop (forthcoming) promote the concept of strategic protection. Strategic protection engages girls and boys as "knowers" of their own worlds and experiences. Girls and boys are key agents in identifying their protection needs and in proposing and evaluating solutions. It also involves attention to the collective empowerment needs of girls and women while acknowledging that women recruited to protect girls may have a somewhat different personal gender empowerment agenda. Strategic protection is also responsive to the changing gender identities of men, women, boys, and girls in the contexts in which they live, and to the dominant forms of masculinity and femininity that prevail. In this way it responds to the work of scholars of gender and conflict and of masculinities and conflict (Enloe 1989, 2000; Whitworth 2004). Strategic protection is attentive to questions such as the following: How do teachers who exploit girl students understand their own personal and professional roles? What are the pressures on these men to assert certain forms of masculinity? Such approaches contrast with the research and practice related to GBV in schools, which has focused on the girls and their vulnerabilities. Even where there are female teachers, classroom assistants, or other women able to provide sex and reproductive health education for young students, strategic protection contrasts with perspectives that focus exclusively on protection, with no space for a positive discussion of healthy and safe sexuality as a dimension of gender identity. Certainly accurate information about their own bodies is of critical importance to adolescents and is understood as a strategic protection need, especially for girls. But strategic protection allows young people to discuss and understand the pleasures and the risks of sexuality in their own particular contexts, and to work together to develop strategies to protect themselves and each other. Such discussions would also engage boys and men in exploring sexuality, masculinity, gender identity, and their roles in eliminating sexual violence. Finally, strategic protection, as suggested above, involves girls as active and knowledgeable participants in the design, implementation, and evaluation of activities and strategies to protect and empower them.

The notion of strategic protection enhances attention to education for peace and equality. The protection mandate remains imperative, but through alternative program approaches, participation and empowerment imperatives are also integrated. Teacher training is an obvious starting point, especially as this is one of the most common program activities in education in emergency contexts. Specific gender training should go beyond questions of increasing girls' access to school. It needs to allow the male and female teachers to openly discuss (in separate groups if necessary) issues such as what it means to be a man, woman, boy, or girl of different ages in the camp or community; if or how this has changed over time; what sort of pressures there are to conform to certain ideals of masculinity and femininity; what the negative results of this might be; and how to create some positive changes. Increased attention to teacher codes of conduct (as recommended in the INEE Minimum Standards, for example) does reflect progress on these issues. But they are inadequate to bring about the changes in the culture of schools, of teaching, and of "being a male teacher," which are necessary to really create protective environments for teachers and students. Activities have to go beyond training teachers on a given code of conduct to complement gender training. Activities need to allow for discussion of sexual and gender identities and power dynamics: how they are both challenged and reinforced in emergency contexts and how teachers may act as agents of change and support their students to do likewise.

Take Holistic Approaches to Protection, Well-Being, Hygiene, and (Reproductive) Health

Lack of access to water and sanitation facilities in schools particularly affects girls' education. Adolescence and puberty can be difficult times for all young people. For girls, however, in emergencies, chronic crises, and early reconstruction contexts, puberty—and especially the onset of menstruation—pose particular challenges, not least this lack of adequate restrooms and water at school to comfortably change sanitary pads or other materials and wash themselves·in private. Refugees, IDPs, and girls otherwise affected by crises may not be able to afford commercially-produced sanitary pads and may not have access to rags or other materials for homemade solutions. The situation may be even more difficult for girls whose clothing is either too small and tight or just torn and worn and who do not have underwear. Both of these factors are known to affect the participation in education of girls in southern Sudan, for example. Menstruating girls may miss classes each month during their period (Kirk and Sommer 2005). Even if they are able to attend school, with limited and makeshift sanitary materials they may be very uncomfortable and unable to fully participate in class. The same may be the case for women teachers who either fail to attend school during menstruation or who attend but are restricted in their activities. Girls who have to use restrooms that are far away from the main school compound, and possibly out of sight of the school authorities, may then risk sexual violence.

In many social contexts these issues are not openly discussed, and there is embarrassment surrounding personal hygiene, health, and menstruation. Particularly where education levels are low, pubescent girls and boys may have very little understanding of what is happening to them and their bodies. Crisis-affected parents may lack the time and energy to talk with their children about puberty and adolescence. Furthermore, school curricula typically do not cover topics such as puberty and menstruation in a very sensitive way and so do not help girls or boys to understand the changes in their maturing bodies. In emergency situations, schools tend to be dominated by male teachers because of difficulties recruiting women. These male teachers may be undertrained with little understanding of or sensitivity to the challenges faced by postpubescent girls in regularly attending school. Where there are women teachers, they are often fully occupied in the lowest grades, and so older girls have no confidante with whom to share questions and concerns.

There is increasing recognition that providing separate, private, and safe restrooms for girls has the potential to improve school access, attendance, and retention, especially for adolescent girls. Safe, adequate facilities, however, are only part of the solution. Girls and boys should be engaged in planning and implementing new sanitation projects. They should have information to understand and cope with puberty. Links should be made between the infrastructure improvements in the school and the nature and quality of teaching and learning for girls and boys.

Build Capacity of Women Teachers and Education Leaders

The above perspectives on strategic protection need to be linked to discussions and policy development on gender-responsive recruitment and deployment and support for male and female teachers. Men and women should have equal status in schools. Both should be able to act as positive role models for girls and boys. The teachers' different opportunities for positive interaction with parents and community members should also be exploited. In training and professional support of women and men, possible priority differences should also be assessed and incorporated into training plans. It may be, for example, that women teachers need additional support to develop leadership and management skills in education to support promotion and career development. In locations where women have fewer opportunities to interact in English, French, or another lingua franca, language skills may be prioritized. Teacher support, development content, and the processes for professional development warrant gendered consideration. Teacher networks and learning groups may provide very supportive development opportunities for women, which can be adapted to fit with other family responsibilities. Other recommendations include ensuring links between women teachers and community-based women's organizations, providing mentoring opportunities to partner a young and new woman teacher with an older and more experienced educator, as well as recruiting and deploying women teachers in pairs (INEE GTT n.d.).

Conclusions

This chapter has presented some of the prevailing gender inequities in education in contexts of crisis, postcrisis, and state fragility. It has highlighted some of the concrete global policy developments that may support increased attention to gender equality and education. These developments include the INEE Minimum Standards for Education in Emergencies, Chronic Crises, and Early Reconstruction and the Education Cluster within the UN humanitarian reform processes. Concrete programming strategies to promote gender equality in education in contexts of crisis, postcrisis, and state fragility described in the final section of this chapter provide strategic directions for policy and program development. The strategic directions exist within an overarching framework of the INEE Minimum Standards, through which the principles and practices of gender mainstreaming in humanitarian action are interwoven.

Annex 10A: Classroom Assistants in Guinea and Sierra Leone

Adapted from INEE Gender Task Team Gender Strategies in Emergencies, Chronic Crises, and Early Reconstruction Contexts: "Preventing and Responding to Gender-Based Violence in and through Education."

The Classroom Assistant (CA) program was initiated by the IRC in Guinea in 2002, and soon afterwards was adopted by IRC Sierra Leone in its education programs for Liberian refugees. Although there was no documentation of actual abuse and exploitation within the IRC programs, a United Nations High Commissioner for Refugees (UNHCR/ Save the Children U.K. report [2002]) drew attention to the widespread manipulation of girls into sexual relationships with teachers in exchange for good grades or other in-school privileges. It was therefore critical to address the male domination of the schools in order to create more protective, conducive learning environments for girls. A long-term gender equality intervention is to recruit more women teachers to the schools. But this was impossible in the short term because of the few refugee or local women with the level of schooling, time, family support, and resources required to become a teacher. Well-educated women are usually recruited for more lucrative positions in the UN, NGOs, or other agencies in the camps. Others are unable to leave family duties or other better-paying income-generating activities. This is especially true for the many refugee women who are single mothers or who have lost their husbands to the conflict in Liberia.

There are flexible entry requirements (grade 9 education) to become a CA, and so the position is open to a larger number of refugee women. Women who are selected participate in a short two-to-five-day training workshop, which includes lesson planning, team teaching, tracking girls' grades and attendance, report writing, prevention of sexual abuse and exploitation, and child rights and child protection topics. Communication and counseling skills are also included in the training. The assistants are then deployed to grades 3–6 classes and expected to be in class with the students all day, every day. They are visited on a regular basis by IRC supervisors to whom they submit monthly reports detailing girls' attendance, activities, and home visits.

The CAs have an explicit mandate to mitigate abuse and exploitation of students. More broadly, the program was also designed to create more conducive, girl-friendly learning environments and support quality learning for all students. One critical task the assistants perform is the collection and safekeeping of the class grades from the teacher. This means that the students do not deal directly with the teacher about their grades, which helps to avoid situations in which teachers can manipulate and exploit girls for sex in exchange for altering their grades. Additionally, assistants monitor attendance and follow up on absences with home visits. They also help the girls with their studies in addition to supporting health education activities and some social club activities such as needlework, games, and sports.

For many of the CAs, the job means an opportunity for them to continue their own education. They are encouraged to attend evening classes to complete their secondary school studies, participate in different teacher trainings, and eventually become teachers themselves.

Research conducted as part of the IRC's Healing Classrooms Initiative highlights the importance of gender training for teachers, head teachers, and CAs. Such training ensures that there are shared understandings of the roles of the CAs and that there is real attention to presenting the complementarity and equal status of men's and women's roles in schools. Also important is working with the CAs to develop protection messages and strategies for the girls that reflect the principles of strategic protection rather than reinforce the message that the girls are "the problem" and that they should just concentrate harder and stay away from the teachers. The lessons learned about the CA program are now being integrated into IRC programming to support education and gender equality in Liberia (see Kirk and Winthrop 2006, 2007a).

Annex 10B: The Gender Equity Support Project of the Sudan Basic Education Program

From INEE Gender Task Team Gender Strategies in Emergencies, Chronic Crises, and Early Reconstruction Contexts: "Recruiting and Supporting Women Teachers."

In south Sudan, it is estimated that women account for only about 6 percent of teachers and about 1 percent of head teachers. This means that education is heavily oriented toward the experiences and needs of boys. There are few role models to promote more girl-friendly school environments and to encourage girls to continue their studies. To increase the number of women teachers, the Gender Equity Support Project of the Sudan Basic Education Program provided assistance for girls in secondary schools and for women in teacher education programs. The program provided a school fee subsidy for girls and money for a school-based committee including girls, teachers, and parents to purchase items to meet the particular needs of the girls and women (for example, soap, basins, schoolbooks, flashlights). A third of the money was then allocated to purchase items or make improvements in the learning environment, which would benefit all students, for example, to purchase library books and stools. To qualify for the money, the institution had to prepare an institutional gender assessment. It also had to go through a process of participatory action planning to ensure that the decisions made about how to spend the money reflected the views of the girls and women and targeted priority needs. All girls and women were given a "comfort kit," comprising reusable sanitary pads, underwear, soap, and a booklet on menstruation and reproductive health. Schools with no female teachers were also encouraged to identify a mentor for the girls, a local woman who could come to the school on a regular basis to share any questions, concerns, and ideas. Communication materials were targeted at young women with positive messages about women teachers and their roles in the new Sudan.

The program achieved significant results, including increased enrollment and retention of girls in participating institutions and increased awareness of teachers and school personnel of the needs of girls. It is hoped that the girls who have been encouraged to stay in school and complete their studies will be encouraged to become teachers themselves. A follow-up of the project should focus on the links between the girls' completing secondary school and the teacher training programs. The follow-up should focus as well on encouraging secondary school girls to team up with any local women primary school teachers to assist them in the classroom and, it is hoped, to be encouraged to also become a teacher.

Annex 10C: An Integrated Approach to Addressing Sanitary Protection Needs: IRC Ethiopia's Intervention

From INEE Gender Task Team Gender Strategies in Emergencies, Chronic Crises, and Early Reconstruction Contexts: "Gender-Responsive School Sanitation, Health, and Hygiene."

The IRC implemented multisector programming to increase girls' enrollment and participation in Walanihby Refugee Camp Primary School. The programming included the establishment of a girls' school council, recruitment of a refugee girls' education specialist, introduction of school feeding, and distribution of school uniforms. To complement this, IRC started production and distribution of sanitary napkins and soap to school girls as an important strategy to increase girls' participation in the school as well as in other nonformal education activities. When IRC started its education program for the Kunama refugees, girls' enrollment in and attendance at the primary school was very low. The findings from focus group discussion with school girls cited that the lack of protection during their menstrual cycle was one of the main reasons for low enrollment and the high dropout rate of girls in school.

The IRC started dialogue with stakeholders and brought this issue to the attention of the UNHCR, including proposed strategies to address the concerns of girls and women in the camp. The UNHCR donated fabrics for the production of sanitary napkin kits. Using women graduates from the tailoring program, the IRC designed and produced sample sanitary napkin kits in its vocational training program and distributed them to a sample group of girls and women in each zone. The sample group provided feedback on the use and quality of the sanitary napkin kits. The women continued to incorporate feedback from the refugee women and girls to improve the sanitary napkin design. The IRC Reproductive Health and HIV/AIDS Program distributes the kits, involving the women association members in each zone. Moreover, following vocational training on soap production, the IRC added the distribution of soap as part of the sanitary napkin package in 2004–05. The IRC purchases the underwear, pads, and bars of soap from the women and distributes the items every three months to girls and women ages 13–49. Each girl and woman receives four pairs of underwear, 12 reusable pads, and 12 bars of soap per year.

The production of school uniforms and sanitary napkins is not solely an opportunity for women to increase their household income. Distribution of these items encourages greater enrollment and retention of girls in school.

Notes

1. Molyneux's (1985) differentiation between the women's practical gender interests and women's strategic gender interests has been particularly influential in the framing of gender and development theory. It draws attention to the differences between responses to the concrete, practical, and more immediate needs of women, and responses that are more strategic interventions, aimed at longer-term, more transformatory goals, such as women's emancipation. Moser (1989) takes up the differentiation and applies it to policy planning, but also suggests the need for more considered policy interventions that, even if aimed at meeting practical gender needs, are aware of longer-term needs and larger, strategic possibilities.

2. These have been translated into French for inclusion in INEE Capacity Building Workshops and the INEE Minimum Standards Toolkit.

3. See: http://www.humanitarianinfo.org/iasc/content/subsidi/tf_gender/genderH. asp

References

Bird, L., J. Dolan, and S. Nicolai. 2006. *Identifying Alternative Financing Mechanisms That Can Be Used to Achieve Education for All Goals within Emergency and Reconstruction Contexts*. New York: INEE. http://ineesite.org/uploads/INEE%20Initiatives/Events%20&%20Activities/CIDA-INEE%20Policy%20Roundtable%20Outcome%20Report%20(Final).pdf.

Enloe, C. H. 1989. *Bananas, Beaches & Bases: Making Feminist Sense of International Politics*. London: Pandora.

————. 2000. *Maneuvers: The International Politics of Militarizing Women's Lives*. Berkeley, CA: University of California Press.

IASC (Inter-Agency Standing Committee) Task Force on Gender and Humanitarian Assistance. 2005. Guidelines for Gender-Based Violence in Humanitarian Settings: Focusing on Prevention of and Response to Sexual Violence in Emergencies. Geneva: IASC Task Force on Gender and Humanitarian Assistance. http://www.humanitarianinfo.org/iasc/publications/asp.

————. 2007. IASC Cluster Working Groups. http://www.humanitarianinfo.org/iasc/content/Cluster/default.asp?mainbodyID=5&publish=0.

INEE (Inter-Agency Network for Education in Emergencies). 2004. *Minimum Standards for Education in Emergencies, Chronic Crises and Early Reconstruction*. Paris: INEE.

INEE GTT (Inter-Agency Network for Education in Emergencies Gender Task Team). n.d. "Gender Strategies for Education in Emergencies, Chronic Crises, and Early Reconstruction Contexts: Recruiting and Supporting Women Teachers." http://www.ineesite.org/ineedownloads/viewall.asp?pid=1387&cp=18.

International Save the Children Alliance. 2006. *Rewrite the Future: Education for Children in Conflict-Affected Countries*. London: International Save the Children Alliance.

Karam, A. 2001. "Women in War and Peace-building: The Roads Traversed, the Challenges Ahead." *International Feminist Journal of Politics* 3 (1): 2–25.

Kirk, J. 2004a. "IRC Healing Classrooms Initiative: An Initial Study in Ethiopia." Unpublished manuscript. International Rescue Committee.

————. 2004b. "IRC Healing Classrooms Initiative: An Initial Study in Sierra Leone." Unpublished manuscript. International Rescue Committee.

————. 2004c. "Promoting a Gender-Just Peace: the Roles of Women Teachers in Peacebuilding and Reconstruction." *Gender and Development* 12 (3): 50–59.

————. 2004d. "Teachers Creating Change: Working for Girls' Education and Gender Equity in South Sudan." *EQUALS, Beyond Access: Gender, Education and Development* 9: 4–5.

———. 2006a. "Roles, Potential and Challenges for Donors of the INEE Minimum Standards in Education in Emergencies, Chronic Crises and Early Reconstruction." http://www.ineesite.org/minimum_standards/CIDA-INEE.pdf.

———. 2006b. *Education in Emergencies: The Gender Implications.* UNESCO Bangkok Advocacy Brief. . Bangkok: United Nations Educational, Scientific, and Cultural Organization. http://www2.unescobkk.org/elib/publications/092/.

———. 2007. "Education and Fragile States." *Globalisation, Societies and Education* 5 (2): 181–200.

———. Forthcoming–a. "Gender, Sexuality and Education: Examining Issues in Conflict Contexts." In *Gender, Sexuality and Development: Education and Society in Sub-Saharan Africa*, ed. M. Dunne. Rotterdam: Sense Publishing.

———. Forthcoming–b. *Building Back Better: Opportunities and Challenges for Education in Pakistan after the 2005 Earthquake.* Paris: United Nations Educational, Scientific, and Cultural Organization and the International Institute for Educational Planning.

Kirk, J., and M. Sommer. 2005. "Menstruation and Body Awareness: Critical Issues for Girls' Education." EQUALS, Beyond Access: *Gender, Education and Development* 15: 4–5. http://k1.ioe.ac.uk/schools/efps/GenderEducDev/Equals%20Issue%20No.%2015.pdf.

Kirk, J., and S. Taylor. 2004. "Gender, Peace and Security Agendas: Where Are Girls and Young Women?" For Gender and Peacebuilding Working Group of the Canadian Peacebuilding Coordinating Committee. http://action.web.ca/home/cpcc/en_resources.shtml?x=73620.

———. 2007. "Ending Sexual Violence against Women and Girls in Conflict Contexts: UN Security Council Resolution 1325." Forced Migration Review 27: 13–14. http://www.fmreview.org/FMRpdfs/FMR27/06.pdf.

Kirk, J., and R. Winthrop. 2006. "Eliminating the Sexual Abuse and Exploitation of Girls in Refugee Schools in West Africa: Introducing Female Classroom Assistants." In *Combating Gender Violence in and around Schools*, eds. F. Leach and C. Mitchell. Stoke-on-Trent, UK: Trentham Books.

———. 2007a. "Female Classroom Assistants: Agents of Change in Refugee Classrooms in West Africa?" In *Women, Education and Development: Structure and Agency Perspectives*, ed. M. Maslak. New York: SUNY Press.

———2007b. "Promoting Quality Education in Refugee Contexts: Supporting Teacher Development in Northern Ethiopia." *International Review of Education, Special Issue on Quality Education in Africa: Challenges and Prospects:* 715–723.

————. Forthcoming. *Creating Healing Classrooms: Education in Crisis and Post-Crisis Transitions* (Working title). New York: International Rescue Committee.

Machel, G. 2001. *The Machel Review 1996–2000. A Critical Review of Progress Made and Obstacles Encountered in Increasing Protection for War-Affected Children.* New York: United Nations.

Manchanda, R. 2001. "Ambivalent Gains in South Asian Conflicts." In *The Aftermath: Women in Post-conflict Transformation*, eds. S. Meintjies, A. Pillay, and M. Turshen, 99–120. London: Zed Books.

Molyneux, M. 1985. "Mobilisation without Emancipation? Women's Interests, States and Revolution in Nicaragua." *Feminist Studies* 11 (2): 227–254.

Moser, C. 1989. "Gender Planning in the Third World." *World Development* 17 (11): 1799–1825.

Nicolai, S., and C. Triplehorn. 2003. "The Role of Education in Protecting Children in Conflict." Humanitarian Practice Network paper, Overseas Development Institute, London.

Obura, A. 2001. *Knowing the Pen Girls' Education in the Southern Part of Sudan.* Nairobi, Kenya: United Nations Children's Fund and Operation Lifeline Sudan.

Qahir, K. Forthcoming. "Training Refugee Afghan Women Teachers in the Female Education Program, Pakistan." In *Women Teaching in South Asia*, ed. J. Kirk. New Delhi, India: SAGE India.

RET (The Foundation for the Refugee Education Trust). 2008. "Size of the Problem." http://www.r-e-t.com/pages/l1/l2/what_we_do/size_of_the_problem.php?itfLG=english&itfVS=html.

Rose, P., and M. Greeley. 2006. "Education in Fragile States: Capturing Lessons and Identifying Good Practice." Draft paper prepared for the Development Assistance Committee Fragile States Working Groups, Service Delivery Workstream, Subteam for Education Services.

Saigol, R. 1995. *Knowledge and Identity: Articulation of Gender in Educational Discourse in Pakistan.* Lahore, Pakistan: ASR Publications.

————. 2000. *Symbolic Violence: Curriculum, Pedagogy and Society.* Lahore, Pakistan: Society for the Advancement of Education.

Smith, A., and T. Vaux. 2002. *Education, Conflict and International Development.* London: Department for International Development. http://www.dfid.gov.uk/pubs/files/edconflictdev.pdf.

UN OCHA (United Nations Office for Coordination of Humanitarian Affairs). 2007. *Appeal for Improving Humanitarian Response Capacity: 1 April 2007–31 March 2008.* New York and Geneva: UN OCHA.

UNESCO and UNHCR (United Nations Education, Scientific, and Cultural Organization and United Nations High Commissioner for Refugees). 2007. "Educational Responses to HIV and AIDS for Refugees and Internally Displaced Persons." Discussion Paper for Decision-Makers, UNESCO and UNHCR, Paris and Geneva.

United Nations. 2001. *Strengthening the Coordination of Emergency Humanitarian Assistance of the United Nations.* Report of the Secretary-General No. A-56-95-E-2001-85. http://www.reliefweb.int/rw/lib.nsf/db900SID/LGEL-5D9CJ4? OpenDocument.

———. 2005. Humanitarian Response Review. An independent report commissioned by the United Nations Emergency Relief Coordinator and Under-Secretary-General for Humanitarian Affairs, Office for the Coordination of Humanitarian Affairs. New York and Geneva: United Nations.

United Nations Security Council. 2000. Resolution 1325 on Women, Peace and Security. New York: United Nations.

Whitworth, S. 2004. *Men, Militarism and UN Peacekeeping: A Gendered Analysis.* Boulder, CO: Lynne Rienner Publishing.

World Vision International. 2001. *Every Girl Counts: Development, Justice and Gender.* Ontario, Canada: World Vision International.

PART III

Experiences from the Field: How Was It Done?

CHAPTER 11

Building a Better Future for Afghanistan through Female Education

Sakena Yacoobi

As executive director of the Afghan Institute of Learning, a nongovernmental Afghan women's organization that provides health and education services to 350,000 Afghan women and children each year, I am often asked how we have been able to bring preschool to postsecondary education to women and girls in Afghanistan and Pakistan. I am asked to explain how we have been able to introduce women's rights, education, and health programs in areas where such programs were thought to be impossible. I am asked how we have been able to maintain and expand our programs over the years, helping hard-to-reach women in both urban and rural areas. I am asked how our work has endured, despite ongoing insecurity and instability.

These questions illustrate a sad irony. Afghan women are one of the most vulnerable groups of women in the world—having endured war, trauma, starvation, the Taliban regime. Yet, despite the international shock, horror, and protest at the hardships Afghan women have suffered, the international community seems to be at a collective loss as to what can be done to improve their circumstances. False biases and assumptions about Islam and an unwillingness to look beyond the burqa to the real, urgent, and immediate problems of Afghan women have skewed responses to this humanitarian crisis. Many well-intentioned programs have been doomed to only negligibly affect the problems faced by the women such programs are intended to help. Indeed, the problems faced by Afghan women are complex and multifaceted. Nonetheless, when solutions are contextualized in Afghan religion and culture, exhibiting a thorough understanding of Afghan history, and are based on a credible assessment of the actual needs of Afghan women (as perceived by the women themselves), programs can successfully empower Afghan women and help them access the education that will prepare them for leadership roles in rebuilding Afghanistan. This chapter presents an overview of the historical and current issues faced by Afghan women, perspectives on Afghan culture, and a successful method for providing education and health services in an Afghan context.

The Situation of Afghan Women Past and Present

For a time, Afghans were categorized as the world's largest refugee population (United Nations High Commission on Refugees 2002). Before the Soviet invasion in 1979, the Ministry of Planning in Kabul, Afghanistan, estimated the country's population to be 15.108 million (Emadi 1991). During the years of war following 1979, an estimated 2 million Afghans died and approximately 6 million became refugees (Hirschkind and Mahmood 2002; Wali 1994, 2002). Today, Afghans have a low life expectancy, and a high percentage are undernourished. Years of drought have left Afghans starving, a condition exacerbated by post–September 11 bombing (Hirschkind and Mahmood 2002; United Nation Development Programme 2001). Afghan women in particular have suffered immensely under these conditions, with millions of Afghan women living in abject poverty. Women and their children constitute a majority—at least 75 percent—of the refugees in Pakistan and Iran (Hirschkind and Mahmood 2002; Wali 1994). When asked to identify their primary problem, 41 percent of Herati women in one study answered that lack of food was their main problem, 18 percent reported lack of shelter, and 14 percent reported lack of clean water (Amowitz, Reis, and Iacopino 2002). Poverty, starvation, illiteracy, poor health care, and high mortality rates all prevailed before the Soviet invasion and Taliban rule in Afghanistan

(Hirschkind and Mahmood 2002). But these conditions have been exacerbated by the past quarter century of strife. In addition, new problems have developed.

Focus on Education

By 2000, Afghanistan's education system was in chaos (UNESCO 2000). Accurate statistics on social indicators for Afghans, including the literacy rate, continue to be difficult to gather. Estimates vary but suggest that 15–20 percent of Afghan females are literate, and 31.5 percent of the total population is literate (UNESCO 2000; World Education Forum 2000). Only 22 percent of school-age children were attending school in 1996 (Callaghan 2002). Since 2001, enrollment in schools has greatly increased. However, among the students who attend school, attendance is often poor and dropout rates are high, particularly for girls. Poor enrollment rates and attrition can be attributed to the lack of acceptable government education; security problems; the lack of teachers, schools, and materials; inappropriate teaching methods and curriculum; and the need for children to participate in the economic activities of their families and villages.

Afghan females have been particularly disadvantaged with respect to education. Although efforts to educate Afghan girls have a long history in the country, they have advanced very slowly throughout the past century. The war with the Soviet Union and the subsequent Taliban regime worsened the already bleak education opportunities of Afghan women and girls. For example, in 1988 only 19 percent of Afghan females were enrolled in primary school (Kurian 1988). Because of Taliban prohibitions, 11 years later the percentage of girls attending primary school dropped to 5 percent, and humanitarian agencies operated 91 percent of the 446 schools for girls (Callaghan 2002).

Focus on Health

Before the 1979 Soviet invasion of Afghanistan, women's medical needs, particularly in rural areas, were grossly neglected and needed immediate attention. Factors contributing to this situation included attitudes toward women's health as interpreted within Islamic law and local customs, poor understanding of women's health needs, reluctance to present women to male doctors, unavailability of vaccines and checkups, lack of accessible medical facilities, preferences for traditional healing methods, and cultural resistance to medical assistance outside the walls of the very private

household (Grima 2002). Recent surveys of the health needs of Afghan
women and Afghanistan's health system offer an even grimmer picture of
Afghan public health today. The current health and human rights status of
women described in two studies suggests that the combined effects of war-
related traumas and human rights abuses by Taliban officials have had a
profound effect on Afghan women's health. The majority of Afghan
women interviewed in one study reported deteriorating physical and
mental health during the last two years of the Taliban regime and also
reported experiencing human rights violations by Taliban officials and
multiple war-related traumas (Rasekh et al. 1998). Eighty-five percent of
study participants living in Pakistan reported that they had migrated after
the Taliban suspended medical services to women in Kabul in September
1997 (Rasekh et al. 1998). Even in post–Taliban Afghanistan, maternal
mortality continues to be high, and a number of constraints on human
rights may contribute to preventable maternal deaths, including inadequate health care services (both access and quality issues), education,
employment, food, shelter, and clean water. Issues of individual freedom,
such as marriage at an early age, inability to negotiate terms of sex, and
lack of access to birth control methods, may also contribute to the high
rate of maternal deaths.

The Current Crisis
This humanitarian crisis in Afghanistan, provoked by larger political
issues in the context of the Cold War, can be traced to policies that supported the most radical, extreme groups of Afghan soldiers (*Mujahedeen*)
to fight the Soviet occupation (Hirschkind and Mahmood 2002; Wali
1994; Wali, Gould, and Fitzgerald 1999). This support, which included a
deluge of weapons and amounted to more than $3 billion, has led to the
creation of opposing political factions and repressive power structures
and has brought about the destruction of the cultural framework that
defined and maintained the time-honored role of women in Afghan society (Wali 1994; Wali, Gould, and Fitzgerald 1999). As a result of U.S.
covert operations and policies organized around oil interests, the arms
industry, and international drug trade (Abu-Lughod 2002), there are millions of land mines still laid inside Afghanistan; a proliferation of
weapons; and frightening increases in drug trafficking, property disputes,
and factional fighting. Additionally, the delicate balance of tribal power
has been radically destabilized, making ordinary people subject to violence on an unprecedented scale.

The Context in Which Afghan Women Live

Despite the fact that the social and familial organizations of their lives have been dramatically altered by war, poverty, and political instability, Afghans have been slow to adapt their traditional customs to the new problems and realities of their present existence. Today, many Afghan households no longer have any men to sanction actions or decisions, because the men either have been killed or have disappeared in war, leaving their surviving women in a difficult predicament. Historically, most Afghan women, particularly those who were rural and illiterate, did not take decisions upon themselves; they either were told by their closest male relative which course of action to take or obtained his permission. The Taliban did not invent this law, although they brought it to the fore. So far, the shifts regarding these customs—designed to keep women safe and preserve the honor of women, families, and tribes—have reinforced the bonds of *purdah* (the separation of males and females in public) and have disregarded the new difficulties of thousands of women left without men to care for them. A combination of war, culture, politics, and religion have strained and exaggerated Afghan customs and forced a stricter version of *purdah* upon Afghan women in the confined environment of refugee villages. Because of continuing security issues, Afghans are not inclined to change their customs. As a result, Afghan women have been obliged to carry out their struggles in isolation, amplifying their vulnerability.

This strain on Afghan cultural norms was particularly evident in the oppressive political reign of the Taliban. During the regime of the Taliban, women were prohibited from working outside their homes, attending school, or appearing in public without a close male relative. They were forced to ride on "women only" public buses, were forbidden to wear brightly colored clothes, and had to have the windows in their houses painted so that they could not be seen from outside. Initially, they could be treated only by female doctors; later, they could be examined—but not seen or touched—by male doctors, in the presence of a male relative (Wali 2002).

Still, to view the Taliban as the root of all Afghan women's problems is an oversimplification (Hirschkind and Mahmood 2002). The narrow focus on Taliban rule by some activist groups, and their silence on the channeling of U.S. aid to the most brutal and violent Afghan groups (of which the Taliban were only one), dangerously reduces a vastly more complicated problem. Conditions of war, militarization, and starvation have too often been overlooked as injurious to Afghan women in favor of an exclusive focus on the lack of education, employment, and most notably in the media, Western dress styles (Hirschkind and Mahmood 2002).

As part of the justification for its invasion of Afghanistan, the United States linked its post–September 11, 2001, attack to the need to free Afghan women from the Taliban (Wali 2002). This rhetoric of saving Afghan women from oppression carries with it some dangerous, Western biases, not the least of which is the danger of utilizing the more acceptable goal of advancing women's rights as a justification for colonialism (Abu-Lughod 2002). A further danger is that the rhetoric perpetuates the inaccurate view that Islamic laws and practices are at the root of the oppression of Afghan women. The disparate currents within contemporary Islam, all of which are lumped together under the rubric of fundamentalism, do not cohere in a singular movement definable by its dangerous regressivity. They differ in their goals, their politics, their models of society, and their understanding of moral responsibility.

It is difficult for people who have lived otherwise to understand *purdah* or the practice of veiling (Kaldor 1989), but it is imperative that those who are truly interested in empowering Afghan women be willing to empower them to live as they choose, even if that is different from what others might choose for them (Abu-Lughod 2002). "Though it [*purdah*] is surely inconvenient and an obstacle that blocks the way for many types of assistance, it is not a 'problem' that needs to be 'solved.' It is a tradition that must be respected and contended with" (Kaldor 1989, 32). Foreign humanitarian aid organizations and the people they employ must recognize that, whatever effect it has had on women who wear it, the veil has also had a radical impact on the capacity of Westerners to recognize Muslim societies for something other than misogyny and patriarchal violence (Hirschkind and Mahmood 2002). The view that veiling is the quintessential sign of women's lack of freedom is reductive (Abu-Lughod 2002). Many Muslim women are deeply committed to being moral and have a sense of honor tied to the family, which they express through practices like veiling (Abu-Lughod 2002).

Improving the Circumstances of Afghan Women

As Afghan communities attempt to cope with trauma, ongoing instability, poverty, hunger, and other hardships, they continue to be plagued by lack of security, dependence on outside relief assistance, and fluctuating levels of foreign aid. Communities are also contending with the incidence of rape; the sale of women and girls; and the rising numbers of orphans, widows, and people handicapped by land mines. Additionally, international guidelines and instruments do not, in practice, adequately distinguish between male and female refugees, although they pay lip service to the differing and distinct needs of men and women in exile (Schultz 1994). As a result, programs to address the urgent and devastating health and education needs of Afghan women are often inadequate, inappropriate, and ineffective in relieving the suffering of these women.

To truly improve the lives of Afghan women, their human rights must be secured. In addition to their right to freedom from the structural violence of global inequality and from the ravages of war, Afghan women must secure their everyday rights of having enough to eat; having homes in which their families can live and thrive; having decent livelihoods so their children can grow; and having the strength and security to work out, within their communities and with whatever alliances they want, how to live and have a good life. This might very well include changing the ways those communities are organized.

Many people and organizations are working to achieve this goal and implementing a wide range of programs and services toward this end. Some programs are focused on improving research and policies that affect Afghan women. Better planning, implementation, assessment of the target population, feasibility studies, and evaluation have also been recommended as keys to improving the quality of life for Afghan women (Schultz 1994). Some advocates have recommended that national governments be pressured to place conditions on reconstruction aid that are predicated on gender sensitivity, and that institutions serving women at the grassroots level be reclaimed and changed to meet the needs and reflect the desires of the masses.

Values embedded in these various recommended approaches include returning to age-old Islamic principles, increasing the level of prestige associated with practicing medicine in rural areas, integrating women into decision-making circles so that they may take part in the decisions that affect them, and promoting economic self-reliance (Grima 2002; Schultz 1994; Wali 1994, 2002). Most women activists, especially those based in Afghanistan who are aware of the realities in the country, are in agreement that Islam has to be the starting point for reform because of its central place within the culture and identity of Afghan women (Abu-Lughod 2002; Ahmed-Ghosh 2003; Wali 1994).

The method for empowering and educating Afghan women presented in this chapter incorporates these values as well as others, operates within the culture of Afghan communities, respects Afghan history, and focuses efforts for change at the grassroots. This method was developed through my fieldwork in Afghanistan and Pakistan over the past 35 years and is articulated in the format of 10 core concepts, described in the next section. These core concepts can guide others interested in empowering Afghan women and girls through education. For illustrative purposes, my work with establishing education opportunities for girls in refugee camps in Pakistan is described within the explanation of each core concept. The core concepts of this method have also been used to

- operate underground home schools for girls in Afghanistan during the Taliban regime;
- offer human rights, leadership, and health education for Afghan women;
- provide teacher training in Afghanistan and Pakistan;
- establish Women's Learning Centers to meet the multiple health and education needs of Afghan women; and
- provide postprimary education to Afghan women.

A Strategy to Empower and Educate Afghan Women

The 10 steps that follow outline the core concepts of an empowerment strategy for women in Afghanistan.

1. Begin at the grassroots with locally identified needs.

When beginning new programs, it is essential to listen to the people and their representatives and to design programs that address their needs as they express them, rather than designing programs to address the needs perceived by the program officials. For the program to succeed in addressing a local problem, the community served has to recognize the problem and request help to solve it.

When I came to the Northwest Frontier Province in Pakistan in 1992 to work with Afghan refugees, only a few girls' schools had been started in refugee camp communities by local people. Although international nongovernmental organizations had recognized the need for more girls' schools, many people who lived in the camps were suspicions of and resistant to the idea of educating girls. To establish a strong foundation for girls' education in the region, the most appropriate starting point for developing such a program had to be identified. School administrators and political party leaders had voiced a need for teacher training and school support. Most important, it had been recognized and articulated by Afghans involved in the existing schools that the female teachers of these girls' schools could benefit from training. This is the starting point we chose for our program to improve education for Afghan girls. It should be noted that the starting point in this instance upgraded the education of teachers, who were women who had already had at least primary education but had no immediate access to further education.

2. Start with the least controversial service in the least conservative area.

When attempting to begin a new program with a focus that has historically ignited conflict, identify the geographic area and type of service that will achieve the desired goal while encountering comparatively less opposition. When I began my work with training teachers for girls' schools in Afghan refugee camps in Pakistan, the focus was on empowering and educating women. Education and teacher training for girls and women has been a historically controversial issue for Afghans with concerns about the need and relevance of education for girls; doubts about the religious and cultural appropriateness of the curriculum; and suspicion about education from foreign agencies, potentially embedded with foreign values and foreign political agendas. Some groups remained staunchly opposed to education for girls and women. However, teacher training had been requested by a few schools. With these issues in mind, we chose the first site for our teacher training in the less conservative, urban area and used a teacher training curriculum that had previously been accepted to train male teachers. This seminar curriculum was acceptable to the community because it was culturally sensitive and based in Islam.

3. Do not impose services on a community.

It is important to make participation in the service offered truly voluntary. Receipt of other services or support for other programs should not be tied to a person's participation in the training offered. To the extent that it is possible, incentives should not be offered for participation. When services are truly voluntary, the amount of participation will be a true measure of the quality and appropriateness of the training.

When we offered the first teacher training in the urban area of the refugee camps, we announced that the training would be offered and invited teachers to participate. The first teacher training program was offered to teachers in three schools who had approached our organization and requested the training. After our organization was approached by these teachers, we explained our training program to the involved political parties and school administrators and obtained their permission for the training.

The first training in the city drew participants from only a few schools, despite the fact that the political parties and school administrators had agreed that training was needed. The reason for the low initial rate of participation was that the community wanted to evaluate the training before determining whether to participate in greater numbers. The first training was well received by participants, who endorsed it and recommended it to the larger community. Soon after, the program had a long waiting list.

4. Offer high-quality, culturally sensitive programs, incorporating feedback from participants.

Respecting local customs is an imperative for successful women's programs, as noted in the literature (Kaldor 1989). A combination of war, culture, politics, and religion has forced a stricter version of *purdah*, the separation of males and females in public, upon Afghan women in the confined environment of refugee villages (Schultz 1994). Keeping this history and the cultural and religious values of Afghans in mind, strategies can be developed to provide health and education services to women and girls. Some examples of strategies used in my work and noted in the literature include establishing all-women facilities; selecting program sites that are close enough to where the women live for them to freely go; and selecting program sites that are among families that know each other and are on friendly terms, so that women will feel comfortable interacting (Grima 2002; Kaldor 1989).

By hiring and working with local staff, we were able to develop trainings that responded to the needs and concerns of the community. We also had staff who understood and respected local customs. Additionally, the teacher trainers who taught the seminar were well trained, credentialed, and highly qualified. They held high expectations for participants and were greatly respected and admired by the participants. Schultz also recognizes the need and benefit of hiring local women, who are best able to understand and attend to the needs of refugee women. Hiring local women also empowers them because it allows them to develop job skills (Schultz 1994).

Additionally, trainers solicited periodic feedback from participants during the training by asking what they liked least and best and why, as well as what they best remembered about the training or seminar as a whole. Trainers incorporated this feedback into future trainings by self-evaluating each training and writing a report detailing changes that needed to be made. These methods for collecting and utilizing the input of local community members about the trainings help ensure that the training is high quality and culturally sensitive. Initially developed and piloted for Afghan male teachers, the 24-day teacher training seminar included intensive application-focused learning activities. The quality of the curriculum had already been tested and evaluated based on participant and teacher-trainer feedback over the course of three years. The seminar had demonstrated results. When teachers trained in this seminar returned to the classroom and began applying their new skills, student performance improved dramatically. Before participating in the seminar, teachers reported that students would learn to read after three years of instruction. Using skills learned through seminar participation, teachers reported that they were able to teach students to read in three months. Both teachers and students were empowered by these successes.

As word spread about the first teacher training workshop that we offered, interest in more training workshops for broader segments of the community quickly mounted. Our trainings developed a reputation for being secure, safe, relevant, and observant of religious and cultural norms. With our demonstrated commitment to quality programs, respect for local institutions, and protection for our staff, we began to attract more and better staff, which improved the quality of the trainings even more. Soon, we were managing waiting lists for future trainings and receiving requests for new services, including support for schools. Requests for training and support began to come from conservative rural camps, not just the urban areas.

5. Act at the request of the community when expanding services.
Acting at the request of the community is similar to the previously discussed principles of beginning at the grassroots with locally identified needs and not imposing services on the community. The basic approach is simply respectful: expand services only to areas that have invited you and your organization. Gather input from all members of the community that you are working with and involve community representatives. Even though a program may focus on women, meet with the men in the community where you are working, encourage their input, listen and respond to their concerns, and gather their support. Afghan women, like women

everywhere, are an integral part of their families and communities and are involved with familial, social, and economic processes hand-in-hand with men. Therefore, it is crucial not to omit Afghan men when working to establish programs for Afghan women. Working with Afghan men includes overcoming their suspicions, giving them a chance to express their concerns, and completing social formalities (Kaldor 1989; Schultz 1994). Incorporate the views of both women and men into the program that you are offering to make sure that the program is relevant, culturally acceptable, and responding to the actual needs of the people. Develop an agreement about the services to be provided and the respective responsibilities of both the organization providing services and the community. Follow through on promises.

Soon after the success of our first teacher training seminars, we began to receive requests to support girls' schools in the refugee camps. Trust had begun. The Afghan communities, having seen that our teacher training program improved the quality of education for their children and was designed within the context of Afghan and Islamic values, were now willing to let us into their communities to support girls' schools.

6. Require that the community contribute to the development of the new program.

When the community is required to donate security, volunteers, space, and other materials to the establishment of a new program, they become invested in the outcome of the program. Community matches ensure the community's support and protection of the program and also contribute to the long-term sustainability of the program. Community donations also raise the self-esteem of the community, as they realize that they have something to contribute and that their contributions are valuable.

When our program agreed to provide school support to communities at their request and invitation, we signed a contract with them that specified their and our responsibilities. Generally, communities were responsible for finding teachers (female teachers were preferred), gathering students, beginning a school, and finding a building for the school. Our program paid the teacher, provided materials to the school, trained the teacher, and supervised the teacher as she implemented newly learned techniques in the classroom. Our programs were always begun with the assumption that local people were capable of contributing to the program, had something valuable to contribute, and wanted to help educate girls. We did not allow stereotypes to interfere with these basic assumptions.

7. Recognize that in Afghan culture, trust and relationships are personal, not organizational.

By implementing these principles, we were able to build trust between ourselves and the communities that we were serving with teacher training and support for girls' schools. However, it was important for us to realize that the Afghan communities we were working with built trust and personal relationships with each individual member of our staff, not just our organization. New staff members were not able to assume that because they represented a credible organization, they would or should be trusted. Building trust takes time, as noted in the literature (Kaldor 1989). Staff members built and maintained trust and personal relationships with the communities we served by modeling the principles discussed in this chapter, as well as by behaving in a way that was consistent with the norms and values of the community in both their personal and professional lives. Staff had to be respectable members of the community, wear the hijab, model Islamic values, treat people respectfully, value the family, and be knowledgeable about scripture. The importance of hiring Afghan women with a good understanding of Islam to provide services was also emphasized by Schultz (1994).

8. Set flexible rules.

Do not lock your program into discriminatory policies or services that are exclusive. Maintain flexibility in policies and procedures so that you are able to respond to emerging needs and issues without delay.

In our program we never refused to provide education services to boys or men. However, because our focus was on women and girls, we implemented a policy of serving our programs with at least half of the available spaces reserved for women and girls. This policy allowed us to maintain our focus on women and girls without risking alienating the community by excluding some people. Additionally, we enforced a policy of nondiscriminatory hiring practices. We did not discriminate in hiring on the basis of age, region of birth, religious sect, or ethnicity. Policies and practices that facilitate inclusiveness foster broad participation and do not fuel existing divisions.

9. Hold high standards, have high expectations, and model them.

By remaining committed to providing only the highest quality of education and by enforcing expectations for staff behavior and community donations, security risks are minimized and the core mission and values of the program are maximized. When the staff and community find that they are able to meet these high expectations, their dignity and self-esteem increases. Although initially it may seem easier to compromise on some issues, it is worth the time and effort required to build relationships with the community up front and help the staff and the community to meet expectations. Compromising standards and lowering expectations is disempowering, alienating, and detracting from the long-term sustainability and impact of the program.

A small example of this concept is our requirement that seminar participants arrive on time and not be absent without a compelling reason (death in the family, severe illness, and so on). Although all participants were told of this requirement, some believed this requirement would not be enforced. Their experience in other programs was that it was not important. I remember the surprise of one participant who had been warned once about being late and then was told the second time that she would not be allowed to attend anymore if she were late again. The reasons were explained to her. Astonished, she noted that she had never encountered a program that truly wanted participants to learn and was willing to exclude those who were not ready to fully participate. She was not late again, nor did she or others object to the preparatory work they were asked to do outside of class.

10. Offer more controversial programs in a voluntary, culturally sensitive way after trust has been established.

When we wanted to expand our program to offer a human rights workshop for women, we revisited the principles discussed above, including core concepts of starting in the least conservative area and making participation truly voluntary. The human rights workshop was first offered in the city to any interested woman. Women were not given stipends for participating, so that it could not be claimed by men or others in the community that they were being paid to attend. Because of our program's reputation for culturally sensitive education and training, the participating women were confident that their participation in the new program would not put them in jeopardy. In human rights workshops, women learn that they have rights and that their rights can be respected within their cultural and religious context. Most important, they learn how to communicate effectively about their rights. Women who participated in human rights workshops returned home to their families and convinced their husbands, fathers, sons, and uncles that it was not only acceptable under Islam but even beneficial for women to be educated. As a result of participation in human rights workshops, women began flocking to literacy, enrichment, and skills training classes and began sending their daughters to school.

Remarkably, all of this was supported by the men in their households. Because of the culturally and religiously sensitive way that our program was conducted, involving the community at every level, demand for human rights workshops increased, even in more conservative areas. The success of the human rights workshops reinforced demand for our education programs for women and girls and resulted in further expansion of these programs. When we began our teacher training program for Afghan women teachers, we were supporting schools for 3,000 female Afghan students. By the end of one year, our program was supporting schools for 15,000 Afghan girls. This tremendous explosion in enrollment would not have been possible if we had not used the principles of community engagement and empowerment outlined in this chapter.

Conclusion

Education is increasingly viewed as a basic human right leading to empowerment and awareness, as opposed to being regarded solely as a means of bringing about economic growth and political stability (Mehran 1999). These core principals have been used to educate Afghan females at all levels, and these women have in turn been able to advance their human rights, establish schools for girls, and build and maintain an organizational structure to ensure that these advances will continue to be available for future generations of women and girls. When empowered through education, women are able to overcome their circumstances and their self-doubt and exercise more autonomy over their lives.

Education is important for Afghan women and girls. In a practical sense, women and girls must learn to read and write and must learn skills that will help them find work. However, it is far more important for women and girls to receive education that will open their minds to analyze, think critically, and consider people and events in new ways. This type of education will allow women to make real choices about their actions and their lives. To be truly empowered, women must also be able to make choices about the type of education that they will have. Education that is developed using these core concepts allows women to make that choice. Because they respond to the women's voiced needs and emphasize what they can do for themselves, these core concepts are a vital part of education that truly empowers women to make decisions for themselves.

References

Abu-Lughod, L. 2002. "Do Muslim Women Really Need Saving? Anthropological Reflections on Cultural Relativism and Its Others." *American Anthropologist* 104 (3): 783–790.

Ahmed-Ghosh, H. 2003. "A History of Women in Afghanistan: Lessons Learnt for the Future: Women in Afghanistan." *Journal of International Women's Studies* 4 (3): 1–14.

Amowitz, L. L., C. Reis, and V. Iacopino. 2002. "Maternal Mortality in Herat Province, Afghanistan, in 2002: An Indicator of Women's Human Rights." *Journal of the American Medical Association* 288 (10): 1284–1291.

Callaghan, S. J. 2002. "Afghanistan." In *World Education Encyclopedia: A Survey of Educational Systems Worldwide,* 2nd ed., ed. R. Marlow-Ferguson. Farmington Hills, MI: Gale Group.

Emadi, H. 1991. "State, Modernization and the Women's Movement in Afghanistan." *Review of Radical Political Economics* 23 (3): 224–243.

Grima, B. 2002. "Women, Culture, and Health in Rural Afghanistan." *Expedition* 44 (3): 34–39.

Hirschkind, C., and S. Mahmood. 2002. "Feminism, the Taliban, and Politics of Counter-Insurgency." *Anthropological Quarterly* 75 (2): 339–354.

Kaldor, K. 1989. "Assisting Skilled Women." *Afghan Studies Journal* 1 (2): 21–34.

Kurian, G. T., ed. 1988. "Afghanistan." In *World Education Encyclopedia,* 3rd ed. New York: Facts on File Publications.

Mehran, G. 1999. "Lifelong Learning: New Opportunities for Women in a Muslim Country (Iran)." *Comparative Education* 35 (2): 201–215.

Rasekh, Z., H. M. Bauer, M. M. Manos, and V. Iacopino. 1998. "Women's Health and Human Rights in Afghanistan." *Journal of the American Medical Association* 280 (5): 449–455.

Schultz, C. M. 1994. "Promoting Economic Self-Reliance: A Case Study of Afghan Refugee Women in Pakistan." *Journal of International Affairs* 47 (2): 557–601.

UNESCO (United Nations Educational, Scientific, and Cultural Organization). 2000. World Education Report 2000: *The Right to Education for All Throughout Life.* New York: UNESCO Publishing. http://www.unesco.org/education/information/wer/.

United Nations Development Programme. 2001. "Focus on Afghanistan: UNDP's Human Development Report Office Presents New Analysis of Socio-Economic Indicators for Afghanistan." Press release, October 8. http://www.undp.org/dpa/pressrelease/releases/2001/october/8oct01.html

Wali, S. 1994. "Repatriation and the Reconstruction of Afghanistan: The Role of Women." *Migration World Magazine* 22 (4): 26–28.

———. 2002. "Afghan Women: Recovering, Rebuilding." *Ethics and International Affairs* 16 (2): 15–20.

Wali, S., E. Gould, and P. Fitzgerald. 1999. "The Impact of Political Conflict on Women: The Case of Afghanistan." *American Journal of Public Health* 89 (10): 1474–1476.

World Education Forum. 2000. *The EFA 2000 Assessment: Country Reports, Afghanistan.* New York: United Nations Educational, Scientific, and Cultural Organization.

CHAPTER 12

The Effects of a Reduction in User Fees on School Enrollment: Evidence from Colombia

Felipe Barrera-Osorio[1]

In several countries, free basic education means that tuition, the fee paid in exchange for education, is zero. Families are nonetheless required to pay for such things as periodic certificates, uniforms, field trips, special materials, infrastructure support, and textbooks, among other things. In a 2005 World Bank survey, 83 percent of the 93 countries studied charged some sort of user fees in public institutions. In some cases, these payments are an important proportion of the consumption of the household (Bentaquet-Kattan 2006; Oxfam 2001).

It is estimated that, since 1994, 15 countries around the globe have eliminated user fees in basic education at the national level (Bentaquet-Kattan 2006). The main objective of programs that abolish education user fees is to increase enrollment by reducing the direct cost of education. Sadly, the direct and rigorous evidence on the effects of user fees on education outcomes is scarce. This chapter presents a succinct review of the effect of user fees on enrollment, and it will present a brief discussion of the potential gender effects of the elimination of user fees programs.

The next section discusses the arguments for instituting or abolishing user fees. Then it presents a short review of the available evidence from programs that reduce or eliminate user fees, with a brief discussion on the potential gender effects. The chapter concludes with a discussion of gender targeting.

The Effect of User Fees on Enrollment

The cost of education can be split into direct costs, such as tuition and materials, and the opportunity cost, which consists mainly of the inferred income from the labor market that is forgone during the time spent in school.

Arguments Against User Fees

Clearly, user fees are a direct cost of education, and families may be deterred from sending minors to school when they cannot afford to pay the price (Al-Samarrai and Zaman 2000; MacJessie-Mbewe 2002; Oxfam 2001, 2002). Moreover, for low-income households the opportunity cost of sending a minor to school is presumably high, because the extra income that they could get from minors working represents an important proportion of total income.

The opportunity cost of education, and therefore the total cost of education, can vary with age and gender. Older individuals are in general more productive than children, and their higher wages reflect this fact. The individual's typical activity (inside or outside of the household) can determine the gender difference in the opportunity cost. For instance, if boys have a higher demand in the labor market, and girls in household activities, then the opportunity cost for each group is different if the implicit price of the two activities is different. Any policy that reduces the cost of education will therefore have different effects across gender and age.

Arguments in Favor of User Fees

The first argument in favor of user fees is that they can increase efficiency in the provision of education. Schools may charge fees to families on a sliding scale based on income: families that can afford to pay higher fees are charged accordingly, and low-income families are charged less. The second argument is that user fees in education are important for financial sustainability of education systems. The fees are direct resources for the schools to finance everyday tasks, and programs that eliminate user fees, without compensating policies, can induce financial problems. Moreover, user fees may increase enrollment if otherwise unfunded schools can charge fees and become operational (Hillman and Jenkner 2002; Jimenez 1990; Thobani 1984).

Evaluating the Evidence

Whether or not charging user fees increases enrollment is an empirical question. Two strands of the empirical evidence on the effect of user fees on enrollment can be found. One measures the potential effect of reducing user fees through estimating price elasticity of education. The second strand attempts to measure the direct effect of eliminating user fees in countries that have implemented user fees programs.

Education is a good that responds to changes in price, and user fees are part of this price. The articles of Birdall and Orivet (1996), Gertler and Glewwe (1990), Jimenez (1990), Mingat and Tan (1986), and Reddy and Vandemoortele (1996) estimate educational demand functions. The models vary in the structural form and the data used. Nonetheless, all of the studies find that education is responsive to changes in prices. The range of the elasticity estimates fluctuates from –0.03 (in Malawi) to –0.98 (in Mali). Therefore, these articles indirectly show that elimination (and reduction) of user fees can yield an increment in the enrollment rate.

Several countries have been implementing programs to abolish user fees. The second strand of literature makes use of these quasi-experiments to assess the effectiveness of the policy on increasing enrollment. These articles usually compare enrollment before and after the elimination of user fees. For instance, when Malawi eliminated fees in 1994, the net enrollment rate increased from 68.3 percent in 1993 to 99 percent in 1994, and the gross enrollment rate increased from 89 percent to 133 percent. Likewise, Kenya eliminated fees in 2003, and the net enrollment rate rose from 63.5 percent in 2002 to 76.7 percent in 2003; the gross enrollment rose from 86 percent in 2002 to 104 percent in 2003 (Oxfam 2001, 2002; see Bentaquet-Kattan 2006 for a general overview). These large changes in enrollments may be detrimental to the whole system if there are no accompanying policies that help schools compensate for the reduction in resources. For instance, the student-to-teacher ratio in Malawi after the elimination of user fees reached 100:1, the repetition rate was between 16 and 28 percent, and the primary dropout rate was between 5 and 10 percent.

The evidence based on "before the policy" and "after the policy" is not very effective in identifying what would have happened in the absence of the policy, measuring the actual size of the impact, or isolating the effects of the policy from other concurrent changes in the economy and the education system. A recent article evaluates the *Gratuidad* (gratuity) program in Bogota, Colombia (Barrera-Osorio, Linden, and Urquiola 2007). In contrast to a before-and-after estimation, this article uses a regression discontinuity approach, relying on the targeting in the program. The *Gratuidad* program targets low-income individuals using a means-test instrument (Sisben) that ranks households by their socioeconomic characteristics on a continuous scale from 1 to 100, and then classifies families into six groups. The lower the score and the group, the more disadvantaged is the family. Under the *Gratuidad* program, user fees are eliminated for basic education (grades 1–9) for children from Sisben 1 households, while others receive no reduction in user fees. For high school (grades 10–11), Sisben 1 children benefit from the elimination of services fees, while Sisben 2 households receive roughly a 50 percent reduction. Households in Sisben levels 3 and higher receive no benefit.

Barrera-Osorio et al. (2007) present evidence that the *Gratuidad* program induces an increment in enrollment similar to the effects found in conditional cash transfer programs, such as Progresa in Mexico (Schultz 2004). These enrollment increases range from three percentage points for basic education to six percentage points for grades 10 and 11. Under conditional cash transfer programs, the money goes directly to the family instead of going to the school, as it does in programs to eliminate user fees. Both types of programs are more effective at the secondary level than at the primary level, presumably because the baseline level of enrollment is higher for primary: the marginal individual is more difficult to reach if the enrollment is higher. The article also presents evidence of the program's effects for different subpopulations, including differential effects by students' gender. The results regarding gender are asymmetrical, depending on the level of education. On the one hand, the results show that the policy is more effective for boys at the basic level, with an increment of 4.3 percentage points in enrollment versus a statistically nonsignificant estimate for girls. On the other hand, the policy is more effective for girls at the high school level, with an increment of 7.6 percentage points versus a statistically nonsignificant estimate for boys (due to a high standard error).

Deininger (2003) also quantifies the effects across gender of a program that eliminated the cost of primary education in Uganda in 1997. He finds that the policy—which was accompanied by other changes, including a complete restructuring of public spending in the sector—had an important effect in equalization of enrollment rates between females and males after three years of implementation.

Some Ideas on Targeting

Primary education is reaching very high enrollment rates around the word. The net enrollment ratio in primary education in developing countries in 1991 was 79 percent, and it increased to 86 percent in 2004. The remaining 14 percent of children who are not attending schools are the most difficult ones to reach for two main reasons. First, the children are from low-income families in which parents or heads face higher opportunity costs for enrolling; and second, these minors come from families in which the parents or heads have very low human capital accumulation, in terms of both education and health. Moreover, there are still major disparities in enrollment across gender, tempting policy makers to target programs based on gender. Indeed, on average for developing countries, the proportion of young people who are school age but out of school at basic education is higher for females (22 percent) than for males (18 percent) (United Nations 2006).

However, the programs of Bogota and Uganda give another perspective to the problem. These two programs do not target based on gender, despite the fact that the Bogota program targets based on income. Estimates from both programs show, first, that the programs did have a differential effect on females and males, reducing the gender education gap. Second, the program in Bogota shows that there can be differential effects across gender *by level of education.* An education program can have a general target based on income, and the families will respond to the program in different ways depending on the incentives that they face. Part of each family's decision may be based on the gender of the child, especially if the opportunity costs are different for boys and girls. In this way, programs that do not use gender as a targeting mechanism can have results that are not gender neutral.

Nonetheless, the case of Bogota shows that income targeting is a first-best solution to reconcile the two strands of the debate about eliminating or imposing user fees. First, if income targeting is feasible, it is possible that families capable of paying for the services do so, and schools may thus receive some important direct resources for their daily operation. Second, income targeting gives a clear mix between sustainability and free access to the families who would not be able to afford sending their children to school otherwise. Clearly, income-targeting instruments, like means-test instruments, should have an important place in the discussion of abolishing user fees.

Elimination of user fees is one method, among others, to reduce the cost of education. Other programs, such as conditional cash transfers or transportation programs, also reduce the direct costs of education. These programs change the implicit price of attending schools, with different implications for family choices and program operations. Conditional cash transfer programs have recently been rigorously evaluated using randomized approaches (for instance, see Attanasio, Fitzsimmons, and Gomez 2005; Barrera-Osorio et al. 2007; Behrman, Sengupta, and Todd 2005; Schady and Araujo 2006; Schultz 2004). Still, we do not know the comparative cost effectiveness of conditional cash transfer programs versus user-fee programs. Moreover, some programs are complements, rather than substitutes. For instance, nutrition and free meal programs at schools may complement programs that directly reduce the cost of education. Despite important advances in the evaluation of independent programs, we are still in the beginning stages in evaluating a basket of programs to determine the contribution each makes and the complementarities among them.

Note

1. This chapter was prepared for the World Bank's Global Symposium "Education: A Critical Path to Gender Equality and Empowerment," October 2–3, 2007, Washington, DC. Harry Patrinos and Katja Vinha provided very useful comments. The author is indebted to Tazeen Fasih for discussions and ideas regarding targeting. All the views expressed are those of the author and should not be attributed to the World Bank.

References

Al-Samarrai, S., and H. Zaman. 2000. *Abolishing School Fees in Malawi: The Impact of Education Access and Equity.* MPRE Paper No.130, University Library of Munich, Germany. Revised 2006.

Attanasio, Orazio, Emla Fitzsimmons, and Ana Gomez. 2005. *The Impact of a Conditional Education Subsidy on School Enrollment in Colombia.* Report Summary Familias No. 01. London: The Institute of Fiscal Studies.

Barrera-Osorio, F., M. Bertrand, L. Linden, and F. Perez. 2007. "Conditional Cash Transfers in Education: Design Features, Peer and Sibling Effects: Evidence from a Randomized Experiment in Colombia." NBER Working Papers Series No. 13890, National Bureau of Economic Research, Cambridge, MA.

Barrera-Osorio, F., L. Linden, and M. Urquiola. 2007. "The Effects of User Fee Reductions on Enrollment: Evidence from a Quasi-Experiment." http://columbia.edu/~msu2101/BarreraLindenUrquiola(2007).pdf.

Bentaquet-Kattan, R. 2006. "Implementation of Free Basic Education Policy." Education Working Paper Series No. 7, World Bank, Washington, DC.

Behrman, Jere R., Pilali Sengupta, and Petra Todd. 2005. "Progressing Through PROGRESA: An Impact Assessment of a School Subsidy Experiment in Mexico." *Economic Development and Cultural Change.* 54 (1): 237–275.

Birdsall, N., and F. Orivet. 1996. "Demand for Primary Schooling in Rural Mali: Should User Fees Be Increased?" *Education Economics* 4 (3): 279–296.

Deininger, K. 2003. "Does Cost of Schooling Affect Enrollment by the Poor? Universal Primary Education in Uganda." *Economics of Education Review* 22: 291–302.

Gertler, P., and P. Glewwe. 1990. "The Willingness to Pay for Education in Developing Countries: Evidence from Rural Peru." *Journal of Public Economics* 42: 251–275.

Hillman, A. L., and E. Jenkner. 2002. "User Payments for Basic Education in Low-Income Countries." IMF Working Paper No.02-182, International Monetary Fund, Washington, DC.

Jimenez, E. 1990. "Social Sector Pricing Policy Revisited: A Survey of Some Recent Controversies." *Proceedings of the World Bank Annual Conference on Development Economics 1989.* Washington, DC: World Bank.

MacJessie-Mbewe, S. 2002. "An Analysis of Free Primary Education Reform Policy in Malawi." *International Journal of Educational Reform* 11 (2): 94–105.

Mingat, A., and J. Tan. 1986. "Expanding Education through User Charges: What Can Be Achieved in Malawi and Other LDCs?" *Economics of Education Review* 5 (3): 273–286.

Oxfam. 2001. *Education Charges: A Tax on Human Development.* Oxfam Briefing Paper No.3. Oxford, U.K.: Oxfam.

Oxfam. 2002. *Every Child in School: A Challenge to Finance and Development Ministers.* Oxfam Briefing Paper No.20. Oxford, U.K.: Oxfam.

Reddy, S., and J. Vandemoortele. 1996. "User Financing of Basic Social Services." UNICEF Staff Working Papers, Evaluation, Policy and Planning Series, UNICEF, New York.

Schady, Norbert, and Maria Caridad Araujo. 2006. "Cash Transfers, Conditions, School Enrollment, and Child Work: Evidence from a Randomized Experiment in Ecuador." World Bank Policy Research Working Paper No. 3930, World Bank, Washington, DC.

Schultz, T. Paul. 2004. "School Subsidies for the Poor: Evaluating the Mexican Progresa Poverty Program." *Journal of Development Economics* 74 (1): 199–250.

Thobani, M. 1984. "Charging User Fees for Social Services: Education in Malawi." *Comparative Education Review* 28 (3): 402–423.

United Nations. 2006. *The Millennium Development Goals Report, 2006.* New York: United Nations.

CHAPTER 13

Holy Alliances: Public Subsidies, Islamic High Schools, and Female Schooling in Bangladesh

Mohammad Niaz Asadullah and Nazmul Chaudhury

Madrassas (Islamic faith schools) are the fastest growing education sector in Bangladesh, which hosts more religious seminaries than any other country in South Asia. The quality of the schools, however, has been questioned: it is alleged that they are churning out thousands of students not worthy of employment outside the religious sector and hard-pressed to function in a market economy. Driven by such concerns, the government of Bangladesh has endeavored to "reform" or "modernize" madrassa education systems. A reform scheme was implemented by the government in the early 1980s. To induce modernization, cash incentives were offered to madrassas as long as they registered and introduced additional classes on subjects such as science, math, and English.

The response of these religious schools to market incentives is unknown. Critiques of market-based reforms point out that religious schools are nonmarket entities that shun formal sources of finance and rely on charity for sustenance. Hence, any conditional subsidy reform initiative is destined to fail. More important, these schools have for many centuries almost exclusively educated boys, so that the opportunity cost to publicly finance madrassa education is significant—funds could be diverted instead to secular private schools, either coeducational or for girls only, to promote female education and close existing gender gaps in enrollment.

Following introduction of the curriculum reform scheme, Bangladesh saw the emergence of a large number of modern, registered madrassas that embraced female students. It is alleged that these are all new madrassas that have been set up to exploit the availability of public funds under the curriculum modernization and female stipend schemes. We do not know to what extent the reform succeeded in converting preexisting orthodox madrassas into modern religious schools. Likewise, the role played by preexisting orthodox madrassas in promoting female education remains unknown.

In this chapter, we draw upon data from a recent census of secondary educational institutes in Bangladesh and describe the profile of madrassas that have chosen to modernize in response to monetary incentives. We show that, indeed, the conversion of previously orthodox madrassas to reformed madrassas was a significant phenomenon. We further highlight the hitherto unnoticed "feminization" of the madrassa sector, which has ensued following introduction of another incentive scheme in the 1990s, namely, the Female Secondary School Stipend Program. Using simple regression analysis, it is shown that as a consequence of the feminization process, Bangladeshi regions that had a greater stock of madrassas experienced higher rates of growth in female enrollment following introduction of the stipend scheme. Regions that saw new madrassas being set up after 1999 also experienced an increase in growth. This was also true for regions that had a larger endowment of "converted" madrassas. We therefore conclude by arguing that with adequate incentives, religious educational institutions can play an important role in achieving development targets, such as removing education gender gaps in Muslim-majority countries.

Madrassa Reform in South Asia

The schooling system in Pakistan, India, and Bangladesh runs in two parallel streams: the private and public secular schools and the religious seminaries. Students can choose mainstream formal education, or they can choose to study at madrassas, which offer Islamic religious education at primary, secondary, and higher levels. Anecdotal evidence suggests that the majority of madrassas are run on the Deobandi line.[1] Historically, these madrassas have relied on their own assets and charities to finance day-to-day activities. This is because financial autonomy features in five of the eight fundamental principles laid down by Maulana Muhammad Qasim at the founding of Deoband in 1867 (Ladbury 2004):

> As long as the madrassah has no fixed source of income, it will, God willing, operate as desired. And if it gain any fixed source of income, like jagir holdings, factories, trading interests or pledges from nobles, then the madrassah will lose the fear and the hope which inspire submission to God and will lose His hidden help. Disputes will begin among the workers. In matters of income and buildings ... let there be a sort of deprivation. (quoted in Metcalf 1978, 113)

Madrassas in the subcontinent, therefore, are alleged to rely exclusively on external finance and private donations made for religious purposes. A majority of these madrassas also house and educate orphans and children from poor families. But it is not known exactly how they differ in their interpretations of religious doctrine. No single curriculum applies to these madrassas, so that some divisions prevail in course contents. These madrassas focus on reciting the Koran and learning the duties of the Maulvi to prepare students for running the mosques' day-to-day operations. In Bangladesh, these madrassas are known as Qoumi madrassas.

The overwhelming majority of secondary schools in Bangladesh are government-aided private schools. All registered and recognized secondary schools, both secular and religious institutions, are eligible for government subsidies. In the early 1980s the government introduced programs to modernize the madrassa education system through curriculum reform. The most important motivation for madrassa reform has been the primacy of life skills acquisition. In the period before modernization, students in all (Qoumi) madrassas in the country were taught Urdu (instead of Bengali), Persian, and Arabic, as madrassa curricula continued to follow the Deoband style. Their registered counterparts, albeit few in numbers, followed a state-approved curriculum.[2]

Consequently, for students graduating in or before 1980, the mosques and the madrassas were their main sources of formal employment. The "religious sector" of the economy continued to remain the primary destination of madrassa graduates after 1980 as well.[3] This has arguably changed in postmodernization years. The modernization scheme of 1980 introduced secular subjects, such as English, Bengali, science, and math, alongside religion-related subjects and languages.[4] Madrassas that accepted this change in the curriculum received government recognition and subsequently qualified for public subsidies to finance the salaries of all teachers, similar to secular schools.[5] These religious seminaries, which are registered with a government board, are known as Aliyah madrassas (Sattar 2004).

In the Aliyah system, primary education is provided by Ebtedayee madrassas, secondary education by Dakhil institutions, and higher secondary by Alim-level institutions (two years of study). There are also a two-year Fazil-level (degree) education and a two-year Kamil-level (master's) education. The government madrassa board is responsible for the design of a national curriculum for all recognized madrassas in the country. The board also conducts public examinations at the end of Dakhil, Fazil, and Kamil levels. Qoumi madrassas are also characterized by a hierarchy similar to the Aliyah madrassa system (such as hafizia, qiratia, quaumi, and nizamia, all under the kharizia system).

A reform scheme similar to that in Bangladesh was attempted in India in 1986, when the Indian government proposed to introduce science, math, English, Hindi, and similar subjects in the madrassa curriculum. Modernized madrassas were eligible to apply for government financial aid. The government also promised to arrange for recognition of certain madrassas by certain state-funded universities.[6] However, the success of this initiative has, so far, been limited. The nature of the incentive is insignificant. Only one teacher is provided and financed by the government to teach modern subjects (Khan, Saqib, and Anjum 2003). Additionally, wary of the state's interventions in religious instruction and their academic and administrative freedom, most of India's 30,000 madrassas[7] have refused to participate in the scheme (Fahimuddin 2004). Moreover, the financial incentive to modernize remains weak. The Indian state only promises to provide financial assistance to madrassas to teach secular subjects, whereas in Bangladesh all teachers of a recognized madrassa qualify for salary payments from the state exchequer. Consequently, most madrassas in India today are traditional and independent of the state for funds.[8]

A more successful and comparable modernization reform experience is that of Indonesia.[9] The share of the madrassa sector, in terms of total number of schools and students enrolled, is large in Indonesia and

Bangladesh. In both countries, the majority of madrassas are privately run. The Indonesian government in 2003 recognized and brought madrassas and other traditional Islamic educational institutions into the mainstream of national education.[10] The madrassas are recognized on a par with "secular" public schools, in the sense that they now follow the national curricula issued in 1995 by the Ministry of Education. Nonetheless, the Indonesian reform experience has been less successful than that of Bangladesh. Indonesian government agencies have not been able to exercise full control of madrassas; the legal framework to enforce national curricula remains weak. Unlike Bangladeshi-recognized madrassas, those in Indonesia do not receive large-scale financial support from the government, so incentives are lacking to adhere to state-mandated curricula. As a consequence, teacher pay and educational quality in private Indonesian madrassas remain low (Azra 2004).[11]

The Madrassa Reform Scheme in Bangladesh

According to government census records for 2003, there are 8,406 registered madrassa institutions at the post-Ebtedayee (primary) level and 17,389 registered madrassa secondary schools, constituting approximately 26 percent of all postprimary education and 32.5 percent of all secondary educational institutions in Bangladesh (see table 13.1). Madrassa enrollment accounts for 15 percent of total postprimary enrollment (1.5 million students out of a total of 10.6 million).[12] The majority of these are, however, Dakhil madrassas (see table 13A.1 in the annex). Most madrassa education takes place in rural locations, and rural learners

Table 13.1   Profile of Recognized Postprimary Madrassas in Bangladesh, 2003

	Percent of madrassas	Percent of female-only madrassas	Percent of female teachers	Percent of female students
Dakhil	71	14	7	52
Alim	14	7	6	44
Fazil	12	2	5	35
Kamil	1	2	4	20
Total	100	11	7	47

Source: BANBEIS, Ministry of Education, Government of Bangladesh.

account for 92.5 percent of madrassa enrollment, compared with around 86.5 percent in mainstream education (see table 13.2).

Clearly, the religious education sector in Bangladesh embraces a large number of educational institutions and students. Today, 30 percent of all secondary-level students are enrolled in (recognized) madrassas. Public aid constitutes 90 percent of teacher salaries in registered privately aided schools and Aliyah madrassas in Bangladesh. More recently, the government has further raised the incentive for Aliyah madrassas in two ways. First, graduates of recognized madrassas are eligible to seek admission in secular universities, as well as employment in public offices. Second, since 1994, female students enrolled in secondary-level Aliyah madrassas are eligible for stipends under the female stipend program. Two features of Aliyah madrassas stand out from tables 13.1 and 13.2. First, almost half of the students enrolled are girls. Second, 6 percent of the teachers are female. Most important, these proportions are roughly the same for both rural and urban areas. These statistics point out the hitherto overlooked role played by these madrassas in spreading female education in the country.

The Bangladeshi reform program gives rise to three basic questions. First, to what extent did the scheme reduce the number of existing orthodox religious schools? Second, do modernized madrassas embrace further reforms, particularly concerning acceptance of female students and teachers? Third, how have modernized madrassas affected the growth of female enrollment overall? We consider these issues below.

Table 13.2   Profile of Recognized Secondary Schools and Postprimary Madrassas in Bangladesh, by Location, 2003

	Madrassas			Schools		
	Distribution of madrassas (percent)	Percent of female teachers	Percent of female students	Distribution of schools (percent)	Percent of female teachers	Percent of female students
Rural	92.49	6	47	86.5	15.0	53.6
Urban	7.51	11	39	13.5	35.4	51.4
Metropolitan cities	1.44	11	28	3.8	42.9	49.1
Dhaka city	0.75	11	29	1.9	44.4	48.3
All areas	100.00	6	46	100.0	19.2	53.2

Source: BANBEIS, Ministry of Education, Government of Bangladesh.

Did Orthodox Madrassas Modernize?

Are the 8,407 Aliyah madrassas in Bangladesh largely new madrassas that have emerged to take advantage of generous government grants, or do they also represent "converts" from old madrassas that previously imparted orthodox and exclusively religious education? One would not normally expect massive conversions of orthodox madrassas following the reforms. Financial autonomy is a fundamental principle of Deoband madrassas (Ladbury 2004). Indeed, the popular perception has been that the so-called modernized madrassas are altogether new religious schools that have mushroomed under government subsidies (Byron and Mahmud 2005). Nonetheless, the nature of the incentive to modernize offered by the government was substantial. Given that teacher pay accounts for most of the recurrent budget of schools in rural Bangladesh, the incentive to convert is significant: recognized madrassas receive regular financial aid from the government on a monthly basis essentially to cover their wage bills.

In the absence of prereform data on all madrassas in the country, it is not known what fraction of the orthodox madrassas actually embraced reform. A lower bound on the number of converts can be obtained by working out the total number of Aliyah madrassas that were established before1980 and operated as orthodox madrassas in the prereform period. This can be ascertained by using data from the year in which a madrassa was established. Such data are available from census records on all registered secondary schools and madrassas in the country.

Figure 13.1 plots the number of Aliyah madrassas and schools by year for 1947–2003. More than half (52 percent, N = 4,393) of all Aliyah madrassas in the country were established in or before 1980 when the reform was introduced.[13] Thus, all these Aliyah madrassas are converts. These converted madrassas accounted for 31.5 percent of all secondary educational institutions in the country in 1980. However, the impact of the reform, measured by the ratio of converts to nonconverts, is unknown, because no reliable historical estimate of the total number of orthodox madrassas is available. Then, assuming that the number of Qoumi madrassas in the country did not exceed the number of secondary schools in 1980, this would also imply that 45 percent of all Qoumi madrassas opted to modernize following the reform scheme.[14]

The significance of the reform is also evident if we jointly analyze data on year of establishment and year in which government recognition was received.[15] Table 13.3 provides cross-tabulation of these two variables in three periods: the pre-1980 reform era, the post-1993 female stipend

Figure 13.1   Growth of Secular Schools and Modern Madrassas, 1947–2003

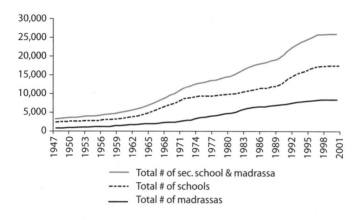

Source: Author's calculation, based on 2003 census of secondary schools, Ministry of Education.

scheme era, and the period in between (1980–1992). It is reassuring to see that 97 percent of the Aliyah madrassas that were set up before the modernization reform indeed received government recognition (following adoption of a modern curriculum) in or after 1980.[16] Another insight obtained from Table 13.3 is that a large number of preexisting madrassas (which are likely to have followed Qoumi curricula) have opted for government recognition after the female stipend scheme was introduced in 1992. As a matter of fact, 75 percent of all Aliyah madrassas that received government recognition during this period were preexisting madrassas. This period also saw conversion of 444 madrassas that were established even before introduction of the modernization scheme. Therefore, the combined effect of the 1980s modernization scheme and 1990s female stipend program suggests that 73 percent of all Aliyah madrassas today are potentially formerly Qoumi madrassas that have opted to modernize in response to economic incentives.

Did Modernized Madrassas Embrace Further Reforms?

As pointed out earlier, a hallmark of Aliyah madrassas in Bangladesh is their acceptance of female students and teachers. At the beginning of the reform program in 1980, 1 percent of madrassa teachers were female.

Table 13.3   Distribution of Aliyah Madrassas by Year of Establishment and Recognition

Year of establishment	Pre-1980	Between 1980 and 1992	Between 1993 and 2003	Total
		Year of recognition		
Pre-1980	120	3,384	444	3,948
	(3.04)	(85.71)	(11.25)	(100)
	[100]	[73.9]	[17.51]	[54.57]
Between 1980 and 1992		1,195	1,477	2,672
		(44.72)	(55.28)	(100)
		[26.1]	[58.24]	[36.93]
Between 1993 and 2003			615	615
			(100)	(100)
			[24.25]	[8.5]
Total	120	4,579	2,536	7,235
	(1.66)	(63.29)	(35.05)	(100)
	[100]	[100]	[100]	[100]

Source: Author's calculation based on census records.

Note: Row percentages in parentheses; column percentages in brackets.

Today, that share stands at 6.9 percent. We argue that the greater openness of Aliyah madrassas applies equally to madrassas established before and after the 1980 reform and is driven by incentives.

The first proposition is easily verified if we compare the sex ratio and gender orientation of converted (pre-1980 reform) and new (post-1980 reform) madrassas. In prereform years, Aliyah madrassas educated mostly boys. Therefore, we would expect this to be true even today if these converted religious seminaries continue to shun female education. Figure 13.2 plots data on gender orientation of Aliyah madrassas established before and after the 1980 reform. As a comparison group, data on schools are also plotted. Clearly, the majority of converted madrassas are coeducational. This is also supported by the fact that only 5.39 percent of the prereform madrassas are single-sex schools (of which only 2.4 percent are boys only), compared with 21.2 percent of postreform madrassas (of which only 0.65 percent are boys only).

Enrollment statistics also confirm that the overwhelming majority of Aliyah madrassas in Bangladesh today admit and educate girls. Per 100 boys, there are 96 girls enrolled in Aliyah madrassas in the country. Once

Figure 13.2   Gender Orientation of Aliyah Madrassas Established before and after 1980 Reforms, 2003

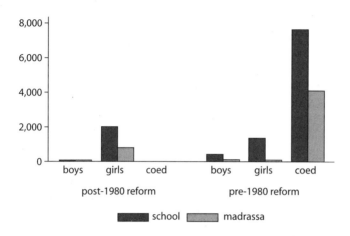

Source: Author's calculation, based on data from BANBEIS, Ministry of Education.

again, converted madrassas, which historically educated boys, today have 85 girls enrolled for every 100 boys (see table 13.4). Altogether, these findings suggest the possibility that converted madrassas have embraced further reform by altering their admission policy and educating girls alongside boys.

Our second proposition is that the change in sex composition of teachers and students in the Aliyah madrassas is rather a recent phenomenon and largely a consequence of cash incentive programs. At the time of the reform in 1980, only 4.9 percent of madrassa students were female. Today, that share stands at 47 percent (see table 13.5).[17] It could be

Table 13.4   Ratio of Girls to Boys in Secondary Schools and Madrassas, 2003

Period	Schools	Madrassas
Prereform	0.90	0.85
Postreform	1.01	1.10
Average	0.94	0.96

Source: Author's calculation based on census records.

Table 13.5   Gender Composition of Students and Teachers in Postprimary Schools and Madrassas in Bangladesh, 1970–2003

	Percent of female teachers		Percent of female students	
Year	Madrassas	Schools	Madrassas	Schools
1970	–	7.2	4.3	18.4
1975	0.1	8.6	4.6	25.0
1980	0.1	10.1	4.9	26.1
1985	0.1	10.1	7.8	32.6
1990	0.8	9.7	7.7	33.9
1995	1.7	13.9	30.1	47.0
2000	3.5	15.1	39.4	52.6
2003	6.5	19.2	46.8	53.2

Source: BANBEIS, Ministry of Education.

Note: Postprimary madrassas range from Dakhil to Kamil.

argued that this merely captures the effect of overall economic development. Over time, there has been a gradual increase in female school participation, which has equally affected secular and religious schools. However, it is clear that over 1980–90 the share of female students in all madrassas had increased by only 3 percentage points. In contrast, over 1990–2003 that share increased by 33 percentage points, implying that female enrollment in madrassas grew by 209 percent (see table 13.6).

The supply-side explanation for the rise of recognized madrassas in the country, namely, the apathy of government policy for educational development, is untenable for an additional reason. Aliyah madrassas, like privately aided schools, charge fees. As seen in table 13.2, a majority of them, even in the rural areas, educate girls who are waived of all tuition payments and additionally qualify for a regular stipend from the government. While gross enrollment (the ratio of total enrollment in grades 6–10 to total secondary school-age population) in secondary Aliya madrassas increased from 7.54 percent to 9.26 percent between 1999 and 2003, this has been largely to the result of the greater enrollment of female students, which rose from 6.63 percent to 9.7 percent during the same period.[18]

Modernized Madrassas and the Growth in Female Enrollment
Our analysis so far has relied on purely descriptive bivariate treatment of administrative data. However, additional insights can be gleaned by analyzing determinants of enrollment growth across regions of Bangladesh in a simple cross-section regression framework. While madrassa-level panel

data on enrollment rates is unavailable for Bangladesh, the existing census (cross-sectional) data set on schools and madrassas contains annual enrollment figures spanning 1999–2003. As mentioned earlier, we have access to this data set, which has been collected by the Ministry of Education. The data set includes information on all secondary educational institutions (25,795 in total) in the 64 districts of Bangladesh for 2003.[19] The data set contains retrospective information on enrollment by gender and grade for 1999–2003. Therefore, it is possible to study growth in enrollment and relate it to changes in the supply of schools.

Given the availability of data on the annual growth rate in enrollment, we want to test whether the presence of madrassas in a region (union) bolsters enrollment of female students.[20] To this end, we follow the empirical income growth literature and specify a regression model of female enrollment growth. To capture the convergence effect, we allow growth during 1999–2003 to depend on enrollment at the beginning of the period. As we also want to know school-type effects, our growth equation includes the level of school availability by type in 1999 and changes therein by 2003. This yields the following reduced-form model of enrollment growth at the region (union) level:

$$G_{ti} = b_0 + b_1 E_{t-4} + b_2 X_2 + b_3 X_{t-4,i} + b_4 \Delta X_{ti} + b_5 W_{ti} + v_t + u_{ti} \qquad (1)$$

where

G_{ti} = Regional growth rate of female enrollment during 1999–2003
E_{t-4} = Regional enrollment in 1999
X_2 = Mean characteristics of educational institutions of the region in 1999
ΔX_{ti} = Change in number of schools and madrassas between 1999 and 2003
W_{ti} = Other attributes of the union (whether an urban region, average age of school/madrassa in the region, presence of a government school in the region)
v_t = Subdistricts (upazilas) fixed-effects
u_{ti} = iid random error
t = Time index
i = Union index

A common problem in equation (1) is that of endogeneity of the number of madrassas admitting females. The presence or emergence of coeducational or girls-only madrassas could be driven by cultural factors: regions where there are fewer cultural restrictions on female mobility are more likely to see the emergence or presence of "liberal" religious schools that also encourage the education of girls. We address the concern over the effect of identification of religious schools by using regional fixed effects. This requires sufficient regional variation in norms and/or a data set with a large number of regions. In 2003, there were 486 subdistricts (upazilas) in Bangladesh, and our data set contains all secondary schools in the country. Within the context of Bangladesh, socioeconomic differences are usually across regions and districts—therefore, we can study growth in enrollment at the union level, controlling for unobservables in a fixed-effect framework.

For our purpose, we create a data set aggregated at the union level. Table 13A.1 in the annex provides a summary of key variables. The period 1999–2003 has seen exceptional growth in total female enrollment in secondary schools. At the union level, the average growth rate is 21 percent. But looking at enrollment in grade 10, this figure is as high as 31 percent.[21]

Table 13.6 reports regression estimates of enrollment growth models using three different dependent variables: regional growth rate in total female enrollment, regional growth rate in female enrollment in grade 6, and regional growth rate in female enrollment in grade 10. For each dependent variable, three regression specifications are used. Specification (1) controls for district fixed effects. Specification (2) controls for subdistrict (upazila)-level fixed effects. Specification (3) replaces the variables—total number of schools in 1999 and total number of madrassas in 1999—by gender-disaggregated versions (coeducation, boys only, girls only).

Four observations emerge from the data in table 13.6. First, regions with higher initial female enrollment in 1999 experienced slower growth than regions where female enrollment was initially lower. Second, between 1999 and 2003, regions with more schools had higher growth rates of female enrollment. But more important, regions with more madrassas experienced higher growth, although the rate was less than that owing to the presence of schools. Third, an increase in the number of madrassas in the region during 2000–03 had a positive and significant effect. Fourth, increase in the mean age of madrassas in the region positively affected female enrollment. We conjecture that older madrassas, which previously

Table 13.6   Determinants of Regional Enrollment Growth, 1999–2003

Determinant	Dependent variable: regional growth rate of total female enrollment in grades 6–10			Dependent variable: regional growth rate of female enrollment in grade 6			Dependent variable: regional growth rate of female enrollment in grade 10		
	(1)	*(2)*	*(3)*	*(1)*	*(2)*	*(3)*	*(1)*	*(2)*	*(3)*
Total female enrollment in 1999 in the region, grades 6–10 (in logs)	− 0.274 (39.57)**	− 0.292 (40.53)**	− 0.296 (40.70)**						
Female enrollment in 1999 in the region, grade 6 (in logs)			−0.336	− 0.354 (39.11)**	− 0.360 (39.25)**	(39.56)**			
Female enrollment in 1999 in the region, grade 10 (in logs)							− 0.370 (41.86)**	− 0.388 (42.12)**	− 0.390 (42.15)**
Number of madrassas in the region, 1999	0.018 (5.55)**	0.025 (7.19)**		0.026 (6.47)**	0.034 (7.63)**		0.037 (7.49)**	0.050 (9.23)**	
Number of schools in the region, 1999	0.054 (20.90)**	0.061 (22.36)**		0.062 (19.32)**	0.070 (20.62)**		0.076 (20.24)**	0.084 (20.93)**	
Change in number of madrassas (1999–2003)	0.057 (2.76)**	0.075 (3.52)**	0.074 (3.49)**	0.095 (3.73)**	0.110 (4.14)**	0.108 (4.09)**	0.025 (0.80)	0.051 (1.57)	0.050 (1.55)
Change in number of schools (1999–2003)	0.085 (7.09)**	0.093 (7.49)**	0.096 (7.69)**	0.133 (8.98)**	0.145 (9.26)**	0.148 (9.51)**	0.012 (0.66)	0.027 (1.43)	0.030 (1.58)
Mean age of schools	− 0.001 (4.39)**	− 0.001 (4.12)**	− 0.001 (3.38)**	− 0.000 (1.32)	− 0.000 (0.60)	− 0.000 (0.10)	− 0.000 (0.15)	0.000 (0.36)	0.000 (1.01)
Mean age of madrassas	0.002 (2.80)**	0.001 (2.32)*	0.002 (2.95)**	0.001 (1.63)	0.001 (1.39)	0.001 (1.84)+	0.004 (4.05)**	0.003 (3.12)**	0.003 (3.63)**
Number of coeducational madrassas in the region, 1999			0.022 (5.25)**			0.031 (5.96)**			0.047 (7.44)**

Number of girls-only madrassas in the region, 1999			0.045			0.053			0.066
			(5.61)**			(5.24)**			(5.31)**
Number of boys-only madrassas in the region, 1999			−0.015			−0.012			−0.019
			(0.68)			(0.43)			(0.56)
Number of coeducational schools in the region, 1999			0.062			0.068			0.085
			(20.32)**			(17.79)**			(18.79)**
Number of girls-only schools in the region, 1999			0.071			0.090			0.095
			(13.28)**			(13.61)**			(11.95)**
Number of boys-only schools in the region, 1999			0.019			0.026			0.015
			(1.69)+			(1.89)+			(0.87)
Govt (=1 if a government secondary school is present)	0.037	0.040	0.058	0.038	0.036	0.049	0.033	0.029	0.060
	(2.08)*	(2.28)*	(3.15)**	(1.72)+	(1.61)	(2.11)*	(1.25)	(1.05)	(2.08)*
Urban	−0.002	−0.016	−0.011	0.009	0.002	0.002	−0.023	−0.026	−0.013
	(0.13)	(1.05)	(0.71)	(0.58)	(0.13)	(0.08)	(1.17)	(1.11)	(0.53)
Constant	1.793	1.873	1.888	1.599	1.647	1.670	1.618	1.648	1.642
	(46.31)**	(46.67)**	(46.45)**	(41.70)**	(41.06)**	(41.14)**	(47.75)**	(46.77)**	(45.73)**
N	4,784	4,784	4,784	4,780	4,780	4,780	4,676	4,676	4,676
R-squared	0.29	0.32	0.32	0.27	0.29	0.29	0.31	0.33	0.33
Fixed-effects	District	Thana	Thana	District	Thana	Thana	District	Thana	Thana

Source: Authors' calculations based on data described in the text.

Note: Unit of analysis is region (union). Absolute value of t statistics in parentheses: + significant at 10 percent; * significant at 5 percent; ** significant at 1 percent. For each dependent variable, specification (1) controls for district fixed effects, specification (2) controls for subdistrict (upazila) level fixed effects, and specification (3) replaces the variables—total number of schools in 1999 and total number of madrassas in 1999—by gender-disaggregated versions (coeducation, boys only, girls only).

educated only boys and have now become coeducational, are driving this result. As a direct test of this hypothesis, we replace the age variable by "fraction of madrassas in the region that are converts (set up before the reform of 1980)" (see table 13A.2 in the annex). Indeed, the variable has a positive, significant impact on enrollment growth. This finding suggests that orthodox madrassas that chose to convert into modern religious schools went beyond curriculum reform by withdrawing restrictions on admission of female students.

It could be argued that our finding of the positive effect of the number of madrassas captures union-specific unobservables. Should this be the case, we would even observe a positive correlation between the presence of schools that do not admit girls and the growth of female enrollment. Disaggregating the stock variables (number of schools and madrassas) by type (coeducation, boys only, girls only) yields a consistent pattern, however (see specification (3), table 13.6). The number of all-boys schools and madrassas in 1999 never has an impact on female enrollment growth. This serves as a placebo test and implies that the observed effect of the presence of madrassas is unlikely to be capturing union-specific variables that are absent in our model.[22]

Another concern over the estimates reported in table 13.6 relates to the problem of reverse causality: many madrassas were newly set up primarily as a response to the stipend scheme immediately after 1994. Between 1995 and 2003, a total of 3,798 secondary educational institutions were set up throughout Bangladesh, of which 24 percent (or 907) were madrassas. If there is a correlation between female enrollment and the presence of madrassas that existed before the stipend reform, that can be taken as a cleaner test of the impact of madrassas on female enrollment. To this end, we restricted data to schools and madrassas established before 1994 and repeated our analysis. Results are reported in table 13A.3 in the annex.[23] However, even for this subsample, there is a robust relationship between the number of madrassas in the region and the growth of female enrollment.

From the results presented in table 13.6 and tables 13A.2 and 13A.3, the positive impact of madrassas on female enrollment growth is evident. We further examine the impact such growth had on achieving gender parity across Bangladeshi regions. To this end, we run regressions using specifications similar to those in table 13A.2 in the annex, but use an indicator variable "whether the region achieved gender parity in 2003" instead as the outcome variable. Reassuringly, we find that regions with greater numbers of madrassas in 1999 are more likely to achieve gender parity by 2003 (see table 13A.4 in the annex).

In sum, it is evident that reformed madrassas in Bangladesh have gone beyond adopting modern curricula by altering their age-old practice of educating predominantly male students to include girls as well. Growth in female enrollment in religious schools is simply reflecting the fact that madrassas, like secular schools, do respond to market incentives and are not beyond reform initiatives.

Conclusion and Policy Implications

The modernization scheme originally initiated in the early 1980s has succeeded in converting a large pool of orthodox madrassas that previously operated with their own funds and eschewed the teaching of modern subjects. These converted madrassas are registered with the government, they adopt state-mandated course outlines and textbooks, and they have become fiscally dependent upon the state. These findings are striking because financial autonomy was at the heart of the orthodox madrassa education system. Our findings indicate that a significant number of formerly orthodox madrassas have converted in response to financial incentives, suggesting that approximately 34 percent of the modernized madrassa system (Aliyah madrassas) in Bangladesh today consists of formerly "orthodox" religious schools.

The Bangladeshi reform experience is unique for an additional reason. Aliyah madrassas have recently embraced female teachers, who are mostly graduates of secular schools. These madrassas today educate a large number of girls and are playing an important role in closing gender gaps in primary as well as secondary school enrollment. They contribute significantly to the government's efforts to expand female education, because they serve the poor, are inexpensive, and operate in rural and isolated areas that offer few other educational opportunities. Nearly half of the student population in these religious seminaries today is female.

These features of the religious education system in Bangladesh provide important policy leverage in harmonizing schooling outcomes among students from diverse educational backgrounds. This scenario is in stark contrast with other countries in South Asia (and elsewhere) with large Muslim populations, where most religious seminaries are of traditional, orthodox types, predominantly single sex (boys only), and still untouched by any significant changes in curriculum.[24] Therefore,

Bangladesh offers an excellent case study for other countries that hope to embark on a modernization scheme to bridge the gap between religious and secular schools.

Secondary madrassas, we find, grew in numbers in Bangladesh in two distinct phases. The modernization scheme of 1980s saw a surge in numbers between 1980 and 1994. The scheme, by providing public grants to finance teacher salaries, offered fiscal incentives for madrassas to modernize course curriculum. After 1994, growth was driven mostly by enrollment of female students and allegedly by transforming formerly all-boy madrassas into centers for coeducation. This feminizing trend of modernized madrassas in Bangladesh dispels the common view that the rise of the religious education sector is explained away only by a lack of public provision.[25]

Regression analysis of data on enrollment growth rates suggests that the presence of modernized madrassas is strongly associated with the boom in female schooling in Bangladesh. This correlation holds even for the sample of older, preexisting religious schools and hence corroborates the hypothesis that madrassas have encouraged greater female participation in secondary education, rather than selectively emerging in regions where households have responded to the stipend scheme by sending daughters to schools. Such contribution of religious schools to social development in Muslim-majority countries has been overlooked by existing critiques of madrassa education (see Ahmed 2005). The impact of the stipend program on female enrollment in religious seminaries provides a partial rebuttal of the hypothesis that madrassas in South Asia predominantly offer free education (see ICG 2004) and hence do not respond to reform initiatives that work by altering relative prices and incentives (such as increased school revenue).

Our analysis demonstrates that with adequate incentives, religious schools can play a useful role in the broader development efforts in Muslim societies. The evidence presented in this chapter echoes Evans's (2006) policy admonition that the majority of madrasas actually present an opportunity, rather than a threat. Therefore, recent calls to isolate all religious schools by eschewing any form of financial assistance by the government and the international community (as made by Ahmed 2005) need to be reexamined. Specifically within the context of rural Bangladesh, the current concern over the proliferation of madrassas (Byron and Mahmud 2005) is somewhat misleading.

There is no question that secondary-level madrassas in Bangladesh are playing a critical role as far as enrollment and gender parity are concerned (two important Millennium Development Goals). Researchers and critiques should instead focus on what is being taught and actually learned in these educational institutions, particularly literacy and numeracy skills. It is expected that the inclusion of modern subjects will not only give the students of madrassas the requisite skills highly valued in a market-based economy, but will also change their attitude toward worldly affairs and members of different religions and ethnicities. Unfortunately, little systematic research has been done yet on the learning aspect of the reform program. Existing survey data do not contain information on labor market outcomes of postreform graduates. Nonetheless, research using test-score data on registered secondary schools and madrassas in rural Bangladesh finds no significant difference in test scores by school type, conditioned upon students' school choice and differences in socioeconomic backgrounds (Asadullah, Chaudhury, and Dar 2007).[26] Interestingly, the only other rigorous study of educational quality in madrassas finds little difference between madrassas and secular schools in Indonesia (Beegle and Newhouse 2005). This highlights the low quality of education in many developing countries, particularly in poor rural areas, regardless of the provider.

Rigorous analytical studies on the influence of madrassa education on socialization and social cohesion are also limited. Recent evidence-based research on madrassas has focused on issues such as the potential links to sectarian conflicts and the political orientation of the curriculum (Ahmad 2004; Ali 2005; IPS 2002; Rahman 2004a, 2004b). These studies offer some description of the worldviews of madrassa students in Pakistan. Rahman (2004a, 2004b) compares opinions of madrassa and school students in grade 10 on matters such as armed conflict, jihad, and minority rights. Rahman finds that madrassa students and teachers in Pakistan have more radical views than their school counterparts. Recently, similar research has been carried out using data on Bangladeshi reformed madrassas. Using survey data on a cohort of girls who recently graduated from rural secondary schools and Aliyah madrassas, Asadullah, Chaudhury, and Dar (2006) examine whether teachers and graduates of religious schools display hostile attitudes toward working women, working mothers, gender equity, democracy, and other socioeconomic values. The authors find that madrassa graduates have perverse attitudes toward desired fertility, favor boys over girls for higher education, and consider housewives rather than working women as the ideal for raising children. Nonetheless, Asadullah, Chaudhury, and Dar show that exposure to female students and teachers in madrassas helps to attenuate these polarizing attitudes.

In conclusion, our study finds that fiscal incentives can indeed modernize madrassas and pry them further open to female students and teachers. The very fact that modernization was possible in Bangladesh, which has the world's second largest madrassa secondary school system, should be encouraging for other countries with large Muslim populations currently grappling with similar issues of curriculum reform and gender equity.

Despite these policy achievements through the skilful use of incentives, the government of Bangladesh has recently decided to recognize postsecondary Qoumi madrassa degrees, without first attempting to induce (via fiscal incentives) or mandate (via threat of closure) reforms in primary Qoumi madrassas. This decision has been widely assailed as a political move by the ruling party to appease its Islamic coalition allies— before the upcoming elections. Thus, although fiscal incentives can induce madrassa reform, as they effectively did in the secondary school sector in Bangladesh, political prerogatives and complex path-dependent factors often trump this potentially powerful policy tool.

Looking beyond these political issues, we argue in closing that, once madrassas are brought into the mainstream, we must systematically measure how good these schools are at teaching literacy and numeracy skills to their pupils. A rigorous quality assessment should be done for schools across the spectrum—public or private, secular or religious—so that it is possible to compare educational service providers. Furthermore, systematic research by a wide array of social scientists on the impact of madrassa education on socialization, political participation, and labor market decisions is essential to assess the overall implications of incorporating religious institutions as service providers.

Annex 13A:
Variable Description, Summary Statistics, and Regression Results

Table 13A.1   Descriptive Statistics

Variable	Additional description	Mean	Standard deviation
Growth rate of female enrollment (grades 6–10) in the region	Ln(enrollment in 2003) – Ln(enrollment in 1999)	0.21	0.29
Growth rate of female enrollment (grade 6) in the region	Ln(enrollment in 2003) – Ln(enrollment in 1999)	0.11	0.35
Growth rate of female enrollment (grade 10) in the region	Ln(enrollment in 2003) – Ln(enrollment in 1999)	0.31	0.45
Total female enrollment in 1999 in·the region	in natural logs	6.56	0.78
Total female enrollment in grade 6 in 1999 in the region	in natural logs	5.27	0.76
Total female enrollment in grade 10 in 1999 in the region	in natural logs	4.53	0.83
Number of coeducational madrassas in the region, 1999		1.73	1.66
Number of girls-only madrassas in the region, 1999		3.54	2.17
Number of boys-only madrassas in the region, 1999		1.50	1.40
Number of coeducational schools in the region, 1999		0.19	0.49
Number of girls-only schools in the region, 1999		0.03	0.17
Number of boys-only schools in the region, 1999		2.74	1.70
Change in number of madrassas, 1999–2003	Change in number of madrassas in the region, 1999–2003	0.70	0.89
Change in number of schools, 1999–2003	Change in number of schools in the region, 1999–2003	0.10	0.37
Mean age of schools		0.03	0.17
Mean age of madrassas		0.08	0.31
Fraction of madrassas in the region (in 1999) that are converts	Converts are madrassas established before 1980	0.39	0.41
Urban	Fraction of urban schools	0.13	0.31
Govt	Whether any government school in the region	0.05	0.22
N		4,784	

Source: Authors' calculations based on data described in text.

Note: Region refers to "union," an administrative unit that is smaller than a subdistrict (upazila) but bigger than a village (usually comprising 10–15 villages).

**Table 13A.2   Determinants of Regional Enrollment Growth—
Alternative Specification, Ordinary Least Squares Estimates, 1999–2003**

	Dependent variable: Regional growth rate of total female enrollment (grades 6–10)	Dependent variable: Regional growth rate of female enrollment in grade 6	Dependent variable: Regional growth rate of female enrollment in grade 10
Total female enrollment in 1999 in the region, grades 6–10 (in logs)	−0.293 (40.54)**		
Female enrollment in 1999 in the region, grade 6 (in logs)		−0.355 (39.23)**	
Female enrollment in 1999 in the region, grade 10 (in logs)			−0.389 (42.23)**
Number of madrassas in the region, 1999	0.028 (8.81)**	0.036 (8.96)**	0.055 (11.32)**
Number of schools in the region, 1999	0.060 (22.82)**	0.069 (21.22)**	0.080 (21.10)**
Change in number of madrassas, 1999–2003	0.075 (3.53)**	0.110 (4.15)**	0.051 (1.58)
Change in number of schools, 1999–2003	0.092 (7.37)**	0.143 (9.21)**	0.024 (1.24)
Mean age of schools	−0.001 (4.29)**	−0.000 (0.65)	0.000 (0.24)
Fraction of madrassas in the region being "converts" (established pre-1980)	0.024 (2.68)**	0.021 (1.81)+	0.057 (4.04)**
Urban	−0.016 (1.03)	0.003 (0.14)	−0.026 (1.09)
Govt (=1 if a government secondary school present)	0.041 (2.32)*	0.036 (1.64)	0.031 (1.11)
Constant	1.882 (47.01)**	1.653 (41.51)**	1.658 (48.15)**
N	4784	4780	4676
R-squared	0.32	0.29	0.33
Fixed effects	Thana	Thana	Thana

Source: Authors' calculations based on data described in text.

Note: Absolute value of t statistics in parentheses. + significant at 10 percent; * significant at 5 percent; ** significant at 1 percent.

Table 13A.3 Determinants of Regional Enrollment Growth, 1999–2003: Sample of Older Schools

	Dependent variable: Regional growth rate of total female enrollment (grades 6–10)			Dependent variable: Regional growth rate of female enrollment in grade 6			Dependent variable: Regional growth rate of female enrollment in grade 10		
	(1)	(2)	(3)	(1)	(2)	(3)	(1)	(2)	(3)
Total female enrollment in 1999 in the region, grades 6–10 (in logs)	-0.222 (32.11)**	-0.230 (32.14)**	-0.233 (32.16)**						
Female enrollment in 1999 in the region, grade 6 (in logs)				-0.283 (32.51)**	-0.292 (32.18)**	-0.298 (32.52)**			
Female enrollment in 1999 in the region, grade 10 (in logs)							-0.358 (40.03)**	-0.375 (40.42)**	-0.378 (40.31)**
Number of madrassas in the region, 1999	0.022	0.017 (4.90)**	0.026 (5.95)**	0.033	(5.91)**	0.041 (6.82)**	0.053	(7.64)**	(9.10)**
Number of schools in the region, 1999	0.051 (17.74)**	0.058 (19.31)**		0.060 (16.56)**	0.069 (18.00)**		0.087 (20.48)**	0.094 (21.20)**	
Change in number of madrassas, 1999–2003	—	—	—	—	—	—	—	—	—
Change in number of schools, 1999–2003	—	—	—	—	—	—	—	—	—
Mean age of schools	-0.000 (0.59)	-0.000 (1.43)	-0.000 (0.82)	0.001 (2.59)*	0.001 (2.45)*	0.001 (2.85)**	0.000 (0.88)	0.000 (0.60)	0.001 (1.26)
Mean age of madrassas	0.002 (4.20)**	0.002 (3.67)**	0.002 (4.08)**	0.002 (2.72)**	0.002 (2.51)**	0.002 (2.81)**	0.003 (4.08)**	0.002 (2.74)**	0.003 (3.18)**
Number of coeducational madrassas in the region, 1999			0.020 (4.70)**			0.031 (5.54)**			0.051 (7.71)**

Number of girls-only madrassas in the region, 1999			0.036 (4.02)**			0.051 (4.43)**			0.062 (4.48)**
Number of boys-only madrassas in the region, 1999			-0.002 (0.10)			-0.007 (0.26)			-0.006 (0.18)
Number of coeducational schools in the region, 1999			0.060 (18.13)**			0.068 (15.74)**			0.098 (19.61)**
Number of girls-only schools in the region, 1999			0.064 (10.91)**			0.091 (12.15)**			0.105 (11.83)**
Number of boys-only schools in the region, 1999			0.019 (1.68)+			0.022 (1.52)			0.020 (1.13)
Govt (=1 if a government secondary school present)	0.018 (1.06)	0.019 (1.10)	0.038 (2.10)*	0.013 (0.58)	0.014 (0.64)	0.029 (1.23)	0.019 (0.71)	0.021 (0.77)	0.057 (2.00)*
Urban	0.015 (1.14)	-0.009 (0.61)	-0.001 (0.07)	0.036 (2.21)*	0.014 (0.74)	0.014 (0.69)	-0.019 (0.96)	-0.024 (1.05)	-0.006 (0.27)
Constant	1.381 (35.75)**	1.417 (35.40)**	1.427 (35.01)**	1.220 (31.59)**	1.236 (30.69)**	1.261 (30.83)**	1.507 (43.81)**	1.555 (43.61)**	1.549 (42.34)**
N	4737	4737	4737	4734	4734	4734	4660	4660	4660
R-squared	0.20	0.22	0.22	0.19	0.20	0.20	0.28	0.31	0.31
Fixed effects	District	Thana	Thana	District	Thana	Thana	District	Thana	Thana

Source: Authors' calculations based on data described in text.

Note: Absolute value of t statistics in parentheses. + significant at 10 percent; * significant at 5 percent; ** significant at 1 percent. For each dependent variable, specification (1) controls for district fixed effects; specification (2) controls for subdistrict (upazila)-level fixed effects; and specification (3) replaces the variables—total number of schools in 1999 and total number of madrassas in 1999—by gender-disaggregated versions (coeducation, boys only, girls only).

234   Girls' Education in the 21st Century

Table 13A.4   Determinants of Gender Parity in Secondary School Enrollment, 2003: Linear Probability Model Estimates

	Dependent variable: Achieved gender parity in total enrollment in grade 6 by 2003? (yes = 1, no = 0)			Dependent variable: Achieved gender parity in total enrollment in grade 10 by 2003? (yes = 1, no = 0)		
	(1)	(2)	(3)	(1)	(2)	(3)
Female enrollment in 1999 in the region, grade 6 (in logs)	−0.104 (10.41)**	−0.100 (9.20)**	−0.103 (9.41)**			
Female enrollment in 1999 in the region, grade 10 (in logs)				−0.075 (6.94)**	−0.088 (7.65)**	−0.091 (7.83)**
Number of madrassas in the region, 1999	0.010 (2.44)*	0.012 (2.47)*		0.003 (0.54)	0.011 (1.75)+	
Number of schools in the region, 1999	0.015 (4.14)**	0.016 (4.17)**		0.020 (4.64)**	0.027 (5.73)**	
Change in number of madrassas, 1999–2003	0.010 (0.33)	−0.006 (0.19)	−0.007 (0.22)	−0.016 (0.43)	0.003 (0.07)	0.001 (0.04)
Change in number of schools, 1999–2003	0.030 (1.73)+	0.018 (0.96)	0.020 (1.06)	−0.023 (1.06)	−0.020 (0.86)	−0.018 (0.76)
Mean age of schools	0.000 (0.39)	0.000 (0.20)	0.000 (0.29)	0.001 (1.26)	0.001 (1.26)	0.001 (1.39)
Fraction of madrassas in the region being "converts" (established pre-1980)	0.040 (3.08)**	0.041 (3.00)**	0.045 (3.20)**	0.046 (2.75)**	0.031 (1.76)+	0.031 (1.75)+
Number of coeducational madrassas in the region, 1999			0.011 (1.91)+			0.011 (1.61)
Number of girls-only madrassas in the region, 1999			0.027 (2.25)*			0.014 (0.91)
Number of boys-only madrassas in the region, 1999			−0.059 (1.84)+			−0.021 (0.51)
Number of coeducational schools in the region, 1999			0.015 (3.26)**			0.023 (4.30)**
Number of girls-only schools in the region, 1999			0.027 (3.38)**			0.043 (4.41)**
Number of boys-only schools in the region, 1999			0.005 (0.29)			0.001 (0.06)
Urban	−0.038 (1.99)*	−0.002 (0.08)	−0.003 (0.14)	−0.092 (3.74)**	−0.049 (1.63)	−0.049 (1.58)
Govt (=1 if a government secondary school present)	−0.026 (1.03)	−0.042 (1.58)	−0.042 (1.51)	−0.011 (0.34)	−0.005 (0.13)	−0.000 (0.00)
Constant	0.604 (13.65)**	0.571 (11.96)**	0.586 (12.12)**	0.507 (12.58)**	0.527 (12.24)**	0.538 (12.22)**
N	4,747	4,747	4,747	4,627	4,627	4,627
R-squared	0.03	0.02	0.03	0.02	0.02	0.02
Fixed effects	District	Thana	Thana	District	Thana	Thana

Source: Authors' calculations based on data described in text.

Note: Absolute value of t statistics in parentheses. + significant at 10 percent; * significant at 5 percent; ** significant at 1 percent. For each dependent variable, specification (1) controls for district fixed effects; specification (2) controls for subdistrict (upazila)-level fixed effects; and specification (3) replaces the variables—total number of schools in 1999 and total number of madrassas in 1999—by gender-disaggregated versions (coeducation, boys only, girls only).

Notes

1. The Deoband (Darul Ulum) system, introduced in 1866 in northern India, is considered by many to be a reaction to the Anglo-Oriental education in colonial India. The Deobandis shun modern scientific and technical education and follow the "Dars-i-Nizamia"—a syllabus comprising authoritative texts that date back to the 11th century. The nature of other learning materials used therein remains unknown. Being unrecognized by the government, the madrassas do not follow the government-approved curriculum and hence are open to exploitation by extremist quarters.

2. The origin of registered madrassas in Bangladesh can be traced to 1780 when, under the British initiative, Calcutta Aliyah madrassa, the first-ever madrassa in the public sector, was established in the subcontinent. The madrassa went through major reorganization in 1850, when it was divided into two separate divisions: the Arabic and the Anglo-Persian. However, only the purely religious side of the Calcutta madrassa moved to Dhaka in 1947. The handful of registered madrassas in Bangladesh between 1971 and 1980 are all inspired by the Calcutta madrassa and hence, are popularly known as Aliyah madrassas (Zaman 1999).

3. Those few who succeed in securing wage employment perform relatively poorly in the labor market. Studies comparing wage earnings of graduates of madrassas and secular schools suggest lower returns to religious education (see Asadullah 2006a, 2006b).

4. All madrassas in Bangladesh are privately owned and managed. There are just three state-run religious seminaries in the country.

5. Recently, humanities, science, and business education have been introduced at the secondary level.

6. In contrast, Aliyah madrassa degrees are recognized by all universities in Bangladesh.

7. This figure is from Kennedy (2004).

8. At present, only seven Indian states (Assam, Bihar, Madhya Pradesh, Orissa, Rajasthan, Uttar Pradesh, and West Bengal) have government-sponsored madrassa education boards, with which a number of madrassas are affiliated.

9. Outside of South and Southeast Asia, Egypt and Turkey are two countries with considerable experience in madrassa reform.

10. This followed amendment of the Indonesian Educational Act No. 2/1989.

11. Another noticeable difference between the two countries is that recognized madrassas in Bangladesh are supervised by the Ministry of Education, whereas in Indonesia they remain under the control of the Ministry of Religious Affairs.

12. In contrast, madrassas in Pakistan account for less than 1 percent of total school enrollment (Andrabi et al. 2006).

13. According to Sattar (2004), however, at the time of independence, there were 1,371 registered madrassas in Bangladesh. However, no basis could be found for this figure; the author used past newspapers clippings as the data source. If one accepts this estimate, the fraction of converts as a percentage of total registered madrassas becomes 34 percent.

14. According to anecdotal evidence, there are today as many as 12,000 Qoumi madrassas in Bangladesh. If one assumes that the growth of the total number of secondary schools and Qoumi madrassas has been similar between 1980 and 2003, then the estimated number of Qoumi madrassas in 1980 would be significantly less than 9,692. This would, in turn, imply a larger percentage of compliant Qoumi madrassas.

15. "Recognition year" corresponds to the year in which a madrassa first received grants from the government. For 14 percent of the madrassas in the census data set, however, this information is missing.

16. The remaining 3 percent constitute preexisting registered madrassas, which were inspired by the Arabic branch of Calcutta Aliyah madrassa and specialized primarily in medieval Arabic and Islamic texts.

17. Indonesia is another Muslim country that has achieved similar gender parity in madrassa enrollment.

18. See table 7 at http://www.banbeis.gov.bd/db_bb/madrasah_education_2.htm.

19. Administratively, the nation is divided into divisions, districts, subdistricts (upazilas), unions, and clusters of households (mouzas).

20. As many as 24 percent (N = 1,179) of the unions in Bangladesh do not have a secondary madrassa.

21. A similar pattern is observed forming gross enrollment statistics. According to BANBEIS, gross female enrollment at the secondary-school level (total number of females enrolled in secondary school/total number of 11- to 15-year-olds in the population) increased from 42.5 percent to 48.4 percent between 1999 and 2003.

22. As an alternative placebo test, we repeated the regressions using growth rate in boys' enrollment as the dependent variable (results available upon request). Once again, presence of girls' madrassas in the region had no impact on boys' enrollment.

23. Exclusion of prereform educational institutions leads to a fall in union-level growth in secondary enrollment (19 percent, as opposed to 30 percent). This implies that newly set up schools/madrassas following the introduction of the stipend scheme contributed more to female enrollment than older educational institutions.

24. Among all countries with large a Muslim population, Indonesia has the largest number of madrassas (38,500, enrolling 5.7 million students or 13 percent of all students). In the Philippines, there are 1,581 madrassas in the country, only 35 of which are accredited by the government.

25. The relevance of this hypothesis for Pakistan is also questioned by some researchers (see Andrabi et al. 2006).

26. This, however, simply demonstrates that quality of education remains very low in rural areas, so private secular schools do not have an advantage over Aliyah madrassas in attracting prospective students.

References

Ahmad, Mumtaz. 2004. "Madrassa Education in Pakistan and Bangladesh." In *Religious Radicalism and Security in South Asia*, eds. Satu Limaye, Robert Wirsing, and Mohan Malik. Honolulu: Asia-Pacific Center for Security Studies.

Ahmed, Samina. 2005. Testimony prepared for the U.S. Senate Foreign Relations Committee Hearing on Combating Terrorism through Education—the Near East and South Asian Experience. Washington DC, April 19, 2005.

Ali, Saleem. 2005. "Islamic Education and Conflict: Understanding the Madrassahs of Pakistan." Unpublished manuscript.

Andrabi, Tahir, Jishnu Das, Asim Ijaz Khwaja, and Tristan Zajonc. 2006. "Religious School Enrolment in Pakistan: A Look at the Data." Special issue on "Education in Islam: Myths and Truths." *Comparative Education Review.*

Asadullah, M. Niaz. 2006a. "Returns to Education in Bangladesh." *Education Economics* 14: 453–468.

———. 2006b. "The Effectiveness of Private and Public Schools in Bangladesh and Pakistan." Unpublished manuscript. University of Oxford.

Asadullah, M. Niaz, Nazmul Chaudhury, and Amit Dar. 2007. "Religious Schools, Social Values and Economic Attitudes: Evidence from Bangladesh." Paper presented at the Northeast Universities Development Consortium Conference, Cornell University, Ithaca, NY, September 29–30.

Azra, Azyumardi. 2004. "Mainstreaming Islamic Education." Paper presented at the United States Indonesia Society 10th Anniversary Lecture Series, Washington, DC, March 31.

Beegle, C., and D. Newhouse. 2006. "The Effect of School Type on Academic Achievement: Evidence from Indonesia." *Journal of Human Resources* 2006 XLI: 529–557.

Byron, Rejaul Karim, and Shameem Mahmud. 2005. "Madrasas Mushroom with State Favour." *The Daily Star,* August 4.

Evans, Alexander. 2006. "Understanding Madrasahs." *Foreign Affairs* 85 (1): 9–16.

Fahimuddin. 2004. *Modernization of Muslim Education in India.* New Delhi, India: Adhyayan.

ICG (International Crisis Group). 2004. *Pakistan: Reforming the Education Sector.* Asia Report no. 84. Washington, DC: ICG.

IPS (Institute of Policy Studies). 2002. *Religious Education Institutions: An Overview.* Islamabad: IPS.

Kennedy, Miranda. 2004. "Rumors of Jihad." *Boston Globe.* April 4.

Khan, Amirullah, Mohammad Saqib, and Zafar Anjum. 2003. "To Kill the Mockingbird." Mimeograph.

Ladbury, Sarah. 2004. *Madrassahs and Islamic Education in South Asia: What the Donor Community Needs to Know?* Washington, DC: World Bank, South Asia Department.

Metcalf, Barbara. 1978. "The Madrasa at Deoband: A Model for Religious Education in Modern India." *Modern Asian Studies* 12 (1): 111–134.

Rahman, Tariq. 2004a. "Denizens of Alien Worlds: A Survey of Students and Teachers at Pakistan's Urdu and English Language–Medium Schools and Madrasas." *Contemporary South Asia* 13 (3): 307–326.

———. 2004b. *Denizens of Alien Worlds: A Study of Education, Inequality and Polarization in Pakistan.* Karachi, Pakistan: Oxford University Press.

———. 2005. "Madrassas: The Potential for Violence in Pakistan?" Unpublished manuscript.

Sattar, Abdus. 2004. *Bangladesh madrasa shikhkha o samaj jibone tar provab.* Dhaka, Bangladesh: Islamic Foundation.

Zaman, Muhammad, Qasim. 1999. "Religious Education and the Rhetoric of Reform: The Madrasa in British India and Pakistan." *Comparative Studies in Society and History* 41 (2): 294–323.

CHAPTER 14

Cultivating Knowledge and Skills to Grow African Agriculture

Richard Johanson, William Saint, Catherine Ragasa, and Eija Pehu

The Context for Agricultural Education and Training in Africa

Until it learns to grow its agriculture, Africa is unlikely to register significant developmental advances. Recognizing this reality, in 2002 African governments adopted a Comprehensive Africa Agriculture Development Program under the auspices of their New Partnership for African Development (NEPAD). This program states that larger investments in agricultural research and extension and education systems are required to achieve the targeted increase in agricultural output of 6 percent a year over the next 20 years. In 2006 NEPAD issued a Framework for African Agricultural Productivity as a guideline to member states for attaining this production goal. These and other recent continental initiatives frequently recognize the general importance of agricultural education and training (AET), but they offer little specificity on what should be done or how to do it. The analysis contained in this chapter aims to fill this void.

To this end, the World Bank initiated a series of studies on AET in 2005, which were compiled into a final report published in 2007 titled *Cultivating Knowledge and Skills to Grow African Agriculture* (World Bank, 2007). The purpose of the report was to synthesize the findings of the studies and propose a set of strategic measures for strengthening the contribution of AET to agricultural productivity in Sub-Saharan Africa. The target audiences are African practitioners and policy makers concerned with boosting food supply and agricultural output, donor representatives, and World Bank staff. This report presents a case for increased investment in AET, analyzes issues in the subsector, and outlines possible options for policies and interventions to build skills and capacities appropriate for the changing circumstances of African agriculture in the 21st century. One of the key issues identified was the need to boost women's tertiary education in agriculture.

Lessons emerging from recent agricultural reform experiences demonstrate that a more nuanced understanding is needed of AET's role in promoting innovation, productivity gains, and growth in agriculture. Insight is specifically needed on how to bring AET into closer, more productive relationships with other actors in the agricultural sector and wider economy. This will allow sharing in the comparative advantages of different actors and institutions to reduce transaction costs, achieve economies of scale, exploit complementarities, and realize synergies in innovation. We adopt an analytical approach guided by an agricultural innovation system framework in the belief that it contributes fresh perspectives to addressing this need.

In essence, an agricultural innovation system is a blending of institutional capacities, coordination mechanisms, communication networks, and policy incentives that fosters innovation-led gains in agricultural productivity. It emphasizes the need to understand key actors, both men and women—their roles, behaviors, and practices—and the institutional context within which they interact. All of these are key conceptual elements in innovation systems analysis.[1] This, in turn, points to issues of institutional structures of governance and management (for greater flexibility and responsiveness), criteria and incentives for professional performance (for improved productivity), and access to information and interinstitutional communication networks (for enhanced competitiveness). All of these issues are relevant to African education and training institutions.

Agricultural Education Is Vital for African Development

Agriculture continues to be Sub-Saharan Africa's dominant economic activity, accounting for 40 percent of gross domestic product (GDP), 15 percent of exports, and 60 to 80 percent of employment. Higher agricultural productivity is a precondition for growth and development in most African countries, and increasing yields is the key to raising incomes in rural areas. Farmers and commercial producers may benefit especially if they can diversify their production into higher-value, knowledge-demanding, specialized crops. Strong AET systems are necessary to underpin such productivity gains. AET directly raises agricultural productivity by developing producer capacities and indirectly increases agricultural productivity by generating human capital for support services. Investments in AET clearly enable research, extension, and commercial agriculture to generate higher payoffs. As stated by NEPAD, "The quality of tertiary agricultural education is critical because it determines the expertise and competencies of scientists, professionals, technicians, teachers, and civil service and business leaders in all aspects of agriculture and related industries." [Forum for Agricultural Research in Africa (FARA). 2006. p. 72. Cited in Framework for African Agricultural Productivity (FAAP). P 19.] Higher agricultural education also contributes directly to research and advisory services. Finally, the case for improving AET systems is compelling in view of their seminal role in agricultural development elsewhere in the world. AET development was an integral part of strategies of countries that grew agriculture successfully, such as Brazil, India, and Malaysia.

African AET in Perspective

Postsecondary AET was established in Africa as far back as 1924. An essentially bifurcated system of agricultural education emerged from the colonial period, in which postprimary vocational education was targeted at the sons of traditional farmers, and postsecondary agricultural education was designed to lead the sons of the middle class into public employment. This dual legacy, and the separate expectations associated with each branch of it, has hindered the development of agricultural education in Africa up to the present.

Extensive institutional infrastructure for AET has been put in place since the 1960s. Africa now has roughly 200 public universities (compared with 20 in 1960), and about a hundred of them teach agriculture and natural resources management. In addition, private universities are beginning to complement these capacities with their own offerings.

The initial institutional building achievements of the 1970s and 1980s have given way to neglect since the 1990s. Donor assistance to African agriculture has declined sharply, and within that total, support for AET in Africa has largely disappeared. Assistance for *formal* AET declined to just 0.7 percent of agricultural sector aid between 2000 and 2004 (Johanson and Adams 2004). Government funding has tended to follow donor priorities. The ultimate cost of the government and donor pullback from AET has been to distance African professionals from knowledge networks, global information resources, and the cutting edge of technology transfer. This has left a severely depleted human resource pool in African agriculture. The low number of women among this human resource pool is especially alarming.

Women play multiple roles in agriculture and account for more than half of agricultural output in Sub-Saharan Africa. But women have continuously received a less-than-proportionate share of investment in agriculture. For example, women farmers receive only a 5 percent share of extension services, even though it has been shown that farm productivity increases by 22 percent when women receive the same advisory services as men (Udry et al. 1996).

Constraints on Building AET Capacity

AET supply is often out of synch with labor market demands for knowledge and practical competencies, especially in agribusiness, basic management, and problem solving. AET is not realizing its potential contribution to agricultural development because of poor links with research and knowledge sources. External problems—such as fragmented organizational responsibilities for AET—and internal problems—such as underfunding, unattractive working conditions, and consequent staff depletion—contribute to AET underachievement.

AET Enrollment Profiles Are Distorted and Declining

Africa's technical education enrollment pyramid falls short at the upper levels, especially postgraduate enrollments. Females receive far fewer

Figure 14.1   Sub-Saharan Africa: Enrollments in the Agricultural Sciences in Ethiopia, by Gender, 1991 and 2000

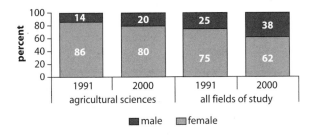

Source: Stads and Beintema 2006.

opportunities than indicated by their important role in agricultural production. Student interest in agriculture is waning, in large measure because it was directed almost exclusively to government employment that is now dwindling. Agriculture enrollments show declining shares at all postsecondary levels, and the share of female enrollment lags behind.

AET Institutions Tend to Be Isolated and Fragmented
AET systems lack strategic alignment to national development priorities and suffer from weak links to stakeholders, employers, and the productive sector—making less than their expected contribution to national agricultural innovation systems. They are also poorly connected to international sources of knowledge. Their isolation often results from overcentralized or divided administration.

AET Curricula Tend to Be Obsolete and Disassociated from the Economy
Curricula are often outdated and focus narrowly on farm production; they do not encompass markets, agribusiness, and processing. In terms of women's interests, the curricula contain very few courses on issues such as household nutrition, sanitation, and hygiene, critical areas for household welfare. The curricula also provide few gender-specific career tracks for female students entering public service. Moreover, little effort is made to use female AET graduates as a means of effecting change in rural livelihoods through gender-specific impact pathways.

Numerous Countries Face Shortages in AET Staffing

Staff shortages are common because of brain drain, a rising tide of retirements, and the attrition caused by HIV/AIDS. High levels of staff turnover because of unattractive working conditions can be a serious issue. Rapid enrollment expansion and the consequent need to hire many junior staff have left staff qualifications weak at many AET institutions.

Teaching Methods and Facilities Are Often Inadequate

Teaching methods are overwhelmingly traditional in their heavy use of classroom lectures. Practical instruction receives insufficient emphasis, and students have little opportunity to develop technical competencies, problem-solving experience, or communication and organizational skills. Learning infrastructure is widely deficient because of insufficient budgets and overdependence on public financing. For women students, special constraints are the lack of physical facilities like dormitories and assurance of personal safety.

African universities ultimately will be responsible for replenishing the stock of human capital in their research and extension services and for providing them with the broader set of skills necessary to grow agriculture in the 21st century. But the universities are ill-prepared to train the continent's next generation of agricultural scientists, professionals, and

---

Box 14.1

A Promising Example of Gender Integration in Training from Benin

In Benin there is a progressive Songhai agricultural training center in Porto Novo. Of the graduates, 65–70 percent settle into agriculture. The college is locally owned and privately managed; has a capacity of 225 boarding places; and offers training in small-scale farming, farm management, and agricultural teaching. About 20–30 percent of the trainees are women, and 60 percent of the trainees come from rural areas. The instruction favors application: more than 75 percent of time is devoted to practical subjects. Innovations in the training include a business center of agricultural products, a soybean marketing chain, and a credit program to help trainees establish themselves after training. Women compose a large share of these new entrepreneurs.

technicians. As stated by NEPAD in the Framework for African Agricultural Productivity, "Urgent action must be taken to restore the quality of graduate and post-graduate agricultural education in Africa."

Priorities for Modernizing Agricultural Education

Seven priorities are proposed for modernizing agricultural education in Africa. First, political will must be generated in support of agricultural development by educating the public about its role in economic growth and poverty reduction, creating capacities for lobbying, joining forces with other stakeholders, and sustaining these efforts over two or three decades. Women's associations and lobbying groups need to join in these advocacy efforts to highlight the importance of training young African women in agriculture. Second, AET institutions should be integrated into the national agricultural innovation system by establishing better institutional and market links. Associated AET reforms ought to be grounded in an analysis of agricultural priorities and market requirements. Changes in organization and management can provide opportunities and incentives for productive external links. Access to international knowledge sources is becoming increasingly easy, but it often requires external assistance. Third, AET enrollment profiles should be assessed and rebalanced away from secondary-level vocational training and toward diploma, degree, and postgraduate levels. Fourth, curricula and pedagogy should be modernized by emphasizing analytical skills, problem solving, agribusiness processes, postharvest technologies, and "soft" but essential skills such as communication and teamwork. Student interest in agriculture could be sparked by recasting programs in more modern and appealing terms, such as applied sciences and technology. The public should be educated on the full range of agricultural career possibilities, keeping in mind the interest of women students. Fifth, it is essential to replenish human capital by strengthening and expanding national master of science (MSc) programs, laying the foundation for doctoral programs, and tackling the conundrum of incentives for staff retention. In Malaysia a focus on national MSc programs with an enhanced enrollment of women students has resulted in 34 percent of today's researchers being women. Sixth, finances must be managed proactively by making more efficient use of existing resources, mobilizing nonpublic resources, and persuading donors to finance operating costs. Seventh, better gender balance must be achieved among AET graduates.

Different Approaches for Different Levels of Training

What can be done to build momentum in the face of existing constraints? Different strategies will need to be pursued at each level of AET.

Secondary-Level AET

Efforts might best focus on preventing premature specialization, especially in lower secondary education, where a solid basic education remains the most important goal. Upper secondary technical programs are most effective when they emphasize the acquisition of specific competencies for properly selected trainees. Programs are least effective when they serve as an alternative pathway to university admission. Greater flexibility in the length of courses would also enable secondary-level AET to meet the training needs of a wider range of potential students. Specific career interests and skills of women students need to be kept in mind when designing the training programs.

Tertiary-Level AET

Reforms in curricula and teaching methods are likely to be the most immediately useful undertakings. In the medium term, modification of institutional governance structures to introduce greater institutional flexibility and increased responsiveness to stakeholders would be a valuable complement. At the system level, a review—and if necessary, a rebalancing—of agriculture enrollments among degree, diploma, and certificate levels could ensure that adequate numbers of competent higher-level technicians are available to meet the increasingly complex demands of the labor market. Conscious efforts to recruit more women students are needed to maintain quality within the technical and professional skills pool. This also ensures that the labor pool possesses the capacity necessary to work with the large numbers of female farmers and traders found in the agricultural sector. Finally, harnessing the potential for agricultural distance education and online provision of technical training will enable lifelong learning to emerge as a way of maintaining workforce competitiveness.

Postgraduate-Level AET

Circumstances call for MSc programs within Africa to be strengthened in quality and expanded in numbers of programs, enrollments of students, and gender balance. This is becoming urgent in order to address local staffing shortages and give impetus to local research. Collaborative regional MSc programs offer cost-effective ways to build professional capacities in a range of important specialized areas. But programs are likely to develop only through sustained financial commitments by donor consortia. Looking ahead, aggressive efforts in staff development at the doctoral level will be necessary to lay the foundation for an expanded number of local PhD programs. Training outside the region will continue to be needed because of limited regional capacities in doctoral-level training, especially in new scientific areas. Different modes such as sandwich training or use of third-country universities could help to keep costs in check and minimize brain drain.

The Time to Act Is Now

AET is a vital, but much neglected, component of agricultural development in Africa. Continuing neglect of AET risks limiting agricultural recovery and restricting the possibilities for economic growth and poverty reduction. Consequently, countries in Sub-Saharan Africa are encouraged to address the shortcomings of current approaches to agricultural human capital formation by training a new generation of professionals with different skill sets. This goal is not amenable to a quick fix. Long-term, patient support over 20 years or more will be needed from government, AET institutions, and development partners to attain this objective.

Short-Term Actions

In the short term, representative actors of the national agricultural innovation system might usefully be convened for a collective exercise in national priority setting. This would include government officials from agricultural research and extension, science and technology, and export promotion; private sector entrepreneurs; nongovernmental organization rural advisory staff; AET institutional leaders; and farmers' organizations. As a basis for discussion, the following six short-term measures are proposed for consideration: (1) create networks and associations that can champion the cause of agriculture and learn lobbying techniques to generate supportive political will; (2) modernize curricula and teaching methods at the tertiary level, along with the necessary teaching inputs; (3) improve institutional links (strategic partnerships, professional networks, collaboration incentives) and knowledge access (The Essential Electronic Agricultural Library [TEEAL], Access to Global Online Research in Agriculture [AGORA], computers); (4) persuade development partners to fund essential operational and equipment maintenance costs; (5) conduct labor market studies and establish a labor market monitoring capacity; and (6) work to make the agricultural professions attractive employment and career options, while recruiting many more women into this field.

Long-Term Actions

In the long term, beneficial actions would include (1) rebalancing AET enrollments away from secondary programs in favor of tertiary-level diploma, degree, and postgraduate programs; (2) strengthening and expanding a selected number of MSc programs in areas of strategic importance to the nation, including associated staff development, so that all major master's programs for agriculture are available in Sub-Saharan Africa within 10 years; (3) broadening the foundation for regional PhD programs by launching a major program of postgraduate fellowships to train 1,000 PhDs, initially abroad and eventually at home, over the next 15 years.

National Political Leaders

National political leaders should consider the following actions to strengthen capacities for skills development in support of agricultural growth: (1) a renewed and sustained political commitment by African governments to building human capital in agriculture; (2) devolving greater authority to AET institutions while strengthening the relevance of their programs by increasing stakeholder participation in institutional governance; (3) avoiding proliferation, or atomization, of AET institutions and programs, which dilutes resources and drives down quality;[2] (4) increasing female enrollment in AET institutions through quotas, earmarked scholarships, professional mentoring, and appropriate facilities to accommodate women; (5) boosting the attractiveness of agricultural careers by advocating their importance for national development to the general public, by creating new career paths that open up a wider range of employment opportunities, and by stimulating student and parental interest in agriculture as a profession; (6) governmental incentives and rewards for AET staff—together with diverse staff retention measures such as merit pay, transparent promotion procedures, and administrative streamlining—to attract better students and facilitate their recruitment as future staff; and (7) outsourcing a portion of public agricultural research to tertiary AET institutions, preferably through competitive research grants.

AET System and Institutional Managers

Actions by AET system and institutional managers to enhance agricultural development in Africa should include (1) creating forums among stakeholders for building institutional links, fostering information networks, and setting priorities in AET in relation to agriculture development plans; (2) improving student selection procedures so that only those with a personal interest in agriculture are admitted to tertiary-level studies (with special recruitment efforts to attract women students); (3) consulting stakeholders, particularly private sector employers, on program definition and conducting periodic employer surveys and tracer studies (disaggregated by gender) to assess the effectiveness of AET programs; (4) linking curricula to the market for graduates, in part by focusing on growth areas and niches in commercial agriculture; (5) introducing, where possible, interdisciplinary programs at the undergraduate level, such as natural resource management, with practical training, contact between students and a range of producers, and focus on solving actual production problems; (6) budgeting for and providing periodic professional updating of staff; (7) creating a conducive professional environment for retaining staff, including the definition of clear career ladders and streamlining administrative procedures to reduce inefficient use of staff time; and (8) mobilizing additional resources and using them for upgrading staff conditions and teaching and research.

Development Partners

Development partners could help to build on the numerous positive experiences that have been generated in AET by assisting in their replication across the continent. The resources of African countries alone are unlikely to be adequate for this task. Thus, development partners are encouraged to make long-term financing commitments to help interested governments replenish their human capital and strengthen the performance of their agricultural innovation systems. Development partner actions are recommended in seven priority areas:

- The most immediate task is to rebuild the human capital base in agriculture, to increase the quality and number of high-level agricultural professionals, by means of postgraduate fellowships to attain the goal of 1,000 new PhDs in agriculture within the next 15 years. This must be preceded by an assessment of current supply capacity and, with

Box 14.2

Examples of Gender Mainstreaming in the Agricultural Professions

- Winrock International has 37 women scholars in bachelor's and master's programs in science; 15 had completed their degrees as of 2004.
- African Women Leaders in Agriculture and Environment (AWLAE), based in Wageningen University, currently supports 20 women in doctoral programs.
- Female Scholarship Initiative, initiated by Makerere University in Uganda and funded by the Carnegie Corporation, provides full scholarships of $1,200 each to 19 women of limited income to pursue studies in agriculture.
- RUFORUM has adopted a similar approach within eastern and southern Africa, awarding 40 percent of its 170 postgraduate fellowships to women.

Source: http://www.winrock.org; http://gender.mak.ac.ug/fsi.htm; http://www.ruforum.org/.

interested governments and donors, the preparation of a feasibility study and detailed plan.

- Support donor consortia for, say, a dozen specialized collaborative regional doctoral programs.
- Fund the operating and equipment maintenance costs that are essential for retaining skilled academic staff and enabling them to teach and conduct research productively.
- Ensure gender rebalancing within the above staff development programs and establish female scholarship programs at the secondary and undergraduate levels to attract more women into agricultural sciences.
- Expand access to international sources of information by funding electronic innovations (such as TEEAL and AGORA) at key AET institutions and by financing the facilities and equipment necessary for increased bandwidth and computer facilities and networks.
- Finance competitive grant funds for tertiary institutions to undertake peer-reviewed research. A competitive fund for institutional development could also stimulate initiatives based on strategic plans generated by AET institutions and faculties.

- Finance experimentation and capacity building in new modes of delivering AET that make use of information and communication technologies, including online degrees and various types of distance learning.

To conclude, given the attention to Sub-Saharan Africa agriculture, there is a unique opportunity to support agricultural postsecondary education and to mainstream gender into these efforts. Political will is needed with advocacy for gendered perspectives. There are already positive examples of effective gender programs in Sub-Saharan Africa, and they can be scaled out.

Notes

1. The interrelated importance of education, research, and extension in enhancing agricultural production and reducing rural poverty is well recognized in many developing countries. However, evidence suggests that the traditional education-research-extension triangle may be increasingly ill-equipped to respond to the new opportunities and challenges now associated with agriculture in Sub-Saharan Africa. The entry of new actors, technologies, and market forces, when combined with new economic and demographic pressures, suggests the need for more comprehensive approaches to strengthening agricultural education, research, and extension.

2. To that end, AET institutions might be integrated under a single governmental authority that could allocate public financing to institutions on the basis of their strategic goals and performance rather than by following historical precedent or equitable sharing.

References

Johanson, Richard K. and Arvil V. Adams. 2004. *Skills for Development in Sub-Sahara Africa.* World Bank Regional and Sector Studies. World Bank, Washington, D.C.

Stads, Gert-Jan and Nienke M. Beintema. 2006. "Women Scientists in Sub-Saharan African Agricultural R & D." Washington, DC: International Food Policy Research Institute.

Udry, Christopher and John Hoddirott, Harold Alderman and Lawrence Haddad. 1995. "Gender Differentials in Farm Productivity: Implications for Household Efficiency and Agricultural Policy. Food Policy. 20 (2): 407-423.

World Bank. 2007. Cultivating Knowledge and Skills to Grow African Agriculture.

CHAPTER 15

Quality and Gender Equality in Education: What Have We Learned from FAWE's 15 Years of Experience?

Codou Diaw

Introduction

As the leading nongovernmental organization (NGO) advocating for African girls' education over the past 15 years, the Forum for African Women Educationalists (FAWE) has significantly contributed to the advancement of gender issues in education in Sub-Saharan Africa. FAWE's initial mandate was advocacy to put girls' education on the policy agenda of African ministries of education (MoEs) and international donors. FAWE's actions have since evolved to include demonstrative interventions, program implementation, and capacity building for its national chapters. This change in vocation occurred while FAWE was maturing into a network of 32 national chapters,[1] each constituted as an NGO in its own right.

There is ample evidence that FAWE's advocacy work has increased awareness among education policy makers, practitioners, and stakeholders about issues affecting girls' education in Africa. FAWE's work has also resulted in the integration of gender equity issues in numerous national education plans. FAWE's current strategies have focused on educational quality issues through gender-responsive models to transform formal schooling processes for better retention and performance of girls in schools. This work has convinced several African MoEs to adopt or mainstream their gender-responsive educational models developed over the past decade.

In the process FAWE, its national chapters, and its partners have learned many lessons about strategies to improve girls' education and gender equity in education in the African context.

Background and Evolution of FAWE

FAWE was founded in 1992 and registered in 1993 as a pan-African NGO. It is headquartered in Nairobi, Kenya, and has national chapters in 32 countries in Sub-Saharan Africa. FAWE is a membership organization consisting of female ministers and deputy ministers of education, female vice chancellors and deputy vice chancellors, and senior female education policy makers and prominent educationalists. Male ministers of education are associate members of FAWE. Membership at the national chapter level includes both female and male education practitioners, researchers, and gender activists.

The mission and mandate of FAWE is to promote female education in Sub-Saharan Africa. The founding members were profoundly disturbed by the gender gaps in enrollment, retention, and performance in African schools. They envisioned national education systems in which gender disparities would be significantly reduced and more girls would have access to schooling, complete their studies, and perform well at all levels.

During the initial phase of FAWE's existence, concerted efforts were directed at convincing national MoEs and other stakeholders to make girls' education a priority. The focus was on girls' access to universal primary schooling. By 1998, in most part as a result of FAWE's efforts, there was increased awareness about the need and benefits of educating girls among policy makers, education practitioners, and communities in many countries where FAWE operated.

By 2000 the world was paying significant attention to quality as it relates to access and gender issues in education. This was encapsulated in the Education for All (EFA) Dakar Framework for Action and the Millennium Development Goals (MDGs). At the same time, an increasing number of African stakeholders sensitized by FAWE were expressing concern about gender disparities in educational processes and within schools.

During the same period, FAWE realized the need to move beyond advocacy to influencing action in the field to substantially reduce gender disparities in access, retention, and performance. It was also clear to FAWE that the gender parity goal in access could not be achieved without addressing educational quality from a gender perspective. Although FAWE's strength and comparative advantage have been in advocacy since its inception, the changing national and international demands prompted FAWE to move from

- advocacy for girls' education at policy level to influencing policies and plans;
- a focus on universal primary education to transforming classroom processes at a basic education level;
- a focus on girls only to a gender-based approach to education;
- scattered single interventions to a holistic model of transforming a school into a gender-responsive school.

It is in this context that FAWE's Strategic Plan (2002–06) addressed these concerns through four objectives and several strategies for transforming schools and education systems using a gender approach:

- Influencing policy formulation, planning, and implementation by increasing access and improving the retention and performance of girls
- Building through advocacy public awareness and consensus on the social and economic advantages of girls' education
- Demonstrating through interventions in the field how to achieve increased access, improved retention, and better performance of girls
- Influencing replication and mainstreaming of best practices from the demonstrative interventions into broader national education policy and practice

FAWE's experiences in its various national chapters also informed the strategies adopted to reach these goals. These experiences highlighted the need to address several dimensions of girls' education simultaneously to make a lasting impact. This called for an educational model that integrates multiple supply-side and demand-side factors. In addition, even though improving girls' education contributes to the improvement of the entire schooling system, FAWE realized early on that a gender approach is necessary to address the educational needs of both girls and boys.

That is why FAWE's gender-responsive models have been implemented in both single-sex and mixed-sex schools, at both primary and secondary levels. At the national level FAWE demonstrates that these models effectively transform schools, administrations, teachers, students, and community stakeholders. It also endeavors to convince MoEs to replicate and mainstream the models within the national education system.

Although much remains to be done, FAWE has been successful because it has well-designed programs that are adapted to the realities of African education systems and societies. It has also managed to adapt to the changing international, regional, and national contexts surrounding girls' education and gender issues in education. But this success could not occur without the voluntary nature of its membership; the steady support of its many donors; and collaboration with its various international, regional, and national partners.

Overview of Girls' Education in Sub-Saharan Africa

The general outlook for girls' education across the African continent is optimistic. Admittedly, there are numerous challenges in closing the gender gap in access, retention, and achievement. Nevertheless, the United Nations Educational, Scientific, and Cultural Organization's (UNESCO) 2005 Gender Parity Index for Sub-Saharan Africa confirms that access has increased significantly at the primary level and that 11 countries[2] have achieved gender parity at the primary level. Another 8 or so countries are making tremendous progress toward parity. However, parity still eludes 26 countries. Average gross enrollment rates for primary schooling in Sub-Saharan Africa remain lower than those in other regions (see table 15.1).

Transition rates from primary to secondary levels are also rather low. According to UNESCO's Global Monitoring Report 2006, only 65 percent of girls and 67 percent of boys who enter primary school in Africa complete the cycle. Only 21 percent of girls attend secondary school on average, compared with 26 percent of boys. Meanwhile the gender parity target in access for EFA and the MDGs was missed in 2005.

While the gender gap in access is still a challenge in many countries, another challenge is quality and equity. In this regard, FAWE has developed good practices and models that, if adopted by governments, could lead to noteworthy advances in educational quality and gender equity in Africa over the next decade.

Table 15.1 Primary Gross Enrollment Rates

	1990/91			2004		
	Male	Female	Total	Male	Female	Total
Sub-Saharan Africa	88.7	68.3	77.1	96	85	91
World	105.7	93.1	99.5	109	103	106

Source: UNESCO 2006.

FAWE's Major Achievements

Through its national chapters and in collaboration with MoEs and other key African education sector players, FAWE has made significant strides in promoting girls' education (see table 15.2). During the past 15 years, some of the major achievements that FAWE can take some credit for include the following:

- Establishing a strong network of grassroots organizations promoting female education in Sub-Saharan Africa. The structure and composition of FAWE's membership at national levels has allowed for more effective awareness raising about the socioeconomic benefits of educating girls at the grassroots level. One successful example is the creation of an FM radio station by the Ghana chapter. Dedicated solely to the promotion of girls' education, its programs reach out to hundreds of communities.
- Mainstreaming gender-fair practices into national education policies and plans in several countries. FAWE's advocacy at a policy level for pregnant girls and young mothers to continue their educations resulted in the adoption of a reentry policy in 13 countries across Sub-Saharan Africa (Burkina Faso, Ethiopia, Ghana, Guinea, Kenya, Malawi, Mozambique, Namibia, Nigeria, Tanzania [Zanzibar], Uganda, Zambia). Because of FAWE's constant lobbying, several countries have adopted the following policies: effective provision of free and compulsory basic education; provision of gender-responsive school infrastructure, especially separate restrooms for boys and girls; an increase in the number of female teachers as role models; affirmative admission policies; sanctions against early marriages and sexual harassment; appointment of more women education managers; and gender-responsive budgetary allocations.

- Empowering youth, especially girls, using the TUSEME (let us speak out) empowerment model in more than 300 schools. This model uses theater to empower students to speak out about the problems hindering their personal and academic development. It equips students with skills to analyze the root causes of the problems they face, find solutions, and take action to address the problems. As a result of the TUSEME process, students, particularly adolescent girls, are also equipped with life skills such as assertiveness, decision making, leadership, and negotiation.
- Creating and developing the Gender-Responsive School or the FAWE Center of Excellence (COE) model. The crux of this model is to create a gender-responsive environment in schools using a holistic approach. The model consists of an intervention package of strategies to effectively address the barriers to girls' education in the academic, social, and physical school environments and surrounding community. This model has been undertaken in nine countries (Burkina Faso, Chad, The Gambia, Guinea, Kenya, Namibia, Senegal, Tanzania, and Zambia).
- Creating and developing the Gender-Responsive Pedagogy Model. As a result of its work in the COEs, FAWE realized the need to build the capacity of teachers in gender responsiveness. The FAWE Gender-Responsive Pedagogy Model has been used to enhance teachers' ability to make teaching and learning processes more inclusive for both genders. This model has now been mainstreamed in teacher training in three countries (Senegal, Tanzania, and Zimbabwe).
- Promoting girls' participation in science, mathematics, and technology (SMT) subjects in 12 countries (Burkina Faso, Cameroon, Kenya, Malawi, Mali, Mozambique, Swaziland, Tanzania [Zanzibar], Uganda, Zambia, and Zimbabwe).
- Documenting seven FAWE best practices in girls' education that have emerged from various demonstrative interventions:
  - Ghana: Peer education to protect girls from HIV/AIDS
  - Kenya: Addressing HIV/AIDS in relation to girls' education
  - Kenya, Rwanda, Senegal, and Tanzania: Transforming an ordinary school into a COE
  - Sierra Leone: Providing girls' education under conflict situations
  - Uganda: Addressing sexual maturation in relation to education of girls
  - Tanzania: *TUSEME* (empowerment of girls)
  - Zambia: School reentry for adolescent mothers

Table 15.2 FAWE's Key Interventions and Initiatives

Model/initiative	No. of Schools	No. of Countries
GRP – gender-responsive pedagogy (TT + manuals + learner-focused methods)	44	12
TUSEME – Girls' empowerment, leadership, and life skills training	300	12
Bursaries to needy girls	+200	17
Boarding and eating facilities (rescue centers for vulnerable girls)	7 (Kenya, Tanzania, Rwanda)	7
Guidance and counseling services (including peer counseling)	7 (Kenya, Tanzania, Rwanda)	7
HIV prevention	+200	7
Sexual maturation coaching	+30	1 (Uganda)
Promotion of girls' participation in SMT	+40	14
Community sensitization (mothers' clubs)	+400	5
Improvement of physical environment of schools	13	10
Close collaboration with MoE (ownership and mainstreaming) – signing of MOU	–	14

- Establishing stronger partnerships between FAWE national chapters and MoEs for the promotion of girls' education through the signing of memoranda of understanding (MOUs). So far 14 national chapters have strengthened and institutionalized their relationship by signing such agreements.

Components of FAWE's Gender-Responsive School or Center of Excellence (COE) Model

A FAWE COE is a school where the physical, academic, and social environments are gender-responsive (see figure 15.1). FAWE's vision for the COE is a school with the following characteristics in each area.

Physical Environment

The physical environment should include such adequate and gender-appropriate infrastructure as separate, private, and secure restroom facilities for girls and boys; secure classrooms with an adequate space utilization ratio; science and information and communication technology laboratories; library space; adequate desks, chairs, and classroom and laboratory equipment; sports and recreation facilities; secure and separate dormitories for girls and boys with nearby matron's houses; adequate dining facilities; amenities such as water, electricity, and health facilities; adequate security such as fencing and lighting.

Academic Environment

Both boy and girl students are empowered with skills in self-expression, assertiveness, confidence, leadership, and decision making; protection against HIV/AIDS; and good academic performance. Girls confidently participate in SMT and perform well. Financially disadvantaged girls have scholarships and access to career guidance. Girls are creative and innovative and think critically. There is an equal number of girls and boys. Where necessary, affirmative action for girls is practiced.

Male and female teachers and managers are adequately trained in gender-responsive pedagogy and methodologies, and they put them into practice. Teaching and learning materials are rid of gender bias and are available in adequate numbers.

Social Environment

Community members participate in school life and in their children's education. They are sensitized about the benefits of educating girls as well as the need to provide a safe, harassment-free, girl-friendly environment for them to learn.

Challenges Related to the Achievement of FAWE's Strategic Objectives 2002–06

Influencing Policy

Despite some achievements in gender mainstreaming in the African education sector, FAWE national chapters could be more involved and influential in making education policies and plans comprehensively gender responsive. Many chapters still lack a full understanding of the bureaucratic processes of national education policy formulation. In addition, many national chapters face obstacles in participating effectively in the wider education reform processes, including sectorwide approaches, Sector Investment Programs, the UN Girls' Education Initiative, Poverty Reduction Strategy Papers, the Education for All Fast-Track Initiative, and the like. Where national chapters have the opportunity to participate in policy-formulation processes, their contribution is sometimes hampered by not using evidence-based information. Many FAWE national chapters have not yet managed to effectively translate gender-responsive policies and plans into action.

Advocacy

Advocacy for girls' education is FAWE's greatest strength. However, now that there is awareness at international and national levels, FAWE's advocacy needs to be better targeted toward the community level, where the barriers to girls' education are most acute. This entails sharpening the national chapters' capacity for community-based advocacy.

Demonstrative Interventions

Many FAWE national chapters have undertaken successful interventions that have demonstrated what works in improving access, retention, and performance. However, many chapters still require additional skills for effective program planning, implementation, monitoring and evaluation, and resource mobilization.

Replication and Mainstreaming

Because of the high demand for action, some national chapters have had to scale up their interventions beyond demonstration, even though FAWE's mandate is to demonstrate rather than undertake large-scale interventions (which is the role of the MoE). National chapters, therefore, need to be equipped with skills on how to document successful models and practices that have emerged from their demonstration interventions so they can use them to influence MoEs. Challenges also relate to the wider socioeconomic and cultural context within African countries.

Overall Challenges

Despite the world's commitment to gender equality and equity in education, the gender parity goals for access, set in the EFA and MDG declarations, are far from being achieved. Although there has been some success in improving access, many challenges remain in improving retention and performance of girls. This calls for FAWE to scale up its efforts while continuing to undertake interventions that demonstrate what works in addressing barriers to girls' education.

Table 15.3   Impact in FAWE's Four Pilot COEs

Academic Performance	Empowerment of Girls
• Improved national exam score for girls 66% in 2000 to 75% in 2002 Kenya—Kadjado Girls' School • 6 COE girls among top 10 students nationally in 2003 Rwanda—FAWE Girls' School • Higher passing grades for more girls 47% in 2001 -> 69% in 2003 Senegal—CEM Gd Diourbel • Better national ranking of COE students in form 2 at national exam 169 in 2002 -> 72 in 2003 Tanzania—Mgugu Secondary School for Girls	• Reduction in teenage pregnancy Less than 1% in all 4 COEs • More girls in school committees and leadership roles • More participation of girls in classroom processes • Higher retention rates for girls • Low dropout rates • Boys in mixed schools with higher gender awareness make gender relationships much easier within schools and surrounding communities

Source: FAWE 2003.

Other cross-cutting or emerging issues also add to the challenges of promoting gender equality in education. For example, armed conflict still constitutes a barrier to the provision of education in a number of African countries. HIV/AIDS is still ravaging the continent, leading to numerous orphans and children heading households, particularly in southern Africa. Socio-cultural gender biases against women and girls still pervade many African societies and are often used to justify early marriage, gender-based violence, female circumcision, and a low value placed on girls' education.

Poverty continues to hamper socioeconomic development and adversely affects participation in education, for both girls and boys. High unemployment rates are rampant across the continent, thus contributing to the perception of schooling being a useless investment. FAWE faces the challenge of moving beyond the formal education system and developing skill and vocational training models that provide girls with an education that prepares them for employment.

African education systems as whole, as well as the environment under which education is provided, are still not gender responsive. Teacher training, for example, has continued to exclude gender in its curricula. Consequently, FAWE needs to constantly respond to all these and other emerging issues.

Lessons Learned

FAWE has drawn lessons not only from the challenges it faces, but also from its successes. These lessons will continue to inform and guide its future operations. Promoting gender equity in education is an uphill endeavor that requires institutional and community-based partnerships. For mainstreaming efforts to be viable and lasting, MoEs must be involved from the initial stages. The signing of MOUs with MoEs helps ensure the institutionalization of FAWE-government relationships, even in the context of frequent changes in MoE leadership. This has also led to garnering political support that is crucially needed for long-term mainstreaming efforts. FAWE will pursue these types of agreements in all countries where it has national chapters.

FAWE has realized that to maximize the effectiveness of its actions, it must apply a multidimensional approach. Combining advocacy with demonstration leads to replication for the final outcome of mainstreaming. Advocacy at the policy level alone is clearly not enough. FAWE must equally target practitioners and all community stakeholders. Likewise, girls' access to primary schooling is not a panacea. Quality and equity in schooling processes as well as gender-fair learning materials are equally if not more important for high rates of retention and performance.

Improving the quality of education for both girls and boys requires gender-responsive approaches that go beyond the school to reach communities and other practitioners. Gender equity and equality in education cannot continue to be considered as limited, local elements, but rather must be mainstreamed, operationalized, and budgeted for at all levels of education policy making and practice.

Transformation of teaching and learning processes are crucial for retention and performance of girls in schools. For transformative education to be achieved, school environments for both girls and boys must be conducive to learning. Female and male teachers and administrators must be continuously trained to integrate gender-responsive processes and methods into their daily work. Otherwise, gender-based approaches will continue to be extraneous to teaching and learning processes and applied on only a limited basis.

To avoid dispersion, duplication, and the "short-term project syndrome," it is crucial to conduct consolidated interventions that address various dimensions of education at once and from a gender perspective. Single interventions may provide immediate solutions, but integrated, holistic, adapted solutions such as the FAWE COE model may yield higher returns in the medium to long term. However, depending on local conditions and realities, specific interventions should be incorporated where needed, particularly in conflict and postconflict situations, in HIV/AIDS-stricken communities, and in communities with practices that are harmful to girls and that impede their retention and performance in schools.

As an organization, FAWE has also learned about its own capacity to deliver and to effectively scale up its models and interventions. Chapters that have better technical and human resource capacity tend to have better results in influencing policy and replicating models at national levels. The weak capacity of some FAWE chapters has led to their overwhelming preference for demonstrative interventions or donor-driven activities at the national and local levels.

Consequently, FAWE has learned that capacity building for its chapters is crucial for strengthening their ability to contribute effectively in policy processes, influencing education-related decision-making, and implementing solid programs in line with FAWE's strategic goals. In addition, strengthening activities must include resource mobilization training to ensure that chapters are able to access needed resources at the national and local levels. The voluntary nature of FAWE's membership base is a great asset that needs to be retained and nurtured.

However, for an NGO like FAWE to pursue its mission, it must build up its human resource base by hiring committed, qualified, well-trained, and well-remunerated staff.

This issue goes to the heart of funding predictability and reliability. The establishment of a donors' consortium, composed of multilateral and bilateral donors and a few foundations, has allowed continuous funding for the implementation of FAWE's strategic plan and annual work programs since 2003. However, the changing context of educational development financing requires widening the donors' consortium to include other types of donors and diversifying funding sources, particularly targeting the private sector and individual donors. To that end, the creation of an endowment fund will contribute to less reliance on restricted institutional funding.

Indeed, seeking out private sector donors is another way of widening FAWE's partnership base, with the goal of advancing girls' education in Africa. Experiences through the SMT program have proven that it is both feasible and fruitful.

Conclusion and Way Forward

FAWE's membership of ministers of education and other senior policy makers in education has ensured that policy reform in favor of girls' education remains a high priority on the agenda of African governments and education stakeholders. FAWE will continue to play an important role as advocate, watchdog, lead demonstrator, and provider of technical expertise on gender issues in African education. FAWE will continue to nurture its relationship with MoEs to replicate, scale up, and mainstream recognized best practices in girls' education. And FAWE will continue to connect with other advocacy partners to keep the girls' education agenda alive at the international, regional, and national levels.

At the program level, FAWE's national chapters will continue to use demonstration interventions as laboratories for generating innovative best practices in girls' education.

But consolidating FAWE's programs from the previous strategic plan may be appropriate. The COE or gender-responsive school model provides a good avenue for integrating most FAWE approaches into a minimum intervention package, supplemented by additional features where and when necessary.

In other words, a basic COE model will include gender-responsive training for teachers, managers, and students; provision of scholarships for economically disadvantaged girls or elimination of school fees; gender-fair manuals and facilities; attention to the physical aspects of the school; empowerment of girls and boys; and links with the community.[3] A supplemental package will include specific interventions to respond to a particular need or context. This may include HIV/AIDS education and prevention, dormitories, rescue centers for girls, counseling desks, vocational training, and the like. However, before going that route, the COE, as well as other FAWE models, will be evaluated on a large scale to ascertain their value added and to validate earlier successful results.

Beyond access, retention, and performance at primary-level schooling, FAWE must continue to focus on transition to secondary school, with a special focus on quality, achievement, and attainment for girls. In that regard, great attention must be given to vocational and professional training and SMT training for girls. This would ensure that girls are channeled into fields that can lead to employment and that girls have not entered in high numbers because of many factors. This could also ensure that girls who drop out of secondary school have other outlets for continuing their education or acquiring skills they can immediately apply in the job market.

FAWE's new programs will emphasize education in conflict or post-conflict situations, especially with the establishment of new chapters (Angola, the Democratic Republic of Congo, Somalia, and southern Sudan). Much can be learned from FAWE's experiences in Liberia, Rwanda, and Sierra Leone. Emphasis will also be put on vocational and technical training for girls who are out of the formal education system.

Given that Early Childhood Development and Education (ECDE) is part of basic education and EFA, it is within FAWE's mandate to focus on this subsector. The education of girls does not start at primary school. Instilling certain values in girls, as well as boys, at an early age can actually help eradicate gender biases and inequities before they pervade children's minds and attitudes. FAWE intends to develop gender-responsive tools for ECDE practitioners as well as work with the Associate for the Development of Education in Africa (ADEA) Working Group on Early Childhood Development to advocate for ECDE policies that are gender responsive.

In FAWE's Strategic Plan 2008–12, the regional secretariat role will be geared more toward monitoring and evaluation and providing capacity building to national chapters to facilitate replicating and mainstreaming of FAWE's demonstrative interventions. This will require increased training delivered by the regional secretariat, which is why FAWE will endeavor to set up a Regional Training and Resource Center for Gender Responsiveness in Education. The center would ensure the quality, uniformity, and reliability of FAWE's training and capacity-building activities. Given that FAWE covers 32 countries, the Regional Training and Resource Center would greatly reduce the travel and workload of FAWE program officers so that they can develop training modules and conduct monitoring and evaluation activities.

Finally, the role of research in informing and contributing to the improvement of FAWE's work cannot be overemphasized. Gender-based action research on FAWE programs, interventions, and national chapters would greatly enhance the impact and outcome of FAWE's action for the promotion of girls' education in Africa. FAWE intends to link up with gender-in-education researchers based inside and outside Africa to harness the potential of research for informing and improving girls' education and gender equity in Africa.

Quality and Gender Equality in Education   267

Notes

Thanks to Forum for African Women Educationalists Program Officers Lornah Murage and Marema Dioum for providing input for this chapter.

1. New chapters are being established in Angola, the Democratic Republic of Congo, Somalia, and southern Sudan.
2. Botswana, the Republic of Congo, Kenya, Lesotho, Madagascar, Malawi, Mauritius, Namibia, Rwanda, Swaziland, and Zambia.
3. The list is not exhaustive.

References

UNESCO (2006). EFA Global Monotitoring Report.

FAWE (2004). Creating a Conducive School Environment: The FAWE Centre of Excellence in Kenya.

FAWE (2007). Programme Implementation Report.

CHAPTER 16

Strategies for Gender Equality in Basic and Secondary Education: A Comprehensive and Integrated Approach in the Republic of Yemen

Tawfiq A. Al-Mekhlafy

Since the birth of the Republic of Yemen in the early 1960s, education has been central to the Republic's struggle for development—a struggle characterized by the lack of a modern teaching workforce, by overwhelming illiteracy and "rurality," by poor management expertise, and by few resources.

The Ministry of Education undertook all possible means to secure free access to education for all children. School enrollment gradually increased. But in a traditional society and in a mostly rural country like the Republic of Yemen, urban children outnumbered rural children in schools, and boys outnumbered girls. It thus became clear toward the end of the 1980s that without government intervention, gender and rural-urban gaps in enrollment would become wider and wider.

The Ministry of Education has adopted a strategic plan to ensure sustainable, integrated interventions aimed at achieving universal basic education by 2015. The interventions focus on both improving the low general enrollment (boys and girls together) and narrowing the gender gap—goals that require integrated, multidimensional, and persistent interventions.

Where Are We Now?

The gross enrollment ratio (GER) for basic school (grades 1–9) jumped from 65.4 percent in 2004 to 75.8 percent in 2006. The rates for girls jumped from 50.9 to 63.7 percent and for boys from 79.7 to 87.0 percent over the same two years. The faster improvement of girls' enrollment has narrowed the gender gap from 28.8 to 23.3 percent—5.5 percentage points in two years (Ministry of Education 2007).

The first-grade gender gap in 2006 was 12.6 percent with a global gender parity index (GPI) of 0.83, projecting a brighter future for girls' education in the Republic of Yemen (Ministry of Education 2007). If one looks at completion rates, girls are doing even better than boys—for every 100 children who start basic school, 67 boys and 75 girls reach ninth grade (Ministry of Education 2007).

This bright picture is mirrored in secondary school (grades 10–12). While the number of girls enrolled in basic school grew by 86 percent and the number of boys by 14 percent in 1997–2003, the number of girls in secondary school grew by 162 percent and the number of boys by 60 percent (Ataa 2005).

The strategies adopted by the Ministry of Education to enhance enrollment in general and girls' enrollment in particular—to achieve the goal of universal basic education by 2015—are apparently working quite well.

But the gender gap, as table 16.1 demonstrates, is much more severe in rural areas, indicating that the problem is more of a development problem than a gender problem. This may be illustrated by the writer's own village (now a town). Two decades ago a girl used to assist her mother with household chores, such as fetching water and wood for cooking or looking after her younger brothers and sisters. So, few girls enrolled in school. Nowadays, drinking water is piped to every house, gas has replaced cooking wood, and mothers have nothing to do but household tasks. Basic school GER is now 100 percent, and all girls of secondary school age, except for those few who have gotten married, are in school.

Table 16.1 Gaps in Basic Education
(2003 gross enrollment ratios)

Gender	Basic	Secondary				
			Urbanization			Urbanization
	Urban	Rural	gap	Urban	Rural	gap
Boys	102.4	84.3	−18.1	79.5	51.6	−27.9
Girls	87.2	36.3	−50.9	63.9	10.8	−53.1
Gender gap	−15.2	−61.0		−15.6	−40.8	

Source: Ataa 2005.

Interventions to increase access to education thus need to focus on the needs of rural communities. Moreover, all development ministries, not just the Ministry of Education, need to invest in the countryside to address the root of the problem.

Current Interventions

Within the framework of the Basic Education Development Strategy (2003–2015), the first Medium-Term Results Framework (MTRF 2006–2010), and the newly launched Secondary Education Strategy (2007), interventions are integrated in their planning and implementation.

Interventions are grouped into three components—access, quality, and institutional capacity—that complement each other, working together toward the global goal of universal quality basic education. This integration was instrumental in the development of the Secondary Education Strategy; fewer girls dropped out of the upper grades of basic school when a secondary school was nearby. Moreover, talks are now underway to incorporate all strategic educational plans in one integrated strategy.

Access

There are several efforts to increase enrollment and reduce dropouts by improving access to education.

School construction. Construction projects include building new schools and additional classrooms, rehabilitating others, and making existing schools friendlier by adding lavatories and rooms for out-of-class activities. Table 16.2 shows the main construction projects implemented and underway in 2006/07.

Table 16.2   Construction Projects in 2006/07

Status	School	Classroom added	Classroom rehabilitated	Lavatories	Fences	Activity rooms	Cost (US$)
Implemented	1,036	4,681	1,603	2,368	207	120	618,943
Underway	3,235	13,380	1,735	5,124	1,176	206	177,597*

Source: Ministry of Education 2007.

Note: *Disbursement by the time of writing the source report.

Financial incentives. Incentives take several forms. In 2006, 412,310 girls and poor students benefited from the supply of school meals. In the same year, school kits were provided for 67,760 children in 361 schools in four governorates supported by Education for All Fast-Track Initiative (Ministry of Education 2007). (Figures of schools supported by the United Nations Children Fund are not available.)

A more universal incentive policy is the government decree to exempt girls in grades 1–6 and boys in grades 1–3 from textbooks fees in 2005/06. Preliminary evaluation of its impact is positive (see table 16.3).

Finally, a conditional cash transfer program is still in the pilot phase. Under this program, all girls in grades 4–9 are eligible for a cash transfer conditional on attending school at least 80 percent of each two-month class period and on being promoted to the next grade. The program allows a girl to repeat a grade once before grade 9, but a second repetition, even in a different grade, will make the girl ineligible for the cash transfer. In addition, girls in grades 6 and 8 are eligible for a bonus if they achieve a 65 percent overall mark in the school grade-end examinations.

More female teachers. A female teacher is a role model and creates a more secure environment for girls, especially for those in grades 4 and above. Female teachers have proven effective in increasing enrollment and reducing dropouts.

The Ministry of Education has taken four measures to increase the number of female teachers, especially in rural areas. First, to keep female teachers from leaving rural schools for cities, teaching positions are tied to a specific school. Thus, while a teacher may leave a school, the position will remain vacant for any potential teacher willing to teach in that school.

Second, a teacher redeployment policy is underway. Presently, some areas, especially urban areas, have a surplus of teachers, while others have too few teachers, particularly female teachers.

Table 16.3   Enrollment Growth between 2005/06 and 2006/07
(percent)

Gender	Grade	Urban	Rural
Boys	1	22.0	27.4
	2	3.8	14.0
	3	–0.1	8.0
Girls	1	23.1	34.0
	2	15.3	13.5
	3	4.3	16.1
	4	2.2	24.9
	5	15.5	20.8
	6	1.7	16.2

Source: Al Mansoob 2007.

Note: The sample is 196 schools—25 urban and 171 rural.

Third, an exception has been made to the civil service law that prevents hiring people without university degrees. The exception allows donors to contract with females who have graduated from secondary school in rural areas and train them to teach in their own areas. After the women have taught for two to three years, the Ministry must employ them permanently.

Finally, the Ministry of Education has allocated more teaching posts to females out of the number of teaching positions allocated by the Ministry of Civil Service.

School management. With a budget of US$8,439,452 for the year 2007, the Ministry of Education's school management program covers training school managers, enhancing community participation, and piloting school-based operational budgeting. Several donors are working on this program, including Germany (Gessellschaft für Technische Zusammenarbeit), Japan (the Japan International Cooperation Agency), the United Kingdom (Department for International Development), and the United States (United States Agency of International Development).

Quality

The five-year MTRF has made the reform of curriculum, learning assessments, and learning support materials a top priority, in addition to continuing teacher and inspector training. The plan is to begin with curricular reviews to develop a relevant, gender-sensitive, competency-based curriculum. Learning assessments and support materials will then be reformed based on the new curriculum—an example of the integration and multidimensionality of strategies.

The Ministry of Education's 2007 plan allocated US$493,185,113 for these reforms, 68 percent of the plan budget. Like any qualitative reform, evaluation of the components' effectiveness will not be feasible for a few years.

Institutional Capacity

The Ministry of Education is being restructured and its central and local managerial staff trained for more effective administration and coordination of planning and implementing development strategies. Staff training is already underway, as is the development of the Education Management Information System and the Monitoring and Evaluation System.

Three years ago, the Ministry set up a girls' education sector, headed by a woman deputy minister. The chief purpose of the sector is to boost girls' education. The sector is staffed mostly by women and is represented in all meetings and task forces having to do with planning, implementing, and monitoring planned activities.

Obstacles to Universal Education

These interventions are taking place in an environment filled with obstacles that affect the rapidity and effectiveness of action, as can be seen from the following.

Poverty—A General Hurdle

Poverty hinders girls' education by affecting individual parents' decisions as well as the government's urbanization and educational efforts. The government of the Republic of Yemen has been doing its best to combat the effects of poverty on individual parents through the incentive programs described previously, even though these programs are a burden on its budget.

Poverty will continue to impede development in the country, however, unless the international community extends its hands. Poverty's most immediate impact is on education—given the fact that education is needed by every household, if not every individual—delaying educational achievement for many. Large rural families will keep giving priority to boys as long as they have more girls and boys. The cost of schooling—textbook fees, uniforms, bags, notebooks, and other supplies—limits how many children a poor family can afford to send to school. Can the pilot conditional cash transfer program succeed in covering such costs for educating additional children? If it does, can it be universalized and sustained, given that the pilot cash transfer program is now funded externally?

The Ministry of Education's budget is already under pressure because of making schools more accessible to girls, covering the textbook fees for millions of children, and serving thousands of small hamlets scattered over a mountainous terrain.

In short, the incentives are clearly working, but are they sustainable? According to Al Mansoob's survey (2007), schools are starting to complain about budgetary shortages created by abolishing textbook fees. Key to sustainability is the development of the rural 70 percent of the state.

Illiteracy—A Challenge to Gender Equality

The illiteracy rate in the Republic of Yemen is one of the highest in the world: 45 percent of the population older than 15 and 60 percent of women are illiterate. In a traditional, mostly rural, society, the value of everything is estimated in terms of money. Thus, because financial returns cannot be expected from most women in rural areas (who do not have their own farms), there is no value in sending girls to school, especially if their schooling will cost their parents and be at the expense of her household and farm tasks. A girl's time is better spent in doing such tasks than in getting an education.

Because it is difficult for illiterate parents to see the value of girls' education, education reform must demonstrate the value of education. Making the curriculum relevant and training educators to value education themselves so that they can convey that message to parents and students will help counteract the effect of illiteracy.

Literacy programs, which used to be tackled separately, are now incorporated into the programs and plans of the Basic Education Development Strategy. Literacy awareness campaigns have been part of several plans in the past, but they did not prove as fruitful as expected. Thus the government is encouraging greater community involvement through community participation programs as an alternative strategy. In the past five years, hundreds of mothers' councils have been set up, and the process continues.

As with poverty reduction, rural development is the more comprehensive and sustainable solution to illiteracy.

Quality Education—A Very Demanding Factor

Quality is essential to the effective performance of all parts of the education system, but quality demands money, time, and expertise. The quality component of the Ministry of Education's 2007 plan is just more than two-thirds of the three-component plan. Time is needed to create quality curricula, assessments, support materials, and training programs. Expertise is also a requirement, as well as an outcome, of quality reforms. The Republic of Yemen's previous curriculum reviews have fallen short of producing modern and relevant instruction materials because the necessary expertise was lacking.

The Ministry of Education has realized that focusing on access to education at the expense of quality education will serve neither. They must go hand in hand. The Ministry of Education can take the time required to develop quality education, but it will need determined support from the international community to have the necessary funds and expertise. And sustainability remains a concern.

Previous curricular reviews were supported by money and expertise from abroad, but much more determined support is needed for the demanding reforms currently planned.

A promising initiative for supporting quality education is the establishment of the Centre of Measurement and Evaluation (CoME). The construction of its building is now complete and its systemic structure has been concluded. Still needed is the financial and expert support to operate a professional Centre of Measurement and Evaluation that can monitor quality reforms throughout the implementation process.

The performance of quality reform programs will surely characterize the performance of the other component programs. Thus, all development partners should work with the Ministry of Education to help make quality a reality.

A Concluding Word

The Ministry of Education has realized that basic education reform will not be effective without secondary education reform. An integrated, multidimensional approach is thus a necessity. The following are the instruments of such an approach:

- The Secondary Education Development Strategy was launched in August 2007.
- The Secondary Girls' Education Project was launched in early 2007.
- The Medium-Term Results Framework and its Medium-Term Expenditure Framework were devised to implement the Basic Education Strategy.
- The annual budget of the Ministry of Education in 2007 was program-based for the first time.
- Preparations are underway for integrating educational strategies—basic, secondary, adult literacy, and girls—in a single development strategy.

References

Al Mansoob, M. 2007. "Household and School Survey on the Impact of School Fee Abolition: Preliminary Results." Paper presented at the Third Joint Annual Review Conference, Sana'a, Yemen, May 7–9.

Ataa, M. 2005. "Statistical Analysis of the Secondary Education Trends and Its Development for the Period 1998/1999–2003/2004." Background paper for the Secondary Education Strategy, Yemen Ministry of Education.

Ministry of Education. 2007. "Annual Progress Report on the Implementation of the National Basic Education Development Strategy." Paper presented to the Third Joint Annual Review conference, Sana'a, Yemen, May 7–9.

CHAPTER 17

Conclusion and Recommendations for the Way Forward

Mercy Tembon

The preceding chapters provide clear evidence that it is possible to improve gender equality in education if the right policies and interventions are put in place, and if the interventions are evaluated on the basis of gender-disaggregated data. Successful interventions span community-level programs attuned to local values and norms (Afghanistan, chapter 11); initiatives to increase the demand for education by reducing or eliminating user fees (Mali and Colombia, chapter 12); programs that use fiscal incentives to achieve the modernization and gender equalization of religious educational institutions (Bangladesh, chapter 13); plans to genderize postbasic agricultural education and training (Sub-Saharan Africa, chapter 14); nongovernmental associations that advocate for female education and gender-sensitive pedagogy (Africa, chapter 15); and comprehensive national interventions that seek to simultaneously strengthen educational quality and reduce gender disparities (the Republic of Yemen, chapter 16).

The evidence presented in this book shows why progress in gender equity has not been more consistent. Significant numbers of children—particularly girls and those suffering from disadvantages such as disability, poverty, orphanhood, living in conflict situations, and belonging to ethno-linguistic minority groups—are still excluded from school. Even where schools exist and children are enrolled, education systems in developing countries are failing to teach the children they have reached. Teachers are often unqualified, teaching and learning materials are either absent or in short supply, and teachers receive little to no support from professional education inspectors because of long distances between schools and urban centers. The playing field at postprimary schools is even less level in terms of educational preparation for the labor market. Wide gender differences persist between the type of studies followed by males and females, with females taking more courses in the social sciences (notably education and health), while males are overly represented in physical science programs (for example, engineering and technology). Upon graduation, the labor market earnings of females are typically lower than those of males.

Failure to address these gender inequality issues by 2015 will result in missed opportunities to increase economic growth and improve a wide range of human development indicators (see box 17.1). In the words of Hanushek, "Women are equal to men in their potential contribution to economic outcomes, and this equality implies a huge untapped reservoir of talent in many developing countries" (chapter 2).

Strategic Directions for the Future

What can be done to accelerate achievement of the gender equality goal by 2015? This chapter builds on the findings of previous chapters to elaborate five strategic directions for future education interventions that will enhance gender equality in education:

- Improve the *quality* of education and *learning outcomes* at all levels.
- Focus on *hard-to-reach, disadvantaged, vulnerable, and excluded* groups, especially girls.
- Invest in *postprimary education* for girls, particularly at the *secondary level*.
- Increase *research* and analysis on links between gender, poverty reduction, and growth, and improve the presentation of *data disaggregated by sex,* which will adequately inform policy and decision making.

Box 17.1

Externalities of Girls' Education

- *Promotes per capita income growth:* Increasing the share of women with secondary education by 1 percent boosts annual per capita income growth by 0.3 percent on average (Dollar and Gatti 1999).
- *Increases women's labor force participation rates and earnings:* Providing an extra year of schooling for girls beyond the average boosts eventual wages by 1,020 percent (Psacharopoulos and Patrinos 2002).
- *Lowers infant and child mortality rates:* An additional year of female schooling reduces the probability of child mortality by 5 to 10 percentage points (Schultz 1993).
- *Lowers maternal mortality rates:* An additional year of schooling for 1,000 women helps prevent two maternal deaths (UNICEF 2003).
- *Protects against HIV/AIDS infection:* Ugandan females with secondary education are three times less likely to be HIV positive than those with no education (DeWalque 2004).
- *Creates intergenerational education benefits:* Each additional year of formal education completed by a mother translates into her children remaining in school for an additional one-third to one-half year (Filmer 2000).
- *Reduces fertility rates:* The fertility rate of a woman drops by almost one birth when she gains four additional years of education (Klasen 1999).
- *Empowers women:* Educated women are likely to participate more in household decisions and take a stand for themselves, thus reducing their vulnerability to domestic violence (Sen 1999).
- *Promotes good governance:* Education improves the chances of a woman's civic participation and improves the prospects for better governance and democracy in their countries (Barro 1999).
- *Enables women to reject adverse cultural practices:* In Egypt women with secondary education are four times more likely to oppose the practice of female genital cutting (El-Gabaly 2006).

- Strengthen ***partnerships*** with development agencies, nonprofit organizations, the private sector, and community organizations to effectively implement sector programs for the achievement of gender equality in education.

The remainder of this chapter discusses recommended priority actions in each of these strategic directions, with examples of innovative and successful experiences used to illustrate the issues. It then concludes with a discussion of recommendations for the World Bank.

Quality and Learning Outcomes
Improve the quality of education and learning outcomes at all levels.
To ensure that education systems adequately prepare girls and boys for effective participation in the labor market and economic development, there is a strong need to focus on delivering results. Interventions seeking to improve the quality of education should be assessed for results in both access and learning achievement. Learning objectives need to be more specifically defined and better linked to specific indicators that can be regularly monitored for girls and boys. Interventions accordingly need to identify a range of inputs, defined as a set of indicators, required to produce the desired outcomes and then measure these indicators during implementation. The following actions are proposed.

Define standards and assess learning outcomes. Standards align curricula with instruction and assessment, serve as a guide for classroom instruction, and provide a measure of accountability. Not only are they intended to make expectations clear and measurable, they also serve as a basis for benchmarking progress. For example, member countries of the Organisation for Economic Co-operation and Development have established standards for their education systems, most of which are reflected and tested in international assessments, such as the Programme for International Student Assessment and Progress in International Reading Literacy Study. Similarly, the Southern Africa Consortium for Monitoring Educational Quality uses standards set by Ministries of National Education to assess and compare learning outcomes against these standards.

Improve the quality of teachers. The quality of teacher-student relationships and the quality of classroom pedagogies (that is, those that encourage children to participate in class, think critically, ask questions, and master the basic skills and competences required by the curriculum) are also extremely important for improving the learning outcomes of girls and boys. Research from Tennessee in the United States, for example, reveals that two students with average performance will diverge by more than 50 percentile points over a three-year period, depending on the teacher to whom they are assigned (Mckinsey and Co. 2007).

Provide a conducive learning environment and address school-based violence. The environment in which children learn can greatly influence their academic performance and well-being in school. Facilities, materials, teacher-student and student-student interactions in classrooms all play a vital role in shaping the learning environment for the child. In addition to making classrooms more child and girl friendly, steps need to be taken to address school-based and school-related violence to provide a safe educational environment for all students. School-based violence and predatory sexual behavior are widespread (if rarely discussed) in Sub-Saharan Africa. Girls often fall victim to sexual advances from teachers for fear of bad grades. In other instances, outsiders such as taxi cab drivers (South Africa) may offer poor girls food and money for school in exchange for sexual favors. Not only is this harmful for the psyche of young girls, it is also dangerous for their physical health. In addition, it discourages families from sending their girls to school.

While existing initiatives, such as the Safe Schools Program funded by the U.S. Agency for International Development (USAID, see box 17.2), are attempting to tackle this issue, more grassroots initiatives involving community organizations and girls' and boys' youth groups are needed to change attitudes and remove the long-held taboo against discussing these problems. In addition, leaders and policy makers alike must advocate against gender-based violence.

Prevent and protect children, especially girls, from the threat of HIV/AIDS and other health issues. Poor health, malnutrition, and social pressures caused by HIV/AIDS are crucial underlying factors for low school enrollment, absenteeism, poor classroom performance, and early school dropout, as reflected in the World Declaration on Education for All (EFA). HIV/AIDS affects the supply of education through increased teacher mortality and absenteeism, forcing education systems to recruit and train more teachers as well as increase their resources for HIV/AIDS care and treatment. The epidemic also reduces the demand for education because orphans and vulnerable children are less likely to attend school as a result of economic and social constraints. Stigma and discrimination from AIDS have been found to be major factors in excluding children, particularly girls, from school. Yet recent studies show that school attendance helps prevents the spread of the disease, and girls' education counts

Box 17.2

The Safe Schools Program: Preventing Gender-Based Violence and the Spread of HIV/AIDS

The Safe Schools Project is a five-year initiative (2003–2008) currently being piloted in Ghana and Malawi by USAID. It works in 40 communities in each country,[a] targeting male and female students in upper primary and lower secondary school between the ages of 10 and 14 years old to reduce school-related, gender-based violence. A central strategy of the project is to examine the gender dimensions of violence by broadening the focus from girls alone to include boys. Safe Schools, which works at both the local and national level, is based on the premise that many types of gender-based violence exist in school settings, all of which contribute to a hostile learning environment. By reducing violence, the program seeks to create a safe and respectful learning environment and thereby improve educational outcomes and reduce negative health outcomes.

Different Levels of the Safe Schools Program

(continued)

Box 17.2

Continued

The program operates via partnerships with community-based organizations. Local participation and ownership are crucial to its success, as is the buy-in of other stakeholders, such as ministries of education, health, and social welfare. Representatives from key national institutions, particularly ministries of education, have, for example, participated in the development of program training materials and the drafting of teachers' codes of conduct.

The program also supports the development of tools and materials that can be replicated and applied by host country organizations without the need for international organizations to deliver services.

As of year-end 2007, the program had trained approximately 30,000 students, 800 teachers, and 240 community counselors in Ghana and Malawi. Within the first month of program activities in Ghana, the percentage of school children who believed they had the right to say "no" to unwanted touching increased from 66 to 72 percent; the percentage of school children reporting violence or abuse at, or on the way to, school decreased from 43 to 39 percent; and the percentage of teachers self-reporting the use of physical discipline on students decreased from 86 to 44 percent.

Source: Swanson, Columbia, and Banashek 2007.

a. The current program is designed as an experiment and is being implemented in a total of 80 communities, of which 20 are control sites and 60 are intervention sites.

among the most powerful tools for reducing girls' vulnerability to HIV/AIDS infection.

In 2002, the Joint United Nations Programme on HIV/AIDS (UNAIDS) Inter-Agency Task Team on Education and HIV/AIDS established a working group—known as the Accelerate Initiative— to address these challenges and support countries in Sub-Saharan Africa as they "accelerate the education sector response to HIV/ AIDS." Key partners of the initiative include governments, United Nations agencies, bilateral partners, and civil society, as well as key stakeholders such as people living with HIV/AIDS, teachers' unions, and the media. More than 37 countries responsible for more than 200 million school-age children (86 percent of all school-age children) and 2.6 million primary and secondary school teachers (74 percent of teachers) have participated in demand-led initiatives that have facilitated extensive information sharing and significant achievements.

For example, the Primary School AIDS Prevention Program in Kenya is a partnership between the nongovernmental organization (NGO) International Child Support, Kenya's National AIDS Control Council, and the Ministry of Education Science and Technology. The program is unique in that it equitably equips girls and boys with the behavioral skills to protect themselves and others from HIV/AIDS infection. The multipronged program involves teachers, parents, and students to deliver prevention education that focuses on the inhibitors of girls' self-esteem, such as management of their menstruation, decision-making skills about their sexuality, and susceptibility to cross-generational sex and sex with their peers.

Underserved Groups
Focus on hard-to-reach, disadvantaged, vulnerable, and excluded groups, especially girls.
Despite the considerable increases in enrollments registered at all educational levels in the past two decades, achievement of universal primary education and gender equality at the primary and secondary levels remain elusive. A significant number of students, particularly girls from disadvantaged and vulnerable groups, are still excluded from school. To accelerate achievement of the gender equality goal, it will be necessary to pay special attention to reaching and providing quality education to these excluded groups. The following actions are proposed.

Scale up best practice interventions and seek creative approaches. Extensive practical experience and research evidence have shown that a number of effective demand- and supply-side interventions (for example, scholarships, stipends, conditional cash transfers, recruitment of teachers, and gender-targeted provision of materials) have increased girls' enrollments in many developing countries. Despite the successes registered to date, some countries are still far from meeting the goal of gender equality in education. It is not the absence of knowledge that is preventing countries from making progress on this goal, but rather, that known effective interventions are not reaching the neediest and excluded groups. Therefore, the strategic way forward is to scale up these best-practice interventions and seek creative approaches to reach the neediest and hard-to-reach groups. For example, tent schools and mobile teachers can significantly increase access to education for nomadic populations.

Develop and implement a policy of inclusive education. To scale up the provision of education to all children, particularly those from disadvantaged groups (for example, the disabled, orphans, the poor, and indigenous and minority populations), governments must develop and adopt inclusive education policies and implementation strategies that ensure equal opportunities for all learners, regardless of age, gender, ethnicity, impairment, attainment, or background. Such policies should maintain minimum standards for all students, seek to prevent social exclusion from occurring in the first instance, and reintegrate excluded students back into the education system. To date, only a limited number of developing countries have such a policy—for example, the governments of Bangladesh, India, Pakistan, and Sri Lanka in South Asia, and those of Namibia, South Africa, Swaziland, and Uganda in Africa.

Incorporate strategies for gender equality in education into a broader, multisectoral development agenda. Gender disparities and inequalities in education are determined by a range of social, cultural, economic, and environmental factors—both internal and external to the education sector. Education policies naturally tend to focus solely on aspects of gender inequality related to the education system and thus do not address important causes of gender disparities. Local laws and customs, for example, may discriminate against female students who get pregnant and affect whether or not they complete school after giving birth. The solution to gender inequality in education thus goes beyond the confines of the education sector, stretching to the legal and health systems, as well as to agriculture and infrastructure.

Allocate public and private resources to priority and neediest groups as well as to priority levels of education, such as preschool and early childhood education and care. Without a deliberate, sustained, and structured policy to prioritize the allocation of resources to marginalized groups within national and state budgets, programs aimed at improving the education of disadvantaged groups will have reduced chances of succeeding. Gender budgeting in countries such as Australia and South Africa is but one example of deliberate, sustained policy prioritization.

Create institutions that strengthen the link between nonformal and formal education programs. To open the doors of education to all, governments and other education stakeholders have to maximize positive links between formal and nonformal education. Opportunities for positive collaboration can be explored when both formal and nonformal education models are perceived as parts of one learning system that serves the educational needs of society. On one hand, nonformal education programs can complement formal educational institutions and provide continuing education for people who drop out of school early or who are working. On the other hand, formal education facilities can be made available after hours to nonformal education programs, teachers in regular formal education programs can also serve as instructors in nonformal education programs, and so forth.

The Complementary Basic Education in Tanzania program caters to the needs of adolescents who have never enrolled or have dropped out of school by giving them a second-chance education option to acquire literacy, numeracy, and vocational skills. The three-year program is adapted to the needs of the learners—classes take place for only three-and-a-half hours a day so that students have time to undertake chores and income-generating activities. In India, a formal educational institution, the Loreto Day School, has taken up the challenge of reaching out to street children, who are not only hard to reach but also at high risk. The school has accordingly adapted its teaching to the needs of these children and embraced local customs to provide them education and shelter (see box 17.3).

Build and equip primary schools, particularly in remote and low-enrollment areas. To enroll excluded and hard-to-reach children, educational capacity and quality must be scaled up in deficient and disadvantaged geographic areas. Specifically, governments need to build schools or provide school places within culturally acceptable distances from home that offer culturally appropriate safety measures (for example, boundary walls) as well as sanitary and water facilities. This will require changes in practice. For example, one-room or two-room schools should be encouraged in some contexts (such as low population density areas) as the best strategy for making school places available to girls. Bigger schools are often situated at greater distances from home and tend to work against the promotion of girls' education.

The Baluchistan Primary Education Program (1992–1999) sought to improve access for girls and to promote gender equity in a very conservative area of Pakistan, one that had low female enrollment and occasional high resistance to educating girls. Funded by the World Bank, the program constructed new and rehabilitated old primary schools for girls; it also built separate classrooms for girls in schools that had previously catered

Box 17.3

Loreto Day School, Calcutta, India: A Safe Haven for Street Children

Loreto Day School originally opened its doors in 1857 as a school for the daughters of Irish and English soldiers in India. It later expanded its mission to include children of well-to-do Anglo-Indian families. However, it wasn't until Sister Cyril Mooney became the headmistress in 1979 that the school opened its doors to everyone.

Today the school has 1,500 students, nearly half of whom are from the slums. The school charges fees from the students of well-to-do families and provides free education to those who cannot afford the fees. The street children typically live in the enclosed verandah on the school's rooftop, which is called the *rainbow roof,* hence the name, *rainbow children.* These students take regular classes during the day and help out with the chores, such as cleaning and cooking, afterwards. When night falls, they all take out their sleeping mats and blankets from their lockers, make their beds, and go to sleep—the same way they would at home. The girls have surrogate mothers who live with them and provide structure and guidance.

The teaching method at Loreto Day School focuses on level of ability, rather than age, to determine where to place a student. Groups of four or five students work together on a given subject or project and in the process learn from each other. New children in the shelter can be brought up to speed with their age-respective grade level within a year following this method. Children in grade 5 also teach lower grades, with each child conducting two classes per week. There is no distinction between upper- and lower-income children. All wear the same uniform and learn from the same curriculum. Children wander in when their daily schedules allow them and find a teacher who is free to teach them. (The school ensures that one or two teachers are available at all times.) Nearly 300 students are receiving an education this way, and more than 40 such girls have made their way to secondary school.

The school owes its success to a dedicated staff and an enlightened student community; its programs show no sign of slowing down. Loreto Day School is also expanding: it now has five branches in the city of Calcutta and plans to reach up to 10,000 street children by 2018.

Source: Loreto Day School documentary 2007.

primarily to boys. The project was extremely successful. Girls' enrollment increased by 102 percent, from 115,000 in 1993 to nearly 233,000 in 1999, while boys' enrollment increased by only 6 percent, from 384,000 to about 407,000. In other words, the gender ratio changed from only one girl for every 3.4 boys in provincial government primary schools in 1993 to one girl for every 1.8 boys. Dropouts, particularly of girls, decreased significantly as well (World Bank 2000).

Postprimary Education
Invest in postprimary education and training, particularly for girls at the secondary level.

In many developing countries, girls still have fewer opportunities than boys to access secondary and tertiary levels of education, as well as scientific and technical courses, because of various social and cultural constraints. Too few girls aspire to pursue higher education mainly because of the low economic status of their families; that is, they have no hopes of financing postprimary education. Women are also subject to discrimination in the labor market. Investing in the education of girls at postprimary education levels is thus the best way to provide them the necessary set of skills and competencies to participate in the labor market and become economically empowered. Secondary education also provides girls confidence and self-esteem and is an effective long-term defense against HIV and AIDS. The following actions are proposed.

Mobilize additional resources and earmark them for girls' postprimary education activities. Additional financial resources are necessary to fund the expansion of secondary schools in remote and underserved areas. Resources for girls' education could be tapped from various public and private sources, such as community groups, churches, alumni associations, and other community fund-raising events for girls education. Local businesses also might donate resources in kind or in cash for girls' education, becoming "champions" of girls' education. Local and international philanthropic organizations, such as Lions and Rotary clubs, can provide additional grants for improving girls' education. Embassies and other international grant-making organizations are other sources of potential funding.

Provide incentives that stimulate demand for girls' postprimary education. Poor parents who cannot afford to educate all of their children have little reason to send their girls to school when fees and other expenses are involved. In some cultures, moreover, girls are married when they reach puberty, which means that they either drop out of secondary school or never enroll. Yet as shown in chapters 4 and 5, secondary education has the potential for increasing girls' returns to education in the labor market. Breaking this cycle requires making it easier for parents to afford schooling for girls. Stipends and scholarships, free textbooks and learning materials, and school meal programs are some of the preferred modalities for spurring demand for education and have proven very successful in certain cases, such as the Female Secondary School Stipend Program in Bangladesh.

Design a package of demand and supply interventions to boost postprimary education for girls. The presence of a secondary school in a locality increases the chances that rural girls will make the transition from primary to secondary education. In cases were secondary schools are far from home, the provision of residential facilities for girls or the provision of safe and affordable transportation facilities, together with a package of other interventions, have worked to improve postprimary education for girls in a number of countries. For example, the World Bank-funded Mozambique Capacity-Building Human Development Project (1992–2001) specifically sought to increase female enrollment in secondary schools by providing incentives in the form of scholarships for girls, particularly those from rural areas. A range of other interventions were undertaken at the same time, including community-awareness programs, construction of dormitories for girls, and the provision of teacher training to increase girls' participation in classrooms. As a result of these programs, female enrollments ended up being four times higher than the original project targets (World Bank 2003).

The Dar Taliba de Qualité project in Morocco (see box 17.4) supports rural girls who live in dormitories far from home so that they can attend secondary school. The program created a network of dormitories that are associated with secondary schools, but operated and managed independently of them, and offers young female residents educational and psychosocial support to help them handle the difficulties of boarding school and sustain their academic achievement.

Link education and skills development to labor market opportunities. A well-educated population leads to a more productive workforce, which can lead to increased economic growth, better social outcomes (for example, better fertility and mortality indicators), and higher returns, particularly for women. Linking education with labor market outcomes is particularly important, because finding appropriate employment is an important end goal of educational attainment.

Box 17.4

Dar Tailba de Qualité Project, Morocco: Boarding Facilities for Rural Girls

Faced with an enrollment rate of 42 percent for rural girls at the secondary level, the government of Morocco invested considerable sums to establish dormitories to broaden access to secondary education. Dormitories are generally located near a secondary school and, although they operate independently, are affiliated with the school. The program has been successful in raising the number of rural girls (and boys) in secondary schools.

The dormitory setting offers special advantages to girls, such as physical amenities and a lighter load of chores (often considerably so), as well as an environment devoted to academic achievement. However, the boarding arrangement is not without challenges. First, girls often arrive with a significant handicap in their academic abilities as a result of poor-quality teaching at the primary level. Second, these young students are away from home for the first time, which takes a toll on their emotional and physical health. Finally, the girls have to conquer a sizable cultural and social divide between Morocco's rural and urban areas (which includes even modest towns).

The USAID/ALEF Project,* in partnership with the *Entraide Nationale* office of the Ministry of Social Affairs, launched the Dar Taliba de Qualité initiative to promote the academic and personal development of girls living in these dormitories. The program works with local associations (NGOs) and assigns monitors (*Encadrantes*) to the 14 participating dormitories. These monitors organize activities to help the girls succeed in their studies and become responsible, confident members of their schools and the larger community. The local association ensures the administration of the dormitory, relying on volunteers and a modest staff, which sometimes includes a resident manager.

Overall, the program has been successful: grade point averages have risen significantly for nearly all the girls in the program, and the average percentage of girls with passing grades has risen to 78 percent across the 14 dormitories, with three reporting a 90 percent completion rate.

Source: Muskin 2007.

*Implemented by the Academy for Educational Development.

The vast majority of secondary school students in South Asia and Sub-Saharan Africa must look for jobs upon leaving school. To improve their employment prospects and earnings potential, schools (and tertiary education institutions) must provide them with skills and competencies needed in the labor market. Linking curricula more tightly with locally available jobs would enhance the incentives of parents and girls alike to enroll, attend, and complete school. The Yemen Education Sector Investment Project (1994–2001), for example, aimed to improve secondary-level access for girls and train women teachers to further advance in their careers as female supervisors, counselors, and heads of schools. The project trained about 250 selected students who, after graduation, filled the need for female teachers in mathematics and science subjects. In addition, the project built a national community college system to respond to labor market needs.

A tracer study of the first 100 graduates of the two financed Yemeni colleges showed that graduate employment rates were above 80 percent, and employers reported being highly satisfied with their graduates' skills. Along similar lines, a new initiative to develop entrepreneurial and managerial talent, especially of women, in developing and emerging economies has just been launched by Goldman Sachs (see box 17.5).

Support girls' competitiveness in the global economy through science, technology, and mathematics education and other skills-development programs. Knowledge has become the driving force in economic development, and labor markets increasingly require more educated, more technologically advanced, and better-skilled workers. Full utilization of the scientific and intellectual capacity of men and women is critical for the scientific and technological development of any country. Yet in many developing nations, the number of females studying or involved in science, mathematics, and technology is proportionately lower than the number of males. Results from national and international achievement assessments, especially in developing countries, consistently show that males perform better than females in science and technology subjects, while females perform better than males in literacy and other social studies. To enhance girls' ability to compete in the global economy, particularly in high-value industries (for example, information technology, biotechnology, semiconductor manufacturing), it is important to support innovative approaches and strategies, such as mathematics-language or technology-arts cross-curricular programs that confound traditional gen-

Box 17.5

10,000 Women: A Goldman Sachs Initiative

On March 5, 2008, the Goldman Sachs Group, Inc., a global investment banking firm, launched an initiative to provide 10,000 underserved women, predominantly in developing and emerging markets, a business and management education. The initiative also seeks to improve the quality and capacity of business and management education through partnerships between universities in the United States and Europe and business schools in developing countries around the world. The initiative, to which Goldman Sachs has pledged US$100 million, is inspired by economic research that shows the powerful effects on economies and societies of greater labor force participation of women.

The initiative seeks to

- *Educate 10,000 women in business and management* through innovative certificate programs, enabling them to develop specific skills, such as drafting business plans, accounting, public speaking, marketing, management, and accessing capital.
- *Build global business sister school partnerships* between business schools and universities in the United States and Europe and business schools in developing and emerging economies. Partner schools will collaborate to train professors, exchange faculty, develop curricula, and create local case study material.
- *Provide mentoring support to women entrepreneurs* by establishing mentoring and networking channels for women and encouraging career development opportunities.
- *Work with research and women's development organizations* to better understand local challenges that girls and women must overcome to access greater economic opportunity.
- *Help disadvantaged women in the United States* through parallel programs and partnerships that will provide business and management education to disadvantaged women in the United States.

Source: Goldman Sachs Web site, http://www2.goldmansachs.com/citizenship/10000women/10000-women-fact-sheet.pdf (accessed April 2008).

dered associations and enhance the learning of girls and boys across a given curriculum.

Research and Data Disaggregation by Gender
Promote research; generate knowledge and disaggregate data by gender to inform policy and practice.
Research provides valuable information for the development of gender policies and strategies. Given the continual changes taking place in education systems as a result of existing interventions, it is important to investigate what does and doesn't work to improve the status of education in developing countries. Numerous important questions continue to need the attention of operationally minded researchers in relatively unresearched fields, such as how to reach marginalized groups. Without more solid knowledge, planners and decision makers at local, national, and international levels will be forced to operate with untested assumptions and dogmas that may be far from reality. The following actions are proposed:

Establish effective monitoring and evaluation systems in all programs to measure progress with clear indicators. Monitoring and evaluations systems should monitor inputs, process, outputs, and outcomes, while incorporating a gender perspective in the collection of data. Gender-disaggregated data should be made regularly available and analytical reports based on this data used to document the impact of policies or individual programs. Such data create a critical foundation for action by key stakeholders, who need to be able to identify evolving problems to decide on crucial strategies, corrective measures, and revisions to plans and resource allocations. Monitoring and evaluation systems also help to establish substantive accountability because they demonstrate whether or not a program is reaching its stated objectives.

Conduct rigorous impact evaluations of interventions to improve the evidence base about interventions that work and those that do not. Governments and development agencies need to bolster efforts to generate and apply knowledge from impact evaluations to education programs. This task includes dedicating adequate resources for impact evaluations, facilitating access to information, and building capacity in developing countries to conduct impact evaluations themselves. The World Bank Human Development Network and the Africa Impact Evaluation Initiative are, for example, engaged in analyzing and supporting more than 20 African countries to undertake impact evaluations in education.

The impact of several interventions, including scholarships, textbooks, school-based management, and locally contracted teachers, are being evaluated.

Partnerships
Strengthen partnerships to address gender equality in education.
The quality of project partnerships determines the effectiveness of resources allocated to the education sector. Ensuring that such partners more consistently take advantage of community structures such as the Education for All Fast-Track Initiative helps reduce the four main gaps of gender equality in education: finance, data, policy, and capacity. By coalescing around education sector plans, partnerships can promote better alignment of donor, nonprofit, and private sector support for developing countries, thereby preventing fragmentation of efforts.

Stimulate the formation of partnerships between international aid agencies and NGOs, governments, and private businesses to mobilize additional resources for girls' education. A global partnership with branches at the national and regional level, such as the United Nations Girls' Education Initiative (UNGEI), could monitor the incorporation of a gender perspective into implementation activities, as well as indicators of success during program preparation and implementation. (See box 17.6 for an overview of UNGEI.)

Partnerships can also be formed between the public and private sectors or within the private sector, such as the Business Partnership for Girls Education in Yemen, which aims to mobilize a large and diverse group of private sector partners to create a sustainable private education sector, as well as to strengthen access to basic education, especially by girls.

Build partnerships between schools and communities. Programs that promote community involvement and management of schools reduce the administrative and financial costs of educating girls and increase institutional accountability and sustainability. A growing proportion of girls' education projects have incorporated some kind of community involvement or management. When such involvement is planned and executed properly, it can have a large impact on the success of the project. Yet proper monitoring is also required to prevent elite capture of program benefits.

For example, the El Salvador Basic Education Project (1996–2001) aimed to promote greater equity by improving access and strengthening the capacity of the government's Education with a Community

Box 17.6

What Is UNGEI and What Does It Do?

The United Nations Girls' Education Initiative (UNGEI) was launched in April 2000 to eliminate gender disparities in primary and secondary education and ensure that by 2015, all children complete primary schooling, with girls and boys having equal access to all levels of education. UNGEI works with governments, donor countries, NGOs, civil society, the private sector, and local communities and families to remove barriers to learning, such as school fees and other educational costs, and to provide access to education in emergency situations. The initiative promotes strategies that give priority to the most disadvantaged, including girls and women, in education policies, plans, and budgets. It also advocates for a cross-sectoral holistic approach to gender equality in education, with balanced investments in education across the life cycle.

UNGEI supports country-led development and seeks to influence decision making and investments to ensure gender equity and equality in national education policies, plans, and programs. UNGEI partners mobilize resources for both targeted project interventions and country programs, as well as large-scale systemic interventions designed to influence the whole education system. The initiative streamlines its efforts by using existing development mechanisms, such as poverty-reduction strategies, sectorwide approaches, and UN development assistance frameworks. Current partners at the global level include UN agencies (International Labour Organization; United Nations Educational, Scientific, and Cultural Organization; United Nations Population Fund; United Nations Children's Fund, and World Food Programme, among others), the World Bank, bilateral donor agencies, and NGOs..

Source: http://www.ungei.org (accessed April 2008).

Participation Program. The program created, legalized, and provided support to parent organizations at the community level. As many rural schools offered only a few primary grades, not a complete primary cycle, the project expanded complete primary schools in rural areas. Expansion automatically targeted girls because they were among the most disadvantaged students. The number of sixth-grade graduates increased by 14 percent, from 95,212 in 1996 to 110,559 in 2000 (World Bank 2002).

Use the media to communicate messages about enrollment and learning outcomes of girls' education. Several countries have succeeded in using the media (radio, television, and newspapers), to communicate key messages about female education. Lessons learned by such countries as Congo, El Salvador, Ghana, Guinea, and Mali, which have used the media extensively to promote girls' education initiatives, include: (1) involving members of the primary audience to develop and disseminate the messages; (2) using influential personalities in the environment to convey the messages; (3) targeting messages to specific audiences and presenting them in a language they understand (for example, local-language broadcasts); (4) reinforcing the messages by communicating them often and in various forms; and (5) using more widely accessible media, such as radio and, in some cases, television (see box 17.7).

Involve mothers. It is essential to include both parents in community action—or, at the very least, ensure that women's voices are heard—at the grassroots level. Box 17.8 highlights the positive impact of community involvement in Benin.

The chapters of this book show that interventions can and do succeed in getting girls into schools and keeping them there. However, they also show that the neediest groups are not sufficiently served by current policies and practices. Consequently, new directions are required to achieve girls' education in the 21st century that will promote gender equality, empowerment, and economic growth. First, we need to recast the education equity and access issues to build the knowledge base and focus attention around disadvantaged groups, the majority of whom are girls. We also need to extend access and equity issues beyond primary education to secondary and tertiary education levels. Second, we need to pay close attention to learning outcomes of girls and boys and ensure that the relevant skills and competencies are developed. Finally, we need to promote closer links between the education system and the labor market to encourage economic growth.

Implications for the World Bank

The Bank has made significant strides in mainstreaming gender into education projects during the past 15 years, and there is now a good knowledge base and best-practice examples of interventions that have worked. However, there is still unfinished business about access and completion at

Box 17.7

Alam Simsim: Promoting Gender Equity in Education from an Early Age in Egypt

Alam Simsim is the Egyptian version of the popular children's educational television series, *Sesame Street,* which has been reaching preschoolers across many cultures and continents for the past four decades. The series seeks to prepare children for school and fosters valuable socioemotional and interpersonal skills.

The series began airing in Egypt in 2000 and focuses on early literacy and math skills, as well as health, hygiene, and gender equality—especially in education. It's principal puppet character, Khokha, is a four-year-old girl with a passion for learning. Khokha and her Alam Simsim friends encourage girls to have positive aspirations and expose both girls and boys to gender-equitable attitudes, which are having a measurable impact on children and caregivers.

Research to date shows that the series has been successful in achieving these goals. A study by Johns Hopkins University, for example, concluded that, even after controlling for household income and parent education, children with high levels of exposure to *Alam Simsim* demonstrated more gender-equitable attitudes than their peers, who had few or no such views. A study conducted by SPAAC, an independent consulting firm, found that Khokha is the most popular television character among both girls and boys and that the show encourages girls to seek education and aspire to have careers.

Mothers in rural areas of Egypt are largely illiterate, but those who were interviewed in SPAAC focus groups expressed how influential *Alam Simsim* has been for their daughters and themselves with regard to education. The mothers expressed a greater understanding of why education is important and said the program had encouraged them to send their daughters as well as their sons to school. Many who were illiterate said that they themselves learned letters from *Alam Simsim* and regretted not having an education. Others expressed regret for having previously taken their daughters out of school.

Source: Alyaa Montasser, Cole, and Elattar 2007.

Box 17.8

Giving Mothers a Voice in Their Children's Education

Parents' associations (APEs) in Benin have had an official role in local management of public education since the 1960s. However, the traditional view in rural areas is that social forums are reserved for men, causing APEs to be dominated by fathers. Mothers' associations (AMEs) were created under a World Education initiative to provide "free space" for women to exchange ideas and views among themselves about the local education needs and issues. The goal of the initiative is to enable women to become more involved in their children's, especially their daughters', schooling and, on a more global level, give women a voice in the ongoing national debate on education policy and reform in Benin.

The World Education pilot project envisioned AMEs as a new branch of the original APEs, which would work in close collaboration with them. Field agents contact a local community and hold a series of meetings to generate support for an AME and determine the best approach for establishing it in a given community. Once the APE accepts the idea of having an AME branch, women interested in joining the association are given basic training by a local NGO on such topics as the roles and responsibilities of an association and its board; how to conduct a census of school-age children in villages; how to develop education plans at local levels; how to develop and implement microprojects; and special topics, such as awareness raising training for HIV/AIDS and other sexually transmitted diseases (STDs).

continued

all levels of education, particularly in developing countries generally and fragile states in particular. Following are 10 things the Bank needs to do going forward:

- Scale up action in all the strategic areas identified.
- Sharpen the focus on girls' education in activities under the three pillars of the Education Sector Strategy Update: Learning for All, Education for Competitiveness, and Education Systems for Results.
- Monitor the focus on gender in operations and economic and sector work.

Box 17.8

Continued

All AMEs are financially independent, cost-effective associations—an important element of their sustainability. Virtually all of their activities, including HIV/AIDS and STD awareness, building or repairing school infrastructure, retrieving victims of child trafficking, or providing birth certificates and school supplies for poor children, are paid for from their own fundraising efforts.

An estimated 500 AMEs are currently operating in Benin, many of which have formed independently of the World Education project. Although their quality varies, the success of AMEs in Benin cannot be underestimated. Where they exist in the country, women are more involved in their children's formal education. In addition, AMEs have had a significant impact on problems associated with girls' education, child trafficking, and student dropouts. They have also helped to greatly increase student enrollment, retention, and academic achievement, particularly by girls. A substantial number of APE boards now include up to four women, which was very rare even two to three years ago. More significantly, women members are no longer relegated to second-tier status, with certain women occupying increasingly influential positions on these boards.

> "The mothers' determination, the interest they had in what they were doing, their mobilization for a cause that was dear to them, and their readiness to help out, despite their being overworked in their daily routines, is recognized [by the school community]."
>
> — Odile Akpaka

Source: Taha 2007.

- Increase the number of rigorous impact evaluations of interventions with results on gender-differentiated impact evidence from 42 to 60 in the next two years.
- Incorporate impact evaluation designs, including those that measure distributional effects, into all projects or programs from the design stage.
- Use evidence from gender-focused research to inform the formulation of Country Assistance Strategies.
- Strengthen the capacity of staff to collect, analyze, and use gender-disaggregated data in education operations.

- Maintain databases populated by gender-disaggregated data.
- Use the Convening role of the Bank to organize more knowledge sharing and dissemination activities.
- Broaden partnerships with philanthropic organizations to new areas, such as information communication and technology, and to other sectors, such as agriculture, water, and sanitation.

References

Alyaa Montasser, Alkarma, Charlotte Cole, and Nada Elattar. 2007. "Promoting Gender Equity and Girls' Education through Children's Media: Lessons from Egypt's *Alam Simsim* (Sesame Street) Project." Submitted to the World Bank Global Symposium on Gender, Education, and Development, October.

Barro, Robert J. 1999. "Determinants of Democracy." *Journal of Political Economy* 107 (6): S158–83.

DeWalque, Damien. 2004. "How Does Educational Attainment Affect the Risk of Being Infected by HIV/AIDS? Evidence from a General Population Cohort in Rural Uganda." World Bank Development Research Group Working Paper, World Bank, Washington, DC.

Dollar, David, and Roberta Gatti. 1999. "Gender Inequality, Income, and Growth: Are Good Times Good for Women?" World Bank Policy Research Report on Gender and Development, Working Paper Series No.1, World Bank, Washington, DC.

El-Gabaly. 2006. "Female Genital Mutilation in Egypt." Presentation at Global Forum for Health Research, "Combating Disease and Promoting Health," Cairo, October 29–November 2.

Filmer, Deon. 2000. "The Structure of Social Disparities in Education: Gender and Wealth." Policy Research Working Paper 2268, World Bank, Washington, DC.

Klasen, Stephan. 1999. "Does Gender Inequality Reduce Growth and Development? Evidence from Cross-Country Regressions." Policy Research Report on Gender and Development Working Paper 7, World Bank, Washington, DC.

Loreto Day School documentary. 2007. Submitted to the World Bank Global Symposium on Gender, Education, and Development, October.

Mckinsey and Co. 2007.: "The Challenge of Achieving World-Class Performance: Education in the 21st Century." Presentation at the World Bank, September 10.

Muskin, Joshua. 2007. "Providing Scholarships and Lodging to Increase Girls' Junior Secondary Enrolment in Morroco, USAID/Morocco ALEF Project." Submitted to the World Bank Global Symposium on Gender, Education, and Development, October.

Psacharopoulos, G., and H. Patrinos. 2002. "Returns to Investment in Education: A Further Update." Policy Research Working Paper 2281, World Bank, Washington, DC.

Schultz, P. 1993. "Mortality Decline in the Low-Income World: Causes and Consequences." *American Economic Review* 83 (2): 337–342.

Sen, Purna. 1999. "Enhancing Women's Choices in Responding to Domestic Violence in Calcutta: A Comparison of Employment and Education." *European Journal of Development Research* 11(2): 65–86.

Swanson, Julie, Richard Columbia, and Sarah Banashek. 2007. "The Safe Schools Program." Submitted to the World Bank Global Symposium on Gender, Education, and Development, October.

Taha, Cynthia. 2007. "Giving Mothers a Voice in Education." Benin Case Study. Submitted to the World Bank Global Symposium on Gender, Education, and Development, October.

UNICEF (United Nations Children's Fund). 2003. *The State of the World's Children in 2004.* New York: UNICEF.

World Bank. 2000. *Baluchistan Primary Education Program (1992–1999) Implementation Completion Report.* Washington, DC: World Bank.

World Bank. 2002. *El Salvador Basic Education Project (1996–2001)* Implementation Completion Report. Washington, DC: World Bank.

World Bank, 2003. *Mozambique Capacity-Building Human Development Project, Implementation Completion Report.* Washington, DC: World Bank.

Index

Malawi, 15–16, 284–285
management education, 294
managers, AET, 249
market-based reforms, 209–210
masculinity, 158
mathematics, 41–52
   gender differences, 43–49
   performance, 47, 50
   PISA scale, 45
   science, technology, and mathematics
      education, 258, 293, 295
meals, 122–123
memoranda of understanding (MOU),
   FAWE and, 263
menstruation, 170–171
Millennium Development Goals (MDG),
   25, 61–62, 64, 127
   Benin and, 145
Mincerian earnings function, 36n.4, 82
Ministries of Education, FAWE and, 259,
   263, 265
models, scaling up, 264
monitoring and evaluation systems, 295,
   300
Morocco, dormitories, 291, 292
mothers, involvement, 298, 300–301
Mozambique
   attainment, 99, 100
   scholarships, 291
multidimensional approach, 263

N

needs assessment, 164
Nepal, 118, 160
New Partnership for African Development
   (NEPAD), 239, 241, 245
news media, 298
Nigeria, social exclusion, 118
numeracy, 69, 71, 80–81, 82, 159
   earnings and, 85
nutrition, 59

O

occupation
   age and, 75
   attainment, 73–82, 88, 89n.5
   categories, 69–73, 89n.4
   choice, 88
   Ghana, 77
   outcome, 76–82, 90n.6
   Pakistan, 69–73, 74, 75, 78

orphans, 95, 105–108, 112, 188
   defined, 105
   enrollment, 106–108, 109
out of the labor force (OLF). *See*
   unemployment

P

Pakistan
   access, 288, 290
   crisis, 159–160
   labor market, 67–93, 89n.1
   madrassa reform, 210–213, 236n.12
   social exclusion, 118
   years of schooling, 101, 102
Pakistan Integrated Household Survey
   (PIHS), 76, 87–88, 90nn.7,8
participant feedback, 192–193
participation, 11, 138, 194
partnerships, 18, 20, 259, 281, 285,
   296–298, 302
performance, 8, 27, 36n.5
   mathematics, 45, 47, 50
   reading, 46
   violence and, 148
Peru, social exclusion, 119
Philippines, madrassas, 237n.24
physical environment, 259–260
policy, 23, 120, 133
   develop and implement, 287
   education in emergencies, 161–168
   FAWE influence, 260–261
   gender-based violence, 149–150
   gender-sensitive, 131, 257
   madrassa reform, 225–228
   mathematics proficiency, 47–51
   objectives, 32–35
political leaders and political will, AET
   and, 245, 248
postgraduate education, AET, 246–247
postprimary education, 18, 19, 280,
   290–295
   Bangladesh, 214, 219
poststructural approach, 12, 13, 127, 128,
   134
poverty, 95, 97–99, 102, 112, 262
   "sugar daddy" phenomenon, 148
   Yemen, 274–275

Poverty Reduction and Economic
   Management Network, World Bank
   symposium, 4–5
power structures, gendered, 130–133

United Nations Girls' Education Initiative
    (UNGEI), 135, 139
  role, 297
United States, educational attainment, 42
universal education, 44
  Yemen, 274–276
urban residence, gender and, 102–105
user fees, enrollment and, Colombia,
    15–16, 201–208
  arguments against, 202
  arguments in favor of, 202–203

V

values, 189–190
victims, awareness, 150
violence, 133, 136–137 156
  defining, 146
  post-conflict, 161
  school-based, 283
  see also conflict and war
violence, gender-based, 13, 154, 155,
    157–158, 188–189, 284–285
  Benin, 143–151
  defining, 146
  implications, 148–149
  myth or reality?, 146–148
  overcoming, 150–151
  protection from, 162
  rape, 150, 157, 161, 188
  response, 151
  sexual harassment and abuse, 13, 14,
    143, 145, 147–148
  variation, 150
vulnerability, 163, 280, 286–290
  Afghanistan, 183–184

W

wage employment, 72, 76, *89n.4*
  earnings and years of education, 87
  literacy and, 81
wages. *See* earnings
war crimes, 161
well-being, 170–171
widows, 188
women-and-girls approach, 162
women in development (WID)
    framework, 12, 127, 128, 129–133
World Bank
  AET studies, 240
  implications for, 298–302
  staff capacity building, 301
  strategic directions, 20
  ten things to do, 300–301

Y

years of schooling, 25, 68, 79–80, *90n.9*
  developing vs industrial countries, 60
  earnings and, 87
  occupation and, 77, *90n.8*
  pattern, 99–102
  poverty and, 97–99
  rate of return, 26
Yemen
  basic and secondary education, 17–18,
    269–277
  Education Sector Investment Project,
    293

ECO-AUDIT
Environmental Benefits Statement

The World Bank is committed to preserving endangered forests and natural resources. The Office of the Publisher has chosen to print *Girls' Education in the 21st Century: Gender Equality, Empowerment, and Economic Growth* on 30% post-consumer recycled fiber in accordance with the recommended standards for paper usage set by the Green Press Initiative, a nonprofit program supporting publishers in using fiber that is not sourced from endangered forests. For more information, visit www.green-pressinitiative.org.

Saved:
- 7 trees
- 5 million BTUs of total energy
- 649 lbs. of net greenhouse gases
- 2,695 gallons of waste water
- 346 lbs. of solid waste